Contents

and Local Government

John Bourn

BSc (Econ), PhD

PITMAN

PITMAN PUBLISHING LIMITED
39 Parker Street, London WC2B 5PB

Copp Clark Pitman, Toronto
Fearon Pitman Publishers Inc, San Francisco
Pitman Publishing New Zealand Ltd, Wellington
Pitman Publishing Pty Ltd, Melbourne

Text set in 10/12 Times,
printed by photolithography and bound in Great Britain
at The Pitman Press, Bath

ISBN 0 273 00989 3

Editor's introduction

The purpose of this series is to continue Pitman's interest in the field of government and administration which first began by their publication of Clarke's *Outlines of Local Government* in 1916. As with the earlier volumes, it is intended that the books in this new series should have a wide appeal. They will be primarily addressed to students in all forms of higher education, to candidates for professional examinations and to the practitioners themselves. They will also provide an essential understanding for the many politicians and elected councillors who control and direct our public services.

The extensive growth of governmental services, the intricate mechanisms set up to administer them, and the vast influence which they exercise over the lives of the citizen and the maintenance of his rights and liberties, the efficient and effective use of scarce resources, and the ordering and regulation of public behaviour in a humane and dignified manner are factors which combine to make it important that both officials and elected representatives shall not only know their jobs, but shall carry them out competently and with understanding of the needs of the people they serve.

The field is vast—it has increased in size and complexity since the end of the second world war. The series sets out to deal with the major institutions and services in a logical and easily assimilated manner. The main volumes will deal with Parliament and the political processes, the central administration and the civil service; the structure of local government, local government finance, and the local government service; and with the main social services such as education, the personal social services, social security, housing, the national health service and town planning.

The authors will represent a wide field of interests. Some come from an academic background, whilst others are practitioners in the field. They all, however, come to their task with a long experience of the subject on which they write and all have an established reputation.

WILLIAM THORNHILL
University of Sheffield

Preface

The purpose of this book is to try to give a clear and straightforward account of the use that has been made of recent management ideas and techniques in central and local government in the United Kingdom and to make a preliminary assessment of their value.

The book deals with ideas and techniques that have actually been used, the problems that they were designed to solve, and the strengths and weaknesses that have been revealed. Most of the examples are drawn from central and local government, but some are taken from the health service and other public bodies. The book also deals with important royal commissions and other committees and inquiries and reports that have implications for the public service. The report of the Committee on the Civil Service under the chairmanship of Lord Fulton is one example.

The book aims to break new ground. There are some excellent works which touch upon its subject but none of them provides the same concentration upon practical issues. For example, there is a large number of books about management theory and about management techniques as usually applied to business and commerce. The book provides relevant coverage of these matters, but concentrates on their use in the public service, paying particular attention to the implications of the political environment for their employment. The book also considers if the recent interest in management ideas and techniques is likely to be a passing phase or a permanent feature of public administration in this country.

It is hoped that this book will be useful for students preparing for examinations in public administration for CNAA degrees at polytechnics and other institutions, and for the degrees of the increasing number of universities which teach public administration as a subject. It is also designed for students preparing for degrees and other examinations in politics and in British Government, and it should also prove helpful to students preparing for professional examinations in local government, for the examinations of the Institute of Chartered Secretaries and Administrators, and for management examinations generally.

Finally, it is hoped that the book will be of assistance to those who are interested generally in the government of the United Kingdom and in the scope for improving the quality of the service it provides.

Some of the material for this book was assembled for classes and lectures organized by the National and Local Government Officers' Association for their members preparing for professional examinations and attending management courses. I am grateful to the Education Department of the National and Local Government Officers' Association for asking me to undertake this work. The Association naturally bears no responsibility for any of the views advanced in this book.

Acknowledgements

I am grateful for advice and encouragement in writing this book from Mr William Thornhill, Senior Lecturer in Political Theory and Institutions in the University of Sheffield, and Consulting Editor of the series of books on Government and Administration of which this volume is a member. I should also like to thank my publisher, Mr James Shepherd, for his help and guidance. None of the organizations or individuals mentioned above or in this book is responsible for any of the views expressed. They are my own.

J.B.B.
March 1978
London

1
Management ideas and techniques in central and local government

There is an increasing interest in management ideas and techniques among government ministers, elected and appointed members of local and other public authorities, and among officials throughout the public service. Indeed, everyone who takes an interest in public affairs will have heard or read of such innovations as: 'think tanks' and planning units, planning, programming and budgeting systems, management by objectives, accountable management, computers and data processing, operational research, the employment of management consultants and job satisfaction studies.

The purpose of this book is to describe the use that has been made of these and other management ideas and techniques, and to make a preliminary assessment of their value. This assessment is much needed. We have sufficient experience of the application of these new ideas to begin to know how useful they are. We can start to determine whether they are a passing fashion, with a few simple lessons now well learnt, or if they have a continuing and expanding contribution to make to the efficiency and effectiveness of the public services of this country.

WHAT IS MANAGEMENT?

Definitions of management abound. It is sufficient for our present purposes to say that the study of management is the systematic examination of the ways in which groups of people organize themselves to achieve goals by co-operative action. The purpose of this examination is to try to develop ideas and suggestions for improving the efficiency and effectiveness of such co-operative activity, whether it be the running of a government department, a local authority, a hospital, a business firm or indeed any other organized group.

In carrying out this examination, students of management consider and analyse successful practical experience and relevant theoretical ideas. They consider, for example, what lessons can be distilled from the experience of

1

successful managers and from organizations that are well run. They also consider the application of theoretical ideas to practical problems. Many of these theoretical ideas derive from other subjects. For example, students of management have considered how far the theoretical ideas about human motivation which have been produced by psychologists can successfully be applied to the problems of running government departments and business firms.

The study of management is therefore both a descriptive study, concerned with explaining the nature of co-operative activity, and a prescriptive study, concerned with suggesting how that activity can most effectively be conducted. It is easy to slide from a description of how a particular organization is run to the suggestion that every organization should be run in the same way. In fact, description and prescription are logically separate activities. The study of management is particularly vulnerable to the temptation to take methods that have been successful in one organization, and to apply them to other organizations without considering carefully enough whether they can be transplanted successfully. There is a special temptation to take ideas that have been successful in industry and commerce and to assume that they will work in the very different political environment of the public service.

The study of management in the sense described here is a relatively recent innovation. It is only within the last 25 years or so, that large numbers of people have specialized as management experts, and have made their careers either in whole or in part in advising on management practices, as management consultants, or teaching future and present managers in colleges and universities, or being directly employed as management experts under such titles as work study engineers, operational research specialists, and personnel managers.

Management specialists claim that their subject is able to make a contribution to the solution of all kinds of management problems, from the most general and large scale problems, such as the structure of central government, down to such small scale but important problems as the organization of typing pools. Examples of all types of problems will be considered in this book.

MANAGEMENT IN THE PUBLIC SERVICE

The main reason for the increasing interest in the application of management ideas and techniques in the public service is the hope that their employment will improve the quality of the services provided by government departments, local authorities, public services like hospitals, and by other public bodies. Many of these bodies were set up in the nineteenth or early twentieth centuries. Many of them were originally designed for the regulation of economic and social activities conducted by business and commerce and most of the rest were concerned with the provision of defence and law and order. For example, among the responsibilities of government departments in the nineteenth century were the regulation of the railway companies, the development of company law and the collection of taxes. Local authorities were mainly concerned with the administration of laws relating to public health, weights and measures, and with building and maintaining roads and other civil engineering work.

These responsibilities have tended to become more complex in the twentieth century, especially since the end of the Second World War; for example, the regulation of dangerous substances has now to encompass not only poison and explosives, as it has done for the last hundred years, but also atomic waste and other hazardous substances that are used in modern industry. And, to give another example, taxation is now vastly more complicated than when it consisted of customs and excise duties, the local rates and income tax at a few shillings in the pound.

In addition to the increasing complexity of traditional and other long-standing responsibilities, public authorities have now to provide more services directly and to run much larger organizations. For example, public authorities are responsible for providing a full-scale health service, and for organizing a comprehensive employment and retraining service. Other public authorities are concerned with research into and procurement of the most complicated modern aircraft, missiles and ships for the fighting services. Other authorities—public corporations—are responsible for running the nationalized industries, which provide such vital goods and services as coal, steel and transport. Government departments and other public institutions, such as the Bank Of England, are responsible for collecting statistical information, making forecasts and advising ministers on the most effective budgetary, fiscal and monetary measures for reducing unemployment, restraining inflation and securing economic growth.

These are formidable responsibilities. The public authorities and the public services which operate them are many in kind and number. They include traditional institutions like government departments, such as the Treasury; local authorities, such as the Greater London Council; public corporations, such as the National Coal Board; and bodies which cannot readily be categorized into any pigeon hole, such as the Northern Ireland Housing Executive. The services which staff these authorities are recruited, managed, paid and superannuated under a wide variety of terms and conditions. They include the traditional Civil Service, which comprises not only the legions of officials that man the local offices of the departments of Health and Social Security and Inland Revenue, but also the keepers of the collections in the national museums and those who constitute the Secret Service. The public services also include, to give further examples, doctors working on contract with the health service, the staff of the Racecourse Betting and Control Board and the many thousands of people who work for local authorities up and down the country.

All these authorities and all those services come within the public sector, and about 7.4 million out of the country's working population of 26.2 million are employed within them. The development of these authorities and services is illustrate by the following figures. The size of the non-industrial Civil Service for the years between 1914 and 1976, excluding the Post Office which counted as a government department until 1969, was as follows:

1914	1935	1956	1966	1976
60,000	137,000	385,000	430,000	563,000

Note that the figures for 1914, 1935, 1956 come from F.M.G. Willson: *The Organization of British Central Government 1914-1964*, edited by D.N. Chester. The other figures come from *Civil Service Statistics 1977*, published by the Civil Service Department.

The non-industrial civil service is however, only part of the total public sector, as Fig 1.1 shows.

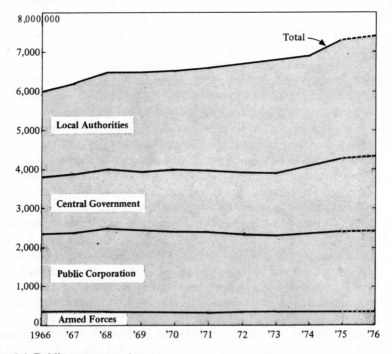

Fig. 1.1 Public sector employees
Source: *J. Rogaly, 'How the monster bureaucracy deceives us', The Financial Times 15 February, 1977*

As a final indication of the increasing size and complexity of government, and the effect of its activities on the lives of the people, it should be noted that in 1900 Parliament added 272 pages to the statute book; in 1930 it added 845 pages; in 1950 it added 1000 pages; and in 1974 over 2000 pages of new laws were added to the corpus of the country's legislation.

The management problems summarized in these statistics are compounded by the fact that most of the authorities and services responsible for dealing with them were set up to deal with different and perhaps easier work. The Civil Service, for example, is in many ways a product of the nineteenth century, because it was in that century that the fundamental principles of its recruitment and organization were laid down. Great changes have been made in recruitment, training and methods of staff management to deal with modern problems. But there is always the difficulty, in all public authorities and public services, of combining the best and still relevant practices of the past with the introduction of new methods. A balance has continually to be struck between experience and innovation, and one of the main reasons for the growing interest in the study of management in the public authorities and services of the United Kingdom has been the belief that they are insufficiently up-to-date in their institutions, their methods of work, and in the skills, training and management of their staff.

CONCLUSIONS AND SUMMARY

(1) The study of management consists of the systematic examination of the ways in which groups of people organize themselves to achieve goals by co-operative action. The purpose of this examination is to try to develop ideas, suggestions and techniques for improving the efficiency and effectiveness of such co-operative action. These ideas, suggestions and techniques are designed to be, in different degrees, relevant to all kinds of co-operative action, including the running of social clubs, business and commercial organizations, and public authorities.

(2) There has been a particular interest in seeing how far managerial ideas can be applied to public authorities and public services because their responsibilities have expanded so greatly in the twentieth century, particularly in the last 20 years; because their methods may be insufficiently up-to-date to deal with these new and enlarged responsibilities; and because important organizational changes have recently been made in the public services. These developments present many problems which the study of management may help to overcome.

2
Four reports concerning management in central and local government

The belief that the application of management ideas and techniques had a great deal to contribute to improving the efficiency of management in central and local government was very much part of the conventional wisdom of the late 1960s and early 1970s. This belief had a variety of sources. At the most general level was the idea, widely publicized in Lord Snow's Rede lectures (1959) *The Two Cultures and the Scientific Revolution,* that British education, and hence the typical British approach to problems, tended to be literary, innumerate and amateur, instead of scientific, numerate and professional. The British approach was further alleged to be insufficiently attentive to the application of new ideas and knowledge to modern problems. At a more specific level, and as an example of the kind of modern knowledge that should be applied to British problems, many argued that one of the reasons why the United States seemed to be economically more successful and competent than the United Kingdom, was because management was taught and studied in universities and special business schools, and because a deliberate attempt was made to apply management principles in business and government. This belief led, for example, to the establishment of management schools associated with British universities, the first of which, the London Graduate Business School and the Manchester Business School, were set up in 1965.

This interest in management ideas was reflected in a number of reports about central and local government published between 1967 and 1972. The reports were: *The Report of the Committee on the Civil Service* under the chairmanship of Lord Fulton (Cmnd. 3638) (1968); the White Paper on the *Reorganization of Central Government* (Cmnd. 4506) (1970); *The Report of the Committee on the Management of Local Government* under the chairmanship of Sir John Maud (1967); the Report of a Study Group under the chairmanship of Mr M.A. Bains on *The New Local Authorities: Management and Structure* (1972).

It is important to take account of these reports because they set the scene for the way that management developments were introduced and explain why certain aspects of management science and certain techniques received more attention than others.

CENTRAL GOVERNMENT

The two major reports for central government were those of the Committee on the Civil Service under the chairmanship of Lord Fulton, which reported in 1968, and the White Paper *The Reorganization of Central Government* that was published in 1970.

The Fulton Committee was appointed in 1966 and was asked 'to examine the structure, recruitment and management, including training of the Home Civil Service and to make recommendations'. The background to the setting-up of the Committee was a general malaise about the performance of the Home Civil Service in the post-war period. It was generally admitted that it had considerable achievements to its credit. The framework and operational machinery of the Welfare State had been successfully introduced. Reforms had been introduced in the management and control of public expenditure following the report of the Committee chaired by Lord Plowden on *The Control of Public Expenditure* (Cmnd. 1432) (1961). This had stressed the importance of taking account of the long-term and resource implications of government programmes, and of their dependence upon the development of the economy as well as underlining the continuing value of the traditional year-to-year accounting contained in the annual budget and estimates presented to Parliament. There had also been developments in management including a greater attention to organization and methods work, the use of work study techniques, and the application of computers. These changes had led to improvements in methods of grading work, simplifications in office procedures, and more efficient ways of undertaking clerical jobs and work in Royal Ordnance Factories, Her Majesty's Dockyards and other government industrial establishments. But in spite of these improvements there was a general belief that the Civil Service had failed to rise to the management challenge, particularly in the development of large-scale government technological projects, several of which, such as the TSR 2 aircraft and the Blue Streak missile, had been cancelled after vast sums had been spent upon them; that the relatively disappointing economic performance of the country must in some way have been the fault of central government; and that personnel management in the Civil Service was generally behind the times.

The Fulton Committee produced a report which echoed this diagnosis. Its general theme is summed up in the opening sentences of the summary of its main findings. 'The Home Civil Service today is still fundamentally the product of the nineteenth-century philosophy of the Northcote-Trevelyan Report. The problems it faces are those of the second half of the twentieth century.' [1] The Committee made four major criticisms. First, they said that the Civil Service was not applying itself to the right task. Most of the top posts were held by 'generalist' administrators, expert in parliamentary procedure and in advising ministers on the political implications of particular policies. These were valuable skills, but they needed to be complemented by a greater knowledge and understanding of the scientific, economic and social problems facing the country in the latter part of the twentieth century. The Committee believed that, if the top jobs in the Civil Service were filled by people who had a knowledge of these problems, then the work of the Civil Service would be more closely directed to the needs of the country today.

Secondly, the Committee claimed that the Civil Service was wrongly organized. The basic form of organization was designed for dealing effectively with parliamentary questions, ministerial correspondence, the application of detailed rules to particular cases and other traditional work. Departments therefore tended to consist of a series of relatively independent hierarchies of officials specializing in their own particular segment of work, paying great attention to detail and to their own segment of administrative reality. But the loose co-ordination of these structures prevented the grasping of the full significance and implications of the problems that confronted modern government and there were too few examples of more appropriate structures as, for example, interdisciplinary project teams formed in order to apply all relevant knowledge to the solution of a problem. Thirdly, as implied by the previous two points, the Civil Service was failing to use its resources of scientific and technological manpower properly and fourthly, and more widely, failing to manage all its human resources effectively. People tended to join a particular class of the Civil Service at entry—administrative, executive, scientific officer, tax inspectorate[2]—and then, with this label around their necks for their entire official lives, plod their way up the particular hierarchies that were the near exclusive preserves of their particular class.

The Fulton Committee made a series of recommendations to overcome these defects. These recommendations were founded on what the Committee called 'a simple guiding principle for the future. The Service must continuously review the tasks it is called on to perform; it should then think out what new skills and kinds of men are needed and how these men can be found, trained and deployed'.[3] To give effect to this principle the Committee proposed first, that a new Civil Service Department should be set up to concentrate on all general questions of Civil Service management and its reform. It should be responsible for the traditional Treasury management function of pay and conditions of service; but it should also spearhead the changes that the Fulton Committee thought were necessary and act as the continuing spur and encouragement to management improvement throughout the Civil Service. Secondly, all Civil Service classes should be abolished and replaced by 'a single unified grading structure covering all civil servants from top to bottom in the non-industrial part of the Service.

The correct grading of each post should be determined by job evaluation'.[4] In other words, instead of categorizing people when they came into the Civil Service by the general kind of work they were fitted to do, all jobs should be individually evaluated and all people individually appraised. Careful personnel management would then ensure the fitting of round pegs into round holes on a Service-wide basis.

Thirdly, this process of staff management and development would require considerable investment in personnel management in order that more should be known about the interests and capacities of each individual civil servant, and that each should feel his career was being individually managed and developed. Accordingly, proposals were made for a considerable expansion in personnel management and training and for the setting up of a Civil Service Training College. Finally, the Committee proposed that each department should have a management services unit with highly qualified and experienced staff; that it should have a planning unit and a senior policy adviser 'to look to and prepare for the future and to ensure that present policy decisions are taken with as full a recognition as possible of likely future developments';[5] and that the work of departments should be organized in accordance with the principles of accountable management. 'This means the clear allocation of responsibility and authority to accountable units with defined objectives. It also means a corresponding addition to the system of government accounting'.[6]

The Government accepted many of the recommendations of the Fulton Committee and a number of changes were introduced both immediately and over a period of time, including the setting-up of the Civil Service Department and the Civil Service College. Some of these changes will be noted later. Indeed, the consequences of the Fulton Report are even yet not fully worked out within central government. However, in 1970, the Government issued a White Paper *The Reorganization of Central Government*. Although this report was not designed as a successor to the Fulton Report, its thinking was formed by the same general principles of management and its recommendations complemented the ideas that Fulton had put forward.

First, the White Paper set out the principles by which the extent of government responsibilities was to be determined and its functions distributed between the departments of government. It proposed that there should be a 'rigorous analysis of existing and suggested government policies, actions and expenditure'[7] to test whether they accorded with the Government's strategic aims, whether they were suitable for government action at all, and to set them out in order of priority. This analysis would yield some dozen major blocs of work, each of which would become the responsibility of a large government department, merged from two or three smaller departments. The White Paper proposed that the emphasis should be on the 'grouping of functions together in departments with a wide span so as to provide a series of fields of unified policy'.[8] The report stated that this was a continuation of the trend which had unified four service departments into one Ministry of Defence in 1964 and produced one Foreign and Commonwealth Office out of the three previously separate departments for Foreign, Commonwealth and Colonial affairs.

The White Paper said that these large departments would offer a capacity to propose and implement a single strategy for clearly defined and accepted objectives; the ability to explore and resolve conflicts in policy formulation and executive decision within 'the line of management rather than by inter-departmental compromise';[9] a capacity to manage and control large 'resource consuming programmes in terms both of formulation and administration within departmental boundaries making possible in turn more effective delegation of executive tasks'[10] and the 'easier application of analytic techniques within large and self-contained blocs of work and expenditure'.[11] The White Paper also said that a few major departments, each responsible for a clear and obvious function of government, would be easier for the public to understand and would consequently improve open government and communication between the departments of state and the public affected by their activities.

The application of this principle both immediately following the publication of the White Paper and in the next few years led to the concentration of government work in a relatively small number of departments. In 1956 there were 24 ministers in charge of separate departments. By 1972 there were only 15, and the major departments were as follows: the Foreign and Commonwealth Office; Ministry of Defence; Department of Trade and Industry; Department of Employment; Department of Posts and Telecommunications; Ministry of Agriculture; Fisheries and Food; Department of the Environment; Department of Education and Science; Department of Health and Social Security; Home Office; Scottish Office; Welsh Office; and the three central departments, i.e. the Civil Service Department, the Cabinet Office and the Treasury together with the Inland Revenue and Customs and Excise whose policy was decided by the Treasury and who were responsible for tax collection.

The White Paper also proposed two particular mechanisms for making sure that future policies and programmes were rigorously appraised. First, a Central Policy Review Staff was set up in the Cabinet Office under the direction of Lord Rothschild who was by training and in early life a university teacher of biology but later entered the Shell Group of companies, finally retiring as research co-ordinator. The Policy Review Staff was set up as an integral element of the Cabinet Office to be at the disposal of the Government as a whole. Under the supervision of the Prime Minister, it was designed to work for ministers collectively. Its task was to enable them to make better policy decisions by assisting them to work out the implications of their basic strategy in terms of policies in specific areas; to establish the relative priorities to be given to the different sectors of their programme as a whole; to identify those areas of policy in which new choices can be exercised; and to ensure that the underlying implications for alternative courses of action were fully analysed and considered. In addition, the Central Policy Review Staff was charged with comparing what the Government was actually doing with what it had set out to do when it was elected. The need for such comparisons arises from the day-to-day pressures on ministers of coping with succeeding crises, of answering parliamentary questions and guiding legislation through the House, of meeting pressure groups and delegations, and of dealing with their own constituency business. In the hurly burly of this energetic life it is easy to lose sight of the main objectives, and the Policy Review Staff was charged with reminding ministers what their goals originally were and what progress they had made in achieving them.

Secondly, the White Paper said that there was a need for regular reviews of Government programmes.

These reviews would be a natural extension of the Public Expenditure Survey system and would support present departmental submissions in the Public Expenditure Survey cycle....they will certainly involve a greater emphasis on the definition of objectives and the expressing of programmes so far as possible in output terms; and the presentation and examination of alternative programmes will be of great importance.[12]

In the House of Commons on 14 January 1971 the Government announced how they were to carry out this intention. They proposed a system called Programme Analysis and Review. The basic idea was that certain of each department's expenditure programmes would be selected for a detailed examination each year. This examination would start with the objective that the programme was designed to achieve; examine the alternative programmes by which it might be attained, including the one either adopted or recommended by the department; would consider the 'outputs' or results of each of these alternatives and make recommendation and conclusions as to which was the best of the alternative programmes for achieving each objective and whether even the best programme represented a justifiable expenditure of resources.

Taken together, the Fulton Report and White Paper *The Reorganization of Central Government* represent a clear managerialist philosophy. The essence of this philosophy is the belief that government objectives should be clearly stated; that organizations should be designed specifically to achieve them; and that, so far as central government is concerned, these organizations should be large departments of government each specializing in a major area of government work. Within each department, however, there should be considerable structural variation to take account of the different aspects of the work. Thus, in addition to the traditional office hierarchy, there should be project teams and inter-disciplinary planning units. In particular, where the work has no direct political significance, as in the case of the procurement of many military supplies and the purchase and maintenance of government buildings, the Fulton Committee suggested that consideration should be given to 'hiving off' to special organizations. These organizations would be freed from having to pay attention to irrelevant political considerations and would be able to concentrate on managerial work on business and commercial lines.

The philosophy also required that special attention should be given within the government service to personnel management to select, train and develop officials with the right blend of modern skills to direct and manage these new departments and other organizations. Finally, work would be conducted on the principle of 'accountable management' which meant that every department, division, section and individual would have a specific aim which it was their duty to achieve, and in the achievement of which their performance would be measured and assessed. In this way, the general and specific objectives of the government service as a whole would be achieved and, by the careful work of the Central Policy Review Staff, by Programme Analysis and Review and by other analytical units and techniques, constant attention would be given to comparing the manifesto on which the Government was elected with the work that departments were actually doing and, within that work, to ensure that each programme was both necessary and effectively executed.

This was indeed a grand design. It was, in fact, a comprehensive programme for the reorganization of departments and for a new approach of civil servants to their work. It might best be illustrated by the following quotation from the report of the Fulton Committee's management consultancy group published as Volume 2 of their Report. This sums up what the Committee felt was wrong with the way in which work had previously been approached in the Civil Service, and how they thought it should be approached in future

> ...we regard it as a valid criticism that few Administrators saw themselves as managers, i.e. as concerned with organization, directing staff, planning the progress of work, setting standards of attainment and measuring results, reviewing procedures and trying to quantify direct courses of action. This in part was because they tend to think of themselves as advisers on policy to people above them rather than as managers of the administrative machine below them.[13]

LOCAL GOVERNMENT

The first comprehensive examination of the management of local authorities was made by a committee under the Chairmanship of Sir John Maud which reported in 1967. The Committee's main argument was that the management of most local authorities was deficient because there were too many committees and departments, each dealing with a specialized aspect of the authority's work, but too inward looking, too concentrated upon over-specialized detail, insufficiently co-ordinated, and consequently failing to look to the general needs of the people within the authority's area. This splintering of local government administration into a plethora of separate committees was both cause and consequence of the elected members' concentration upon detailed matters of administration. Too often they sought to undertake the detailed work for which local government officers were in theory employed, and too seldom did they concern themselves with the general needs of the authorities to which they had been elected.

To overcome these deficiencies, the Committee proposed the introduction of a management board of elected members with responsibility for formulating policy objectives, taking executive decisions and co-ordinating and supervising the work of the authority. The introduction of the management board would facilitate a reduction in the number of committees within each authority, and it was proposed that those remaining should concentrate on deliberative and representative functions; making recommendations to the management board on policy objectives, the means to attain them and upon the progress of plans and programmes. Generally speaking, however, they would not have executive powers, since these would be exercised by the management board. Furthermore, a strict line should be drawn between the activities of elected members and local government officers. The Maud Committee proposed that the management board would be served by a new principal officer possessing authority over the other chief officers and responsible for the efficiency and co-ordination of the authority's work. All detailed routine administration would be delegated to officers.

The Maud Committee's basic idea was, therefore, that the elected members of the authority should concentrate upon the approval and monitoring of broad policy, and upon their deliberative and representative role in connection with its formulation and implementation, while the officers, reorganized under the new principal officer, would be responsible for running the council under the authority of the management board. Each authority would thereby become, it was hoped, a co-ordinated and purposeful organization, instead of a series of more or less separate departments loosely pulled together as a by-product of the Clerk's general responsibilities for legal matters and the finance committee's and treasurer's interest in and responsibility for the authority's budget and the audit of expenditure.

The Report of the Maud Committee was soon followed by the bringing to a head of the 50-year debate about the need for a fundamental reorganization of the structure of British local government. The main argument of the reformers was that there were too many local authorities, many of which were held to be too small to provide efficiently and effectively the growing range of services required by a modern community. This, it was claimed, was the root cause of the progressive removal of many responsibilities from local government to other authorities, such as nation-alized industries, and to the increasing assistance from and control by central government. The currency of local government was thereby devalued, and the declining interest of the ordinary citizen was measured by his increasing unwillingness to vote in local government elections, or to take much interest in the work of local authorities with the notable exception of council house allocation.

Examination of this problem culminated in the work of the Royal Commission on Local Government in England from 1966–1969, under the chairmanship of Lord Redcliffe-Maud (as Sir John Maud had by now become). Considerable discussion and negotiation by successive govern-ments with local authority associations and other interested parties led finally to a reorganized system, differing from the Commission's detailed proposals, though influenced by many of their ideas.

This was introduced in England in 1974 following the Local Government Act 1972. The main aim of this reorganization was to reduce the number of local authorities. In England there had been, outside London, 79 county boroughs, exercising all local government responsibilities, and 48 adminis-trative counties with duties divided between the county authorities and nearly 1100 district councils and 10,000 parish authorities. In their place, a new structure was introduced with six metropolitan counties covering the main conurbations outside London, viz. Tyne and Wear, West Midlands, Merseyside, Greater Manchester, West Yorkshire and South Yorkshire, and containing a total of 36 metropolitan districts. The rest of the country consisted of 39 non-metropolitan counties with powers divided between the county authorities and 296 non-metropolitan districts. A somewhat similar concentration of authorities had been introduced in London with the setting-up of the Greater London Council and its 32 Greater London boroughs in 1965. Arrangements in line with the general principle of reducing the number of authorities were introduced in Wales under the 1972 Act and in Scotland under the Local Government (Scotland) Act 1973, whereby Scotland was divided for local government purposes into nine regions and three island areas. Within the regions there were 53 second tier authorities.

The setting-up of these new and larger authorities naturally concentrated attention on the problem of how they were to be managed. The ideas of the Maud Committee were therefore taken up for re-examination and adapta-tion to meet the needs of the new authorities in a report on *The New Local Authorities, Management and Structure* (1972). This was the report of a Study Group under the chairmanship of Mr M.A. Bains, the Clerk of Kent County Council, which had been appointed jointly by the Secretary of State for the Environment and the local authority associations to examine management structures in local government. The Bains report accepted the general diagnosis and recommendations of the Maud report. But its proposals were set out in language and ideas which bore the imprint of management ideas and techniques which had become more powerful and influential forces since the Maud Committee had reported some five years before. The watchword of the Bains report was the 'corporate approach'. This approach was explained in the following way.

The ingrained departmental approach to management (in local government) is no longer appropriate. We urge authorities to adopt a corporate approach to their affairs in order to ensure that their resources are most effectively deployed. They have an overall interest in the economic, cultural and physical well-being of their communities and should set up consultative machinery for frequent discussions with other local authorities and statutory organizations.[14]

To give effect to this corporate approach the Committee proposed a number of innovations. First, there should be a policy and resources committee of elected members, which should be responsible for formulating and carrying out the overall plan for the community, for setting appropriate objectives and priorities, for co-ordinating and controlling their implementation, and for monitoring and reviewing the performance of the authority in their achievement. Secondly, and in order that the policy and resources committee should deal only with major matters, the more routine questions were to be handled by three resource sub-committees dealing with finance, manpower and land and there should be a fourth sub-committee on performance review. Thirdly, in addition to the above committees, authorities should reorganize their committee system in the light of their overall plan for the community's development. The Bains Report agreed with the Maud Committee's support for the reduction in the number of committees and, while saying that each authority should determine its committee structure for itself, remarked that:

After considering their main objectives [many authorities] have divided their work into spheres of activity, each with its own objectives and programmes for meeting those objectives. Committees have been made responsible for each programme and for the allocation of resources within it…. The advantage of building the committee structure on this basis is that it becomes directly linked to the main needs and objectives of the authority. It encourages a corporate rather than departmental approach so that each programme area committee can call upon and be serviced by the skills and experience of a number of different departments. The heads of the individual departments will, of course, have the right of direct access to the committee.[15]

At the official level, the Committee recommended that:

Each authority should appoint a Chief Executive who should be of outstanding managerial ability and personality. His role would be very different from that of the traditional Clerk. Free of all departmental responsibilities, he would clearly be the head of the paid officials; he would lead a team of chief officers to secure overall co-ordination and control and, in many ways, would set the whole tone and tempo of the authority.[16]

Furthermore, it was proposed that the chief executive should be the leader of a management team of principal chief officers (which would not necessarily include the heads of all the departments in the authority) and, through his responsibility to the policy and resources committee, he was to be the authority's principal adviser on matters of general policy. 'As such it is his responsibility to secure co-ordination and advice on the forward planning of objectives and services and to lead the management team in securing a corporate approach to the affairs of the authority generally'.[17]

Finally, the study group emphasized the need for improvements in personnel management, including recruitment, training and career development and also expressed their support for the further development of management services in local government. The study group reviewed the various management services available to local authorities and mentioned, in particular, the criticism that local authorities had usually given too much attention to operating the services for which they were responsible and too little to planning them. The study group accordingly stressed the contribution that might be made by a corporate planning group, comprising the deputies of all departments of the authority and which could act on behalf of the team of chief officers as the focal point for the identification, formulation and review of objectives; the evaluation of short-term programmes aimed at achieving these objectives; the consideration of priorities within those programmes as between different services; the formulation of proposals for linking presentation of objectives, programmes and budgets; the development of longer term plans; and the monitoring and review of progress as against plans.

It is clear from this account that the Maud and Bains reports were based on much the same managerial philosophy as lay behind the report of the Fulton Committee and the White Paper *The Reorganization of Central Government*. There is the same concern with the importance of setting clear objectives; the same insistence upon having a structure which reflects those objectives and facilitates their achievement; and there is the same claim that existing structures, procedures, methods and approach need considerable modification.

The traditional departmental approach to administration in local government was condemned as focusing too much attention on the details of administration rather than upon objectives and performance. But no single blueprint was suggested for all local authorities, just as Fulton avoided setting blueprints for central government departments. The Bains report, for example, recognized that one of the results of implementing the study group's proposals would be that in many authorities the committee and departmental structures would no longer coincide. In some cases, there would be one department clearly serving one committee. But in other cases the Committee recommended that it should be the responsibility of the chief executive and his management team to set up the necessary interdisciplinary working groups to serve the relevant programme committees. They said:

> This combination of the traditional 'vertical' structure and the 'horizontal' interdisciplinary working group is known as a matrix form of organization. This type of structure can operate both through programme teams giving advice and service to committees concerned with the general administration of particular programmes, or at the more detailed level of execution through teams working on specific projects. The membership of teams at either level can be amended or supplemented, new teams can be set up and existing ones disbanded as circumstances require. Herein lies one of the great advantages of this matrix system of management. By its nature it is flexible and adaptive, unlike the rigid bureaucracy which we suggest that it should replace.[18]

Other variants in organization were suggested in the report *The New Scottish Local Authorities: Organization and Management Structures* (1973) and, while broadly in line with the managerialist philosophy of the Bains report it suggested a different form of organization for planning; the executive office.

> We favour the concept of the 'executive office' whereby the chief executive is assisted in his tasks of co-ordinating policy planning, monitoring the effectiveness of the authority's programmes and managing the central services by two or three officials of chief officer status. These will be a director of finance, a director of administration and, in the largest authorities of all, a director of policy planning. These offices could be designated as deputy chief executives.[19]

MANAGEMENT AS CONCEIVED IN THE FOUR REPORTS

The four reports were alike in a final respect. Although the detailed ideas and recommendations they contained might appear on first inspection to provide specific and comprehensive guidance on how to run central government departments and local authorities they were, in fact, reports on first principles with illustrative examples.

All the detailed work of applying these principles to the operation of central and local government remained to be done and it will be clear from the above analysis that if central government departments and local authorities were to operate on the lines proposed in these four reports then special attention would have to be paid to the following activities:

   (i) forecasting, setting objectives and planning;
   (ii) the definition of the problems that need to be solved to achieve these objectives;

(iii) the search for various solutions that might be offered to these problems;

(iv) the determination of the best or most acceptable solutions;

(v) the securing of agreement that such solutions should be implemented;

(vi) the preparation and issue of instructions for carrying out the agreed solutions;

(vii) the execution of the solutions;

(viii) the devising of an auditing process for checking whether such solutions are properly carried out and, if they are, that they do in fact solve the problems for which they were devised;

(ix) the design, introduction and maintenance of the organizational structures which are most appropriate for these activities;

(x) the selection, training, development and management of the appropriate staff.

Faced with the task of improving the efficiency and effectiveness with which these activities were conducted in central and local government, all concerned—ministers, elected members and officials alike—looked for particular, though not for exclusive, assistance from the students and practitioners of 'management science'. And these experts naturally saw the possibility of helping to implement these four reports as a prime opportunity to demonstrate their professional competence at a time when public interest in their work had never been higher.

The succeeding chapters will therefore discuss the application of management ideas and techniques under the following headings: forecasting, setting objectives and planning; analysis, value and choice; organization; personnel and audit review and control.

Nevertheless, we must note from the start that there are difficulties in the conception of management that underly the four reports described above. By presenting management as largely concerned with the solving of problems, it may suggest that problems solved once so remain, and that perfect systems of management can be developed and introduced. As this book shows, there is no such finality. The tasks and responsibilities of public administration are constantly changing, and the study of management can never utter the last word on how they should be conducted.

CONCLUSIONS AND SUMMARY

(1) Interest in management ideas and techniques in central and local government in the United Kingdom was fostered by four reports:

(a) Central government

The Fulton report on *The Civil Service* (1968);

The White Paper on *The Reorganization of Central Government* (1970).

(b) Local government

The Maud report on *The Management of Local Government* (1967);

The Bains report on *The New Local Authorities: Management and Structure* (1972).

(2) These reports presented management as concerned mainly with the following activities: setting objectives, defining problems to be overcome to achieve them; searching for solutions; selecting the best or most acceptable solution; securing agreement to its implementation; issuing instructions; executing solutions; auditing and reviewing; designing appropriate organizational structures for these activities; selecting, training and managing appropriate staff.

(3) In order to improve the efficiency and effectiveness with which these activities were conducted in central and local government, ministers, elected members and officials turned for help to the management experts.

3
Forecasting, setting objectives and planning

Forecasting, setting objectives and planning have been central ideas in management in central and local government in the last 15 years. They are not new ideas. Forecasting and planning are obviously involved in running any organization, and attention has always been paid to them in the sense that a view must be taken on what the future will hold and plans made to continue existing activities or to start new ones. What has been new in the last 15 years has been the emphasis upon trying to forecast the likely demand for and availability of resources to supply public services in central government and local authorities, to set objectives in the light of these forecasts, and to make plans and programmes for achieving these objectives as effectively and efficiently as possible.

These changes have a number of implications. First, if more attention is to be paid to forecasting, setting objectives and making plans, then more people will have to be employed in these activities, and they will need the relevant skills and expertise to carry them out. This has led to the increasing employment in central and to some extent in local government of experts drawn from such fields as economics, sociology, accountancy, statistics and other social and natural sciences.

Secondly, changes will be required in organizational arrangements to bring the forecasters, and those responsible for determining and evaluating the various means of meeting the objectives that might be adopted, into the centre of their organizations. Planning staff can no longer be looked upon as backroom experts producing interesting studies incidental to the main purposes of the organization. Instead, such experts must be closer to the heart of policy making and the monopoly over this process previously enjoyed by general administrators in central government and specialist officers with executive responsibilities in local government must to some extent be shared.

Thirdly, changes in techniques will be needed, especially in the methods of presenting and analysing forecasts and objectives, in the plans made to achieve them and in the monitoring of performance. In particular, changes will be needed in the way that financial information is analysed and deployed in order to show the cost of the plans and programmes being carried out by the organization as well as the traditional analysis of the cost of the goods and services purchased by the organization.

If a complete system of forecasting, objective setting and planning had been introduced in central and local government in line with the ideas of management theorists of the 1960s and early 1970s it would have taken the form of a comprehensive scheme of corporate planning centred upon a system of 'output budgeting' or a 'planning-programming-budgeting' system.

THE PRINCIPLES OF OUTPUT BUDGETING AND PPBS

A typical system of output budgeting or a planning-programming-budgeting system (PPBS) normally involves the following activities and processes. The key terms are in italics.

First, the authority's *objectives* must be determined and set out as a series of programmes. The series of programmes or *programme structure* for a local education authority might be nursery education, primary education, secondary education and higher education. These programmes might be expressed in terms of *strategic programmes* for the next, say, seven years, *medium term programmes* for the period up to three or four years ahead, and *short term programmes* for the next year. Each *programme level* will be logically connected; the second deduced from the first and the third from the second. And each will be expressed in terms of resources—money, staff, and other relevant factors—directed to the achievement of *goals*. These resource expressions are known as *programme budgets*. The short-term programme will usually take the form of an *operating budget* or annual estimate. As such it will conform to the traditional accounting format of the organization and will often be expressed in *input* terms, e.g. wages and salaries, cost of purchases. But for management purposes it will also be expressed in *output* terms, e.g. hours of tuition in primary schools. These operating budgets will also be expressed in the form of *targets*, i.e. they will state the objectives of the staff to whom the financial allocation has been made in *performance terms* (i.e. terms that can be measured). For example, they will state that the objective of the nursery education division will include the production of x new nursery schools, y new teachers, and so on. The division will therefore be judged on its actual measured achievement. This usually (though not necessarily) implies that the authority as a whole will be organized in a way that coheres with its programmes, e.g. in the instance of the educational programme of a local authority, an education department with divisions for nursery education, primary education, and so on, and not a school building division, a teachers division, etc. This system of allocating the work of an organization into specific targets is often called *management by objectives*. Thus management by objectives can be thought of as a means by which the authority's programmes are broken down into manageable tasks for particular units with measurable targets.

Changes in the environment, and success or failure in meeting objectives, will feed back into changes in the programme structure. Thus taking one year with another, changes will be made in the allocation of resources to particular programmes. These will be the result of rigorous *analyses* (often called *systems analyses* because of their concern with the complete cycle of planning, execution and control) of the nature of the objectives, the problems to be overcome, the *alternatives available* and the best way to carry out the selected solution. In carrying out these analyses there must be a rigorous setting of *priorities* between and within programmes and attention must be paid to the difference between *effective* solutions, i.e. those that solve problems, and *efficient* solutions, i.e. those where the ratio of inputs to outputs meets prescribed standards. *Systems analyses* will comprise:

(*a*) *cost/effectiveness* analyses of each alternative within each programme to determine the most efficient set of alternatives for each programme's goals; and

(*b*) *cost/benefit* analyses to determine whether even the most efficient solutions are worth their cost.

Full use should be made in this work of relevant techniques, not only to test the effectiveness and efficiency of existing programmes but also to examine the consequences of possible changes in crucial factors, to consider the vulnerability of plans to changes in assumptions about the environment, and generally to examine in detail as many as possible of the implications of the present programmes. Such examinations are also concerned with factors of organization, staffing and control, and with the effectiveness and efficiency of the *information system* of the organization for facilitating the passage of accurate and relevant information both within the organization and in its dealings with its environment.

Models often have an important place in such analyses. A model is an abstraction of the system under study. It is focused upon those elements of the system relevant to decision making. There are four key steps:

(*a*) definition of the problems, selection of success criteria, identification of alternatives;

(*b*) formulation of the structure of the model;

(*c*) collection of data;

(*d*) substitution in the model, evaluation of the alternative courses of action, and possible outcomes of chance events.

Models come in many shapes and sizes. In the teaching of anatomy and physiology, skeletons and physical models of the circulatory system serve as models. They help the medical student to learn his trade and the surgeon or doctor to decide on the form of medical treatment. In geography, models may take the form of maps. They help, for instance, the traveller to decide on his route. In accounting, balance-sheets and financial forecasts are examples of models.

In recent years mathematical models have often been suggested by specialists in management services and operational research. For example, a particular problem might be represented by a set of equations and numerical values assigned to the variables in order to develop alternative courses of action. Once a system has been so described, and numerical values have been assigned, the problem can be solved with the appropriate mathematical technique.

Models, in fact, can be broadly characterized as qualitative or quantitative. There is often a transition in the model-building process from the first to the second. A start may be made with a qualitative model followed by an attempt to set it out in the more precise quantitative terms. The symbolic language of mathematics provides a means of doing this, and there are technical approaches available which enable very sophisticated models to be constructed. The great problem, of course, is that in the construction of these precise models too big a gap will emerge between the awkwardness of the administrative reality and the smoothness of the administrative model. Thus fairly precise and useful models can often be made to help a local authority with problems of keeping stocks of supplies at economic levels, but such models have seldom been helpful with more general problems except as a means of delineating the relevant factors.

A key concept in the preceding analysis of planning and decision-making is the idea of rationality. Under this notion, the completely rational decision-maker has:

(a) complete knowledge of the environment which he is operating;

(b) the ability to measure his preferences between alternatives according to some yardstick. In commerce this can very often be money or profit; in government administration there is often no such obvious yardstick because objectives have to be stated in general terms;

(c) the ability to choose those courses of action which maximize the degree to which objectives are achieved.

Although this is a very simple and straightforward view of rationality, which most people would probably accept, it is in fact very difficult for people to be rational in this sense. This is partly because they usually do not have all the relevant information, but it is also because they do not always know their order of preferences. In political life there is often an unwillingness to have a complete ordering of preferences in case politicians get committed to one programme that they subsequently desire to revise, or for fear of offending influential groups. Thus few local government councillors would be prepared to say that for example, housing newly-weds is more important than the care of the old, and they will often not admit their preferences to themselves, preferring to change emphasis in the light of their assessment of the current situation. This may be achieving objectives in a way, but not in the straighforward way of the apostle of rational decision-making.

Summary

A comprehensive system of output budgeting for public administration as a whole would have incorporated a forecasting capability; machinery for selecting the major objectives of the government as a whole, and the subsidiary objectives of the central departments and the local authorities and other public bodies; analytical units for assessing the effectiveness and efficiency with which programmes were discharged and recommending appropriate changes; and an information system to enable the whole system to respond quickly to changing events and thereby to revise forecasts, objectives and plans rapidly and expeditiously.

These requirements have only to be spelled out for it to be obvious that such a system was beyond the bounds of political possibility—for it would have involved the subordination of all public authorities to the central government—and also of administrative feasibility—for it would have required greater technical capacity in the design and working of a comprehensive system than existed or, perhaps, ever could exist.

FINANCIAL PLANNING IN CENTRAL GOVERNMENT

Instead, the introduction of these ideas proceeded in a more piecemeal fashion. It will be convenient to discuss them in the order in which they occurred and to take central and local government in that order. The first step, which provided the setting for the others, was the introduction of medium to long term financial planning in central government, following the report of the Plowden Committee on the Control of Public Expenditure (1961).[1] This Committee pointed out that many government programmes were continuous and depended upon long term factors, in the way that the school building programme depends upon the number of children. They suggested that, in addition to the preparation of annual estimates on the traditional basis, it would also be valuable for government departments to work out each year the annual cost of their present policies over the next few years. These costings could be assembled centrally and placed before ministers together with an assessment of the medium-term development of the economy. Ministers would then be able to compare the cost of their present policies with the resources available to meet them. They would be able to make judgements about the relative size of the public and private sector; to determine a balance between programmes so that, for example, they could take account over succeeding years of increasing demands for some kinds of services and decreasing demands for others. They could allow for improvements in the light of rising prosperity. The Committee hoped it would thereby be possible for government departments, and the Government as a whole, to assess the needs of public policies against the resources likely to be available to meet them. By looking at expenditure in this long term way, it should be possible to analyse continuing expenditure as closely as new programmes and to avoid sudden changes in plan, and the waste arising from the cancellation or adjustment of programmes at short notice because developments had not been anticipated.

The system was introduced and continues to run up to the present day. In broad outline it works as follows. In the early months of each calender year the government departments prepare reports setting out what they expect to spend in constant price terms in each of the next four years on each of their current programmes assuming that no changes are made in government policies. In addition, departments normally submit bids for additional resources for new programmes or change of programmes and, if requested by the Treasury, estimates of possible savings on the assumption of policy changes which they are asked to consider for the purposes of the exercise.

These returns are grouped together by the Public Expenditure Survey Committee (PESC), which is a committee of officials under Treasury chairmanship who prepare an annual report to the Cabinet about the end of June. The Cabinet then has to decide, in the light of the general economic prospects what changes, if any, it has to make in either the total composition of public expenditure as set out in the report, or on the programmes that go to make it up. It might decide, for example, to abridge plans because the economic growth rate is declining. Decisions might therefore be taken to reduce planned expenditure on, say, health, education and defence. Some of the savings on defence might, for example, be applied to education and health so as to make the cutbacks smaller than they would otherwise be.

When the Cabinet has reached its decisions, they are set out in an annual White Paper on public expenditure, which is usually debated by the House of Commons and analysed in more detail by the Select Committee on Expenditure and its various programme sub-committees.

The PESC system was not, of course, the first attempt to introduce long-term assessments of public expenditure. Some departments, particularly those in the defence field, had been making long term calculations of their likely expenditure for a number of years. These departments had been the first to undertake this work because many of their aircraft, missile and warship projects took from five to 10 years to complete and it was therefore necessary, right from the beginning of these projects, to have some idea of their likely financial implications. However, the PESC system was the first attempt to apply this approach to government work as a whole and, by working in terms of constant prices, it removed from the calculations the effects of pay and price increases, thereby allowing for comparisons in real economic terms. Furthermore, since public expenditure covers more than the expenditure of central government departments and includes, for example, the expenditure of local authorities, and some of the expenditure of public corporations, the expenditure survey system shows the impact of public expenditure on the economy. It is thus more comprehensive than the annual estimates.

The PESC system was a considerable improvement upon previous methods of estimating public expenditure. But it was not directly concerned with assessing the value of the existing programmes. In short, it provided a helpful guide to the financial and resource implications of these programmes but it did not provide the means for assessing the value the community gained from carrying them out, or for deciding whether each one was carried out in the most effective way.

OUTPUT BUDGETING, PPBS AND CORPORATE PLANNING IN CENTRAL GOVERNMENT

To deal with these problems the government turned to systems of output budgeting, planning—programming—budgeting systems, corporate planning and corporate management. One practical example of these techniques was the Department of Education and Science's plans for a system of output budgeting set out in *Output Budgeting for the Department of Education and Science* (1970). The case for output budgeting was put as follows:

> Traditionally budgets have categorized expenditure by the type of resource on which it is to be spent—staff, building, materials, etc.—rather than by the purpose for which it is to be spent. The aims of an output budgeting system may briefly be stated as being to analyse expenditure by the purpose for which it is to be spent and relate it to the results achieved. It is a formal system for establishing:
>
> (i) what a department is aiming to achieve—what its objectives are—in the areas of policy for which it is responsible;
> (ii) which activities contribute to these objectives;
> (iii) what resources or imputs are being devoted to these activities;
> (iv) what is actually being achieved or what the outputs are.[2]

The paper explained how the system would fit into the work of the Public Expenditure Survey Committee.

> The PESC forecasts are considered in conjunction with annual assessments of the economic prospect over the same period. Output budgeting can take this further in particular areas by relating expenditure to objectives, rather than simply to functions, by looking at what is being

achieved, and by taking into account, where appropriate, costs other than public expenditure costs.... The whole system is intended to ensure that the objectives underlying the programmes are reviewed regularly, that the necessary studies are carried out to establish the effectiveness of what is being done, and that alternative policies are properly examined and costed. The nature of the system is perhaps better described by the name used in the United States, with Canada the only country which has applied the technique on a significant scale outside the defence field, a 'planning-programming-budgeting system'   The name emphasises that it links expenditure with a planning process and with the attainment of objectives.[3]

The system proposed in the paper set three objectives for the Department of Education and Science: to provide education, to promote research and to improve the quality of cultural and recreational opportunities. Each of these objectives was described as a 'block of work' and within each block a series of programmes were set out. So far as education was concerned, there were seven programmes as follows:

(1) Compulsory education
(2) Nursery education
(3) Education for the 15-year-old
(4) Education for the 16-19-year-old
(5) Higher education, not leading to a degree or equivalent
(6) Higher education leading to a degree or equivalent
(7) Post-graduate education.

The charts in appendix 1, which are taken from the paper, set out the details of the compulsory education programme, showing the main objective, the detailed programmes by which it was to be achieved and the proposed measures or indicators of success by which it was hoped to judge how far the programmes were successful and the objectives achieved.

As will be clear from these charts, the proposed output budgeting system would have entailed the preparation of an enormous amount of information involving every aspect of the educational system, including those within the direct control of the Department of Education and Science, and those which were the responsibility of the local education authorities. It would also have provided a complete framework for analysing the relative success and failure of existing educational activities, showing what they would cost and suggesting areas in which improvements would be necessary. At the same time, it is significant that it was not possible to propose 'success' indicators for every programme, and that those proposed were in some cases vague and hard to measure, e.g. 'appreciation of cultural values by school leavers'.

This programme structure reflected the particular responsibilities of the Department of Education and Science within the British educational system. The major programmes were classified by the groups for whom the education was intended, e.g. those in nursery schools; those in compulsory education. This was not, of course, the only feasible form of classification. It would have been possible, for example, to have specified programmes of technical education, commercial education and scientific education. The detailed programmes were not in fact lists of the activities that would contribute to the objectives of the major programme. Instead, these detailed programmes were in effect, expenditure headings based on distinctions between expenditures required:

(*a*) to provide existing standards for existing numbers;

(*b*) to take account of changes in the population;

(*c*) because of changes in the proportion of the population receiving education, e.g. because of more children staying longer at school or to raise the school-leaving age;

(*d*) because of changes in the proportion of the school and college population at different stages in their education and at different types of educational establishment;

(*e*) to make improvements in building and for improvements in the pupil/teacher ratio.

Thus the detailed programme structure was designed to distinguish those factors over which the Department had no control, such as population changes, from those over which it might be able to exert some control, such as the disposition to stay longer at school, and from those over which it had substantially more control, such as standards of school building, for which it provided the bulk of the money. It was thus a programme structure which fitted in with the Department of Education and Science's customary analysis of its work and activities. This was not necessarily wrong—there is, after all, no set of programmes that is objectively superior to any other. But the point is that the programme structure was designed around the existing powers, methods and perceptions of the Department, and was in a sense a snapshot of how it viewed its work and responsibilities.

How far was this system introduced? In 1972 Mr J.G. Bagley[4] gave a report on the progress made with the system in its early years. By 1972 there were nine major programmes, the existing seven plus the division of compulsory education into primary and secondary and the addition of an 'educational intra-structure' programme to cover the cost of administration and other costs which could not be specifically allocated to other programmes. These changes were made in the light of experience and to 'reflect the inevitable changes in emphasis over the years, in the objectives and priorities of the Department'. It was pointed out, for example, that the raising of the school-leaving age to 16 would eliminate the 'education for the 15-year-old' as a separate programme, and that the increasingly close attention being given to the improvement and replacement of primary school buildings and possible changes in teacher education and training would be reflected in changes in the structure of some programmes. It was also explained that the Department aimed to produce an 'integrated management system' to provide both the Department's contribution to the PESC system and the information required for the Department's own planning functions. It was also hoped that the system would enable the cost of alternative policies to be calculated quickly. The article also said 'the main function of the programme budget is to provide the groundwork for a systematic analysis and review of policy. A planning organization for this purpose was set up within the Department early in 1971. It is headed by a policy steering group with the Permanent Secretary as Chairman, and it brings together the heads of the various operational branches (schools, teachers, further education, universities, etc.)'.[5]

Two years later, further information on the development of the system was given in an article on *Corporate Planning for Education in the Department of Education and Science* by Sir William Pile, then Permanent Secretary of the Department.[6] Sir William placed his main emphasis upon the way the educational planning system in the Department of Education and Science operated within the framework set by the Public Expenditure Survey Committee. Sir William also showed how the Department's work was influenced by other institutions, such as local authorities and universities, which are part of the educational system but not under its direct control. He made clear that the Department of Education and Science was basically concerned with questions of broad scale organization and cost rather than educational content. It concentrated upon trying to make sure that resources were available for existing programmes, and that ministers were able to see in good time what scope existed for possible changes in the nature and content of the educational system given the resources that might be available. Sir William explained that the machinery involved was the policy steering group under his chairmanship, which determined the planning programme in consultation with ministers. There were also several policy groups within the Department, usually under a deputy secretary, each concerned with a major block of activities, and the steering and policy group were serviced by a planning unit headed by an under secretary.

Further comments on the Department's planning system and its concentration on traditional activities were made in a report by the OECD (1975).[7] This report made three major criticisms: that the planning was too secretive and not sufficiently open to public scrutiny; secondly, that it was confined very largely to 'identifying existing trends'; and, thirdly, that the planning was too inward looking, too much conerned with the educational world and insufficiently concerned with the contribution that education could and should make to industry and the community as a whole.

These criticisms were echoed in 1976 by Lord Crowther-Hunt who had been a Minister of State in the Department.[8] Lord Crowther-Hunt, who had been a member of the Fulton Committee, said that the planning unit in the department

> does not fulfil the role that we of the Fulton Committee believe such a unit should fulfil. This is because the long range planning in the Department is not in fact done by the planning unit but by what is called the departmental planning organization, a flexible network of committees established in February 1971....[This means that]....the departmental planning organization is overwhelmingly dominated by, and almost entirely composed of, those who are heavily immersed in the problems of here and now; the permanent secretary, the two deputy secretaries, the heads of the operational branches and so on. And this planning organization is simply serviced by the planning unit which has a sort of secretariat co-ordinating and supporting role.

> It will already be clear that these arrangements for long-term planning are the very anthithesis of those recommended by Fulton. The Fulton Committee saw planning as something to be done by a planning unit largely detached from day-to-day administration and crises.

> The DES sees long-term planning as something to be done by those mainly engaged in day-to-day operational and administration questions—with a planning unit operating as a piece of servicing machinery.

> Certainly, therefore, as far as nearly all the members of the departmental planning organization are concerned, the Fulton criticisms still apply, that in the press of daily business long-term planning and research tend to take second place.

Lord Crowther-Hunt made further criticisms. He said that a Fulton-type planning unit in the DES would have contained

> a professor of education as the department's senior policy adviser, with a status not inferior to that of permanent secretary. And it would have included educational psychologists, educational economists, sociologists of different specialisms and those with other relevant discipline and fields of expertise. But the department's planning unit is naturally not at all like this. Its 14 members consist of an under-secretary and an assistant secretary, three principals, three higher executive officers, two executive officers, one clerical officer, one clerical assistant and two secretaries. Now all these are traditional 'administrative' civil servants each of whom does a two- or three-year stint in the planning unit as part of his or her general work within the department.

Lord Crowther-Hunt also pointed out that, in his opinion, the members of staff change too often. In the 15 months that he was in the Department, three different officers were moved in succession into the planning unit to fill the under-secretary job at the head of it, hardly a recipe for being able to develop an awareness of new educational thinking, let alone being able to contribute to it.

	£m.	Percentage
1. Expenditure on Personnel:		
a. Pay, allowances, *etc.,* of the Armed Forces	1,492.2	
b. Armed Forces' retired pay, pensions, *etc.*	397.4	
c. Pay, *etc.,* of civilian staff (i)	1,107.0	
Total personnel	2,996.6	43.3
2. Expenditure on Equipment:		
a. Sea Systems	858.1	
b. Land systems	619.1	
c. Air Systems	1,024.3	
d. Other (ii)	268.0	
Total equipment	2,769.5	40.0
3. Other Expenditure		
a. Works, buildings and lands	316.7	
b. Pay of DOE civilian staff	72.9	
c. Miscellaneous stores and services (iii)	763.1	
Total other	1,152.7	16.7
Total	6,918.8	

Notes:
(i) Includes pay, *etc.,* of civilian staff of the Procurement Executive and of civilian staff of the Royal Dockyards, net of receipts.
(ii) Excludes personnel and other expinditure associated with the procurement of equipment—see notes (i) and (iii).
(iii) Includes movements, general and accommodation stores, clothing, victualling, fuel and other administrative expenses.

Fig.3.1 Division of the defence budget by inputs 1978–79
Source: *Statement on the Defence Estimates 1978,* Cmnd 8099. HMSO (1978).

Some of these criticisms were repeated by the Expenditure Committee of the House of Commons in a report published in September 1976[9] which referred to the secrecy of planning and the fact that it was very largely undertaken by those with operational responsibilities. However, it may well be that changes are in prospect. This is suggested by details of departmental reorganization announced in December 1976. The keystone of the new organization is an enlarged planning unit led by a deputy secretary. Its task is to concentrate on long-term development and its staff will include statisticians and economists and a research unit to take up the latest thinking outside Whitehall and to apply it to departmental needs. The planning division will also be responsible for monitoring the performance of schools in meeting the requirements of such outside bodies as industry, the professions and, within the educational system, of the universities and polytechnics. It will also consider the implications of changes in population for school building, teacher supply and places available in higher education.

The conclusion of this analysis is that the Department's system of output budgeting, while fashioned around the traditional concern with the allocation of resources to existing institutional sectors, nevertheless provided a framework for analysing the complete range of educational and research activities throughout the country and for trying to assess their effectiveness. In practice, the parts of the system that would have enabled this path to be followed were left in embryonic form and the system was developed mainly for use in connection with the Government's long-term financial planning arrangements and, in particular, the operation of the PESC's system. Furthermore, the Department's planning arrangements were largely, though not exclusively, directed to assessing the implications of immediate problems and their financial impact.

It would, of course, be wrong to base general conclusions about planning systems on a single example. It will therefore be useful to look at the output budgeting system used by the Ministry of Defence. Initially, the Ministry's long-term costings took the same form as their annual estimates and set out the cost of the inputs of personnel and equipment needed to carry out defence plans over a number of years. In 1964, however, 10 year forecasts were introduced on the basis of a 'functional costing'. The functional costing was divided into 13 major programmes. Changes have been made over the years and Figs. 3.1, 3.2[10] give a comparison for 1978/79 of the defence estimates drawn up on the traditional and functional bases.

The first five programmes contain all the costs attributable to fighting units and their immediate support. The other programmes cover various activities which contribute to these frontline programmes, such as training, and research and development. The major programmes are divided and sub-divided into smaller parts. The information is stored on a computer, so that individual elements can be extracted in order to answer questions posed by defence planners. For example, if it is necessary to calculate the cost of a particular operation involving a combination of battalions of soldiers and squadrons of aircraft the appropriate figures can be extracted from the computer.

The programmes in this system are not the final outputs of the defence system but its intermediate outputs. The system does not show, for example, the cost of battles won and operations conducted, but the cost of the squadrons, battalions and warships that are used to carry them out. The programmes also correspond broadly to the divisions between the three armed services. The output budgeting system used by the Ministry of Defence is in this way similar to the one planned by the Department of Education and Science in that programmes are closely linked to the existing organizational structures of the armed services and the educational system respectively. The Ministry of Defence also provides for

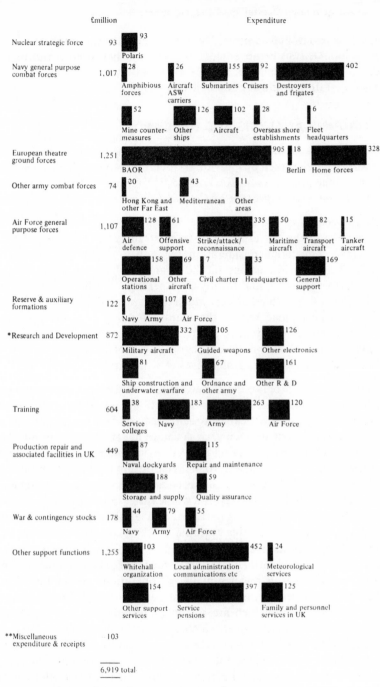

£million   Expenditure

Fig.3.2 Division of the defence budget by outputs
Source: *Statement on the Defence Estimates 1978,* Cmnd 7099.

programme review and analysis. The Ministry has, for example, a Defence Operational Analysis Establishment, whose primary task is to examine the efficiency and effectiveness of various ways that are and might be adopted to meet operational and logistic objectives.

PROGRAMME ANALYSIS AND REVIEW

In order to look in more detail at the effectiveness and efficiency of the programmes undertaken by individual Government departments a system of Programme Analysis and Review (PAR) was announced in the White Paper on *The Reorganization of Central Government* (1970).

> The objectives of the Programme Analysis and Review are, first, to contribute to the Government's overall strategy by focusing issues for collective ministerial consideration; secondly, and perhaps conversely, to be itself an instrument of the strategy by testing departmental objectives against it; and thirdly (and perhaps a rather different role, since the others both relate very much to Ministerial decision taking) to bring under regular review the major on-going programmes, even though apparently no immediate decision may be called for, because we all know that any big programme carries a risk of its own inertia and the regular spring cleaning of objectives is a fundamental part of PAR.[11]

The annual PAR programme is determined by discussion between the Treasury and the Central Policy Review Staff and is subject to ministerial approval. It is neither practicable nor sensible to study every programme of every department in detail each year. A choice has therefore to be made of which issues should be the subject of PAR reviews and, in this connection, the question is bound to arise as to the relationship between PAR reviews and other reviews. The Government is constantly commissioning reviews of problems and policies by way of a whole range of methods from Royal Commissions down to working parties of officials. In what ways, if any, do PAR reviews differ from other reviews?

Since PAR reviews are not published, it is difficult to answer this question. But it would probably be fair to say that the main features of the PAR system are that its reviews involve co-operation between the Treasury, CPRS and other relevant departments, and are directed to existing or planned commitments which are of central importance to the Government's current strategy; or likely to require more expenditure in the near future; or relate to services which are complex and inter-departmental or inter-authority; or which have recently been the subject of other investigations, for example, by the CPRS, but where it is clear that more work remains to be done; or where there is *prima facie* evidence that existing objectives and policies need re-examination. Possible subjects by these criteria include inner-city rehabilitation, urban transport, and technical education, though there is no direct knowledge that these subjects have been reviewed in this way.

What is important, however, is that some mechanism should exist for co-ordinating all the various major reviews in hand, under whatever heading, so that ministers can reach decisions on whether the total investigatory effort is directed to the right subjects; to consider whether there is any duplication and wasted effort; and to decide whether the reviews are worth their cost. This would be an appropriate task for the Public Expenditure Survey Committee and the Central Policy Review Staff. Indeed, there is a clear need for the application of Programme Analysis and Review to the PAR system itself and to associated methods of undertaking reviews of government programmes.

THE CENTRAL POLICY REVIEW STAFF, ADVISERS AND PLANNERS

The Central Policy Review Staff was introduced as proposed in the White Paper on *The Reorganization of Central Government* of October 1970 as a 'small multi-disciplinary central policy review staff in the Cabinet Office'.[12] It was set up to discharge two functions. First, to review the Government's progress in carrying out the promises in the manifesto on which it was elected and to suggest ways of filling any gaps between objectives and performance. Secondly, to examine particular problems and policies and consider if they are being sensibly tackled. The Central Policy Review Staff was originally headed by Lord Rothschild. He was succeeded on his re-tirement in 1974 by Sir Kenneth Berrill, who had been Head of the Govern-ment Economic Service and Chief Economic Adviser to the Treasury since 1973. He had previously been an economics don at Cambridge University, Chairman of the University Grants Committee and economic adviser to various foreign governments and international organizations.

The staff of the Central Policy Review Staff numbers about 15 and is drawn both from within the Civil Service and from outside. The Civil Service members usually work in the CPRS for two or three years before returning to their departments. The outside members have included Professor C. R. Ross, who had been a Professor of Economics at the University of East Anglia and a consultant to the OECD, and other economists and social scientists. During its early years, the staff also included a number of people, such as Mr William Waldegrave, who had active connections with the political party in power.

When the CPRS was set up, some observers believed that it would be quickly reduced to impotence by the unwillingness of departments to supply it with information and by the jealousy of ministers who might fear the infringement of their responsibilities. Other critics, taking a contrary view, saw the CPRS as a likely forerunner of a new Prime Minister's department taking over the co-ordinating functions of the Treasury, Civil Service Department and of the Cabinet Office itself.

Experience has suggested that both these forecasts were wide of the mark. For a time the CPRS produced regular reports for the Cabinet, usually presented at six-monthly meetings held at Chequers, in which they attempted to assess the Government's success in meeting its aims. The need for meetings of this kind is very much for the Prime Minister of the day to assess. Mr Edward Heath is on record as finding them helpful, but they have been discontinued in recent years.[13]

As for its special studies, the CPRS has by now carried out a large number of enquiries, including studies of the Concorde airliner, energy policy, regional policy and population problems. Not all the studies have been published, but the reports which have appeared from the CPRS show a greater concern than the usual White or Green Paper with sketching out the nature of the problem and listing a wide range of approaches. This is brought out in the CPRS report on *The Future of the United Kingdom Power Plant Manufacturing Industry* (1976). The report outlined the difficulties of an industry which contains only a small number of firms and receives only intermittent orders, because the growth of demand for electricity is hard to estimate and there is an inevitable tendency for customers to place orders only when they are as certain as they can be that they will have a need for new plant. The report concludes that 'on grounds of the country's present industrial strategy, the need to sustain employment and the needs of the balance of payments, there is a strong case for maintaining in the United Kingdom a power plant manufacturing industry which can both supply the home market and compete successfully overseas'. In spite of this clear statement of need, the report avoided firm recommendations. It recognized that final decisions must be taken by the Government on factors which are bound to be highly political. Conclusions were therefore expressed as a series of interlinking options each with its own advantages and disadvantages.

A similar approach was taken in the CPRS report *A Joint Framework for Social Policies* (June 1975). The report analysed the way in which social policy is devised and administered by central government. It pointed to the division of responsibility, with separate authorities being responsible for financial benefits, the health service and for practical assistance. This complexity militates against efficiency and promotes confusion amongst the staff as well as the clients. Difficulties have been exacerbated by the tendency of Government to respond to particular crises by piecemeal measures with unexpected and unplanned effects.

To overcome these difficulties, the CPRS recommended regular meetings of senior ministers responsible for social policy. Co-ordination should be the main aim of these meetings, and it suggested that new plans should be presented with particular reference to the connections and possible conflicts between one policy and another. The CPRS also recommended that close attention should be paid to monitoring the outcome of policies on an inter-departmental basis and with the aid of improved statistics. But firm recommendations on the form of future social policies were carefully avoided.

To sum up, it seems fair to say that the CPRS has developed a role in modern government that no other institution could easily fill. It has not threatened the independence of ministers; it has not taken over the role of the Treasury; it has not dominated the Cabinet Office; it has not revolutionized the art and science of government. Yet it has made a number of useful analyses and proposals. Its continuing success depends upon drawing the right mixture of staff from inside and outside the Civil Service and in taking care not to infringe the responsibilities of departments and ministers. For in this way it can be seen as a colleague rather than a rival by those ultimately responsible for the detailed work of government.

When the Labour Party returned to power in 1974 they maintained the CPRS. In addition, Dr Bernard Donoughue, a Senior Lecturer in Political Science at the London School of Economics, was appointed to head a new advisory unit on short-term domestic policy. His colleagues initially included a lecturer in social administration at the LSE; a lecturer in social work and social administration at Glasgow University; economists from Oxford University and the Centre for Environmental Studies; and the manager of domestic trunk services at British Airways. There is no direct evidence of this unit's work since its reports have not been published. It is likely, however, that its main task is to analyse subjects of current concern from the viewpoint of the Government's political interests and standing at home and abroad. This political analysis supplements the recommendations put forward by civil servants from their traditional position of political neutrality. It is theoretically the task of ministers to add the necessary political dimension to the work of civil servants, but given the heavy pressure of modern government there is a case for helping the Prime Minister to look at policy recommendations from a more specifically political standpoint.

This unit therefore provides the Prime Minister with the same kind of service that other ministers receive from the special advisers which they are able to appoint in their Departments. Special advisers from outside the Civil Service are no new phenomenon; in the First World War, for example, Mr Lloyd George had a small team of advisers who operated from some temporary buildings in the garden of 10 Downing Street and therefore became known as 'Lloyd George's Garden Suburb'. In 1970 the Conservative administration under Mr Edward Heath appointed a much larger number of advisers than had previously been customary and this practice was continued by the Labour Government in 1974. Arrangements for these advisers have now been put on a more permanent footing; they are classified as temporary civil servants; and their appointments normally end with the departure of their ministers. There are currently about thirty special advisers, some half-a-dozen of whom serve in the Prime Minister's policy unit.

Some commentators have been suspicious of these advisers, alleging that they are concerned with abstract political ideas rather than administrative realities. It is said that they can easily form a buffer or filter between the department and the minister, and distort the advice submitted to him in order to bring it into line with their pre-conceptions.

Other views have been stated by experts who have served in this capacity.[14] Professor Maurice Peston, an economist from the University of London who served as an adviser to the Department of Education and Science has been quoted as believing that

> by virtue of being expert in a field of policy and sympathetic to the political aspirations of the party in power, special advisers can offer ministers the kind of policy advice that it is impossible for the politically neutral civil servant to give, as well as keeping ministers in touch with party feeling at local level. In that capacity they are invaluable to ministers of both parties and are here to stay.

Mr Terry Pitt, who was attached to the Lord President's Office in 1974, and had served for nearly 10 years in the Labour Party Research Department, was quoted as favouring the appointment by the Prime Minister and senior ministers of about 10 people to act as their eyes and ears in keeping in touch with the work of their departments as well as to keep abreast of party policy. 'You need them because the Civil Service is a status quo organization. They are extremely able people but they will not pursue any sort of radical policy. If ministers are going to pursue radical policies they need people who will help them to push the Civil Service'. Finally, Dr Stuart Holland, an economist who had served as an adviser in the Cabinet Office from 1966 to 1967 and in the Ministry of Overseas Development from 1974 to 1975 argued in favour of adopting the French Cabinet system throughout Whitehall. Under this system, the minister's cabinet constitutes in effect the senior directing staff of the department. The cabinet of a French minister usually contains a number of civil servants as well as outside members and therefore combines a knowledge of the government machine with an understanding of and sympathy with the minister's viewpoint. The cabinet is therefore well placed to put the minister's personal stamp on the work of the department. Dr Holland also proposed arrangements for the party in opposition. 'During Labour's period in opposition, I recommended that a counter-Whitehall structure should be established, each minister having his own cabinet and with regular meetings of special advisers in parallel with inter-departmental committees of permanent officials.'

General opinion has not yet moved in favour of the fundamental organizational change that would be implied by the adoption of the French Cabinet system, if only because the close liaison that traditionally exists between a minister's private secretary and senior officials provides very much the same kind of link that is secured by the Cabinet. The case for the special advisers is, however, increasingly recognized and has been endorsed by the Government.[15] In the last analysis, their justification derives from the fact that government departments, like other organizations, inevitably have a particular view of the area of administration for which they are responsible. This view is formed on the basis of hard practical experience in getting work done and negotiating with interested pressure groups. Yet it is nonetheless a partial view. It may therefore be helpful for ministers to have access to people who are able to state the problems in slightly different terms and suggest other policy options. In theory, ministers can do this for themselves. But they are often too hard pressed to be able to find the time, given the number of meetings they have to attend, the time to be spent in Parliament and the need to represent their departments and the Government at national and international functions.

The system of special advisers depends for its success upon the quality of those appointed. They must be sufficiently intelligent and sympathetic to understand what the department is trying to do and to co-operate with its officials. In making suggestions to ministers they must not seek to cut them off from access to departmental advice or to try to usurp the role of departmental civil servants. If they can avoid these dangers, special advisers can add a new dimension to policy thinking in government departments.

In addition to the work of the Central Policy Review Staff and special advisers, a great deal of planning work is undertaken by other staff in Government departments. Indeed, regular civil servants engaged in planning work far outnumber those appointed from outside the Civil Service, and they have grown in recent years. The number of economists and statisticians, for example, rose from about 100 and 180 in 1967 to over 350 and nearly 500 respectively by 1976.[16] The planning that is undertaken can be divided into three main fields: the provision of information and data as a contribution to continuing inter-departmental planning including the preparation of public expenditure survey material, vote and manpower estimates, participation in inter-departmental reviews of policy and contributions to economic forecasting; reviews of departmental policies to analyse their costs and benefits including the analysis of options for new policies that might be undertaken and the review of existing policies; and the management of resources including the assessment and allocation of financial and manpower resources in the light of the outcome of the decisions taken as a result of the first two kinds of planning work. The Fulton Committee's discussion of planning largely concentrated on the second of these activities. As the development of the Public Expenditure Survey Committee, the system of Programme Analysis and Review and the work of the Central Policy Review Staff has shown, however, all three kinds are necessary in the work of government.

The various kinds of planning are undertaken in a variety of organizational structures; indeed, as our analysis of the Department of Education and Science showed, it is often unrealistic to look for a precise distinction between policy division and executive divisions. There is a spectrum; at one end are small divisions, working closely with ministers and senior officials, and largely concerned with analysing the strengths and weaknesses of the department's current programme and the opportunities for undertaking new programmes. At the other extreme are divisions largely concerned with a continuing executive task. Yet there will be occasions when these 'executive divisions' have to undertake a great deal of planning and policy making as when, for example, a new piece of legislation has to be introduced within their field, or a new scheme worked out for which the division has special knowledge and responsibility. Other experts will be consulted and brought into this work; parliamentary counsel will be concerned, for example, if it is necessary to draw up new legislation; economists, statisticians and research staffs will be drawn in if their special skills are needed. The staff and structure of divisions will be altered to accord with the changing balance of work.

Just as there is no single design for a policy planning division, there is no single job specification for a department's senior policy adviser. The Fulton Committee recommended that the senior policy adviser should, usually, be a youngish man or woman, usually with a social or natural science background, and with the same status as the permanent secretary, the chief official in the department. But while there is no uniformity, and the position of the chief adviser varies, as well as the kind of work he does, there is no doubt that recent years have seen a great increase in the number of scientific and research staff, from all disciplines, working in policy making fields. We shall consider in later chapters some of the different organizational forms which have been adopted for their participation. But the general lesson is already clear—the conclusions of scientific and other research cannot be the sole or even the major constituents of the policy making process. Financial constraints, political necessity, international obligations and the views of pressure groups are all likely to play as big a part as 'pure science'.

OUTPUT BUDGETING, PPBS AND CORPORATE PLANNING IN LOCAL GOVERNMENT

In looking at the use of output budgeting and associated techniques in local government it may be helpful to look at examples from the educational field in three major authorities; Liverpool, Coventry and Gloucestershire.[17]

A planned programme budgeting system was introduced in Liverpool following the engagement of McKinsey & Co. as consultants in 1968. The consultants recommended that a PPB system should be introduced for the whole of the corporation's services. By the autumn of 1968, a planning budget on a programme basis was being prepared for 1970/71 and subsequent years, a traditional type budget being maintained for control purposes. The basis of the system was the existing institutions and activities of the educational system of Liverpool. Four institutional sectors made up the four constituent programmes of the 'Education Programme Area'. Each one had a 'prime objective'. The schools programme and the further education service programme were so large that they were divided into two and five sub-programmes respectively; primary schools and secondary schools were sub-programmes of the schools programme; and the Liverpool Polytechnic, the Colleges of Education, the Colleges of Further Education, the Community Service and the Youth Employment Service were sub-programmes within the further education service programme.

Each programme and sub-programme therefore had a prime objective. Each one was also divided into a number of 'elements', each with its own 'element objective'. Each 'element objective' had a number of relevant activities, whose discharge was designed to achieve the 'element objective' and, in total, the objective of the sub-programmes and programmes. The charts at Appendix 2 show the programme structure as a whole and give, as an example, the sub-programmes and elements of the schools programme, plus some of the element objectives and associated activities within the primary and secondary schools sub-programmes.

In Coventry, a different system was adopted. A planned programming budgeting system was introduced for the city as a whole and aligned with the city's structure plan. Within this system there was an 'education programme area'. The prime objective for this area was 'to enrich the lives of other people by the optimum personal development of each individual in the community'. The community was conceived for educational purposes as consisting of five user or client groups; viz. under fives; children of five to 11; children of 11 to 16; the over sixteens; handicapped children. In addition to these five client groups, each with its own objective, sub-objective and programme of activities, there was a general programme of development, research and consultation. Details are set out in the charts at Appendix 3.

In Gloucestershire, yet a third pattern was adopted. In July 1969, the County Council embarked upon a two-year feasibility study into the possibility of introducing PPBS in seven areas of the Council's work including education. The Council's educational work was defined as the 'educational hemisphere' and three programme areas were distinguished, viz. 'scholastic services', 'vocational assistant services' and 'recreational and leisure services'. In these programme areas a number of separate programmes were distinguished, some relating to groups of people, such as babies and older children, others relating to particular activities, such as research. The pattern is set out in Appendix 4 together with notes on the programme for 'older children'.

It is clear from this material that three very different systems of planning were adopted in the three local authorities, with Liverpool concentrating upon educational institutions, Coventry upon client groups and Gloucestershire on kinds of services. They all claim that the systems have been useful. Liverpool has not used its full PPBS system in recent years but the programme area structure still remains and it is claimed that it has been useful in helping 'separate departments to work together in fields where the programmes of different programme areas overlap'.[18] In Coventry it is claimed that, in spite of the apparent vagueness of the exact meaning of the term 'optimum personal development', and what might seem to be the difficulty of deciding which activities are most conducive to its achievement, a workable system of corporate planning has nonetheless developed in the city, and the education services, in common with the rest of the city's local government activities, are covered in a series of long-term plans.

> In this system the undertaking of annual programme analysis exercises is not dependent on the measurability of progress towards the objectives and the authority find that they can in fact rationally allocate resources and choose between alternatives open to them without over-precision in defining either where they are going or how far along the path they have reached at a given point in time.[19]

This is *prima facie* a surprising statement since if work is proceeding without reference to 'the measurability of progress towards the objectives', it is difficult to see what help the programme system can be to the elected members of the council and to the officers concerned. But no doubt the concentration upon objectives and the activities which are relevant to their achievement is still helpful. It may well be that it is more useful to have an eye to these objectives than to concentrate simply upon the cost of the inputs to the educational system, such as buildings, maintenance and teachers' salaries, which is the inevitable basis of budgeting under the traditional system.

As for Gloucestershire, it is stated that

> The time has not yet come when the elected members are prepared to abandon the traditional method of budget presentation. Nevertheless significant advances have been made and work is now proceeding on the possibility that, as a half-way house, an options budget might be produced covering at least some of the authorities programme areas to give members the opportunity of determining future policy and resource allocation on the basis of an appraisal of alternatives, derived from the planning-programming-budgeting approach.[20]

It is also important to note that all three authorities have retained the traditional form of revenue estimates and that the need to relate programmes and budgets to these traditional accounting classifications take up a good deal of staff time and resources. Both officers and elected members continue to look at the activities of their councils in traditional terms. This tendency has been reinforced in recent years by the importance of restricting expenditure. In local government, as well as in central government the original plans for planning-programming-budgeting systems and output budgeting have not been carried through over the years. They do not govern the detailed administration or planning of the services. But they have widened the traditional concern with input costs to include at least some attention to objectives and programmes to meet them.

More generally PPBS systems seem to have been more attractive to large rather than small authorities. This may be a consequence of the fact that the more developed forms of corporate management, including the use of a chief executive officer and a chief officers board, are more usually found in large authorities, particularly large urban authorities, rather than in smaller and rural local authorities. Furthermore, it is the large urban authorities who have to face more of the major problems involving co-ordination and collaboration between a number of council departments, such as dealing with poverty, traffic congestion, twilight areas and race relations. These call for schemes of action running across various departments.

Again, as with the educational examples we have looked at in detail, a variety of ways of adopting PPBS are seen.[21] Some authorities sought to apply the system to all their departments from the start: examples here include the GLC, Islington, Greenwich, Liverpool, Manchester, Coventry and Gloucestershire. All these authorities made an attempt (which they did not all persist in) to appraise all their objectives, and the relevance of existing activities to their achievement, and to define programme structures across the whole range of their responsibilities. Other authorities preferred a more limited approach, examining single services and trying to set up a PPBS or output budgeting system, within the confines of a particular area of the council's work, although in nearly every case the area selected involved more than one of the authority's departments. Indeed, PPBS applied within a self-contained department would lose a good deal of its potential worth.

There have also been other differences beyond the range of services covered by the system. Some authorities have given priority to the development of programme budgets and long-term financial plans. Others have put the main emphasis upon the analysis of major issues. Others again have been concerned to improve policy implementation, and have concentrated on developing management accountability, management accounting systems and measures of performance.

The variations of approach owe something to the origins of PPBS and output budgeting in different authorities. In many of the larger urban authorities the interest in these systems began with the arrival of a Conservative majority interested in introducing modern management methods and employing consultants with the idea of trying to gain for the public sector some of the benefits that new management methods were believed to have brought to private business. This was at exactly the same time as a Conservative Government was carrying out a similar programme in central government by employing management consultants and restructuring the departments.

This interest in modern management methods in local government led, as the previous chapter showed, to the introduction of organizational ideas based upon corporate planning, usually including, following the Bains report, a chief executive officer and a management board. So far as PPBS and output budgeting is concerned, most of the authorities adopting these systems have felt that each programme area required its own committee. There is less similarity of view on the question of whether each programme requires its own department. Many programme areas cover large parts of several departments; thus a 'protection programme' might include police, fire service, trading standards, roadworks to prevent accidents and so on. Clearly a common department would not be sensible here. Programme areas and departments serve rather different purposes. Programme areas and structures are aids to planning, and departments are organizations for implementing decisions efficiently. Indeed, the general lesson of PPBS and output budgeting in local government is that they are useful devices for helping to plan and look to the future, and in arranging for inter-departmental co-operation. But they have on the whole proved less useful and successful as guides to the implementation of services and to the measurement of performance.

The extent to which ideas about corporate planning and research and intelligence have been introduced into local government has been analysed by R. Greenwood, C. R. Hinings and S. Ranson.[22] They analysed the structure of a large number of local authorities: 39 (100 per cent) county authorities, 5 out of 6 metropolitan authorities, 33 (91 per cent) metropolitan district authorities and 212 (64 per cent) county district authorities. They defined corporate planning as being concerned with:

(a) improvement of the technology for taking decisions involving two or more services, e.g. through use of PPBS, programme budgets, position statements, etc; (b) carrying out research into the local authority's environment; and (c) reviewing the effectiveness of local authority activities in terms of their impact upon environmental problems.[23]

The result of the research was to show that by 1975 41 per cent of the counties, 13 per cent of the county districts, 48 per cent of the metropolitan districts and 20 per cent of the metropolitan counties had corporate planning units or departments; 55 per cent of the counties, 9 per cent of the county districts, 37 per cent of the metropolitan districts and 40 per cent of the metropolitan counties also had research and intelligence units or departments concentrating upon the second activity distinguished in the definition of corporate planning.

These figures show that a considerable proportion of local authorities have set up units for corporate planning and research. More units have been set up in urban than rural authorities. This probably reflects the fact that the problems of urban environments and the need for co-operation between local authority departments are more obvious in the towns. It should not be assumed, however, that the problems of local government in towns are more difficult than those in the countryside. Indeed, it may well be the case that the problems of local government are even greater in rural areas, but that we have so far at least been unable to set about their analysis and solution effectively.

GENERAL LESSONS

The insistence of students of management upon the importance of forecasting, objective setting and planning, has certainly had an effect upon central and local government. Greater attention is now paid to these activities than 10 to 15 years ago. More staff are employed upon them, and more units, departments and organizations have been set up to make surveys of future prospects, to suggest the objectives that central government and local authorities should adopt in the light of developing social and economic needs, and to indicate the various programmes of work that might be undertaken to achieve them in the most effective and efficient manner.

The greater attention to these activities has brought a number of advantages. First, both central departments and local authorities have become more expert and aware of the complexities of the society which they are responsible for administering. Simple rules of hunch and common sense are an inadequate basis for developing policy, because they do not correspond with any convincing explanation of how society works and therefore fail to anticipate and help us to understand new developments. Increasingly, central departments and local authorities need to have an idea about the functioning of the part of society for which they are responsible. Difficulties certainly arise. In the field of economic planning, for example, the following problems have been underlined by the attempts made in the last 10 to 15 years, to produce more specific and expert economic plans.

(a) Society changes as we study it; thus the rate of personal saving has risen in recent years and nobody is certain whether this is a consequence of faster inflation, anxieties about employment, or changes in attitudes to the stock of savings.

(b) The economic cycle is less regular, and there are also quantum jumps as in the five-fold increase of oil prices in 1973–74.

(c) There are great difficulties in getting all the accurate information that is needed, both to make and then to operate the planner's economic models.

(d) Judgements must be made about the risks and potential damage of being wrong and judgements must be made about the likelihood of being wrong by various margins. This means that the safest policy may be very different from the one that would have been adopted if we could have been sure that the forecast would have turned out correctly.

(e) The PESC system may be vulnerable to what might be called 'tactical bidding'. Once claims for resources are accepted and included in the costings for future years it may be difficult to revise them, though it is not impossible to do so. Furthermore, the system has had to be changed to cater for the response to sudden crises and high rates of inflation. A system of cash limits was introduced in 1976,[24] whereby departments and other agencies can no longer expect to receive, as they have done in the past, supplementary provision beyond their estimates to compensate for rising prices. The expenditure information system has been improved; 'profiles' of expenditure out-turn are drawn up for all voted items and some other expenditure. The profiles are compared with monthly expenditure returns so that deviations from the expected course can be quickly identified. The monitoring system also produces frequent returns during the financial year showing the effect of pay and price increases upon the out-turn of expenditure. Finally, new arrangements have been introduced for financial co-operation between central government and local authorities. The Government does not have direct control over local government expenditure, but has sought through a system of detailed discussions and consultative councils to secure a greater means of agreement over the extent of local authority spending.[25]

Difficulties and complexities also arise in physical planning, where there are several objectives in view and the needs of many social groups to take into account. Some of the problems were brought out in studies, prepared by consultants, which dealt with the inner areas of Liverpool, Birmingham and of Lambeth and showed how the efforts so far made, by central and local government, to plan for the sensible dispersal of people and jobs away from crowded cities, have led to unforeseen problems in the city centres.[26] Instead of these centres becoming more interesting and satisfactory places to live and work as they become less crowded, other problems and difficulties have arisen which place substantial if different strains upon those who remain and those who are responsible for government administration. The removal of jobs, accelerated by the country's economic difficulties, has led to high unemployment rates in the city centres and large numbers of those who remain are poor, recent immigrants and old. These relatively disadvantaged members of our society therefore tend to be concentrated in areas with poor housing, which was usually designed for large households and is unsuitable for the small family units often to be found in city centres.

This unhappy state of affairs should not necessarily be seen as conclusive evidence of the failure of planning; it might, after all, have been reasonable enough to disperse people and jobs to new areas. We cannot be certain that the general welfare and satisfaction of the people would have been greater if these changes had not been made. Furthermore, attention has been drawn through the planning mechanism to the difficulties here described and the further work that has to be done has now become clearer. There is nothing in the philosophy of planning to guarantee that the right answer will be found immediately; indeed the assessment of developing events and the working out of their implications for present policies and the consequent adjustment of plans and objectives is implicit in the planning process that we have described. However, doubts about the ability of planners and planning systems to investigate all relevant alternatives and to anticipate all the consequences and evaluate their advantages and disadvantages, have led a number of commentators to suggest that planning should be more open and diffuse.

In his study of social service budgets[27] Mr H. Glennerster advocates 'pluralist social planning' which would provide for 'open, political and explicit decisions' about resource allocation at all levels in the social services. Explicitness in this context is taken to lie in combining a clear knowledge and analysis of the net beneficiaries of existing programmes, with an evaluation of past results and forward planning for the future. Because of the contentious nature of social service goals, and of the difficulties of assessing the value of the consequences of the actions taken in trying to achieve them, such information and analysis should derive from as many sources as possible, and be subject to political debate. In his study of cost benefit analysis[28] Professor P. J. O. Self claimed that the political process, operating within constitutional limits and prescriptions, allows the voter at large, pressure groups, experts, and elected members of local authorities and of Parliament, to contribute in a defined way to the taking of subsidiary and ultimate decisions about public policies and the evaluation of their implementation. Professor Self argues that the political process, with all its faults, offers at least the prospect of avoiding the artificial distortions that may arise from too slavish an adherence to particular techniques and from the discussion of policy alternatives among a restricted group of officials and ministers.

In similar vein, there is a current interest in setting up bodies outside the government machine to undertake policy studies. Dr Dahrendorf, the Director of the London School of Economics, has suggested that an independent institute should be set up to look at socio-economic problems from the viewpoint of a number of academic disciplines, keeping its studies in close relationship with the non-academic world.[29] Again, the establishment was announced in 1977 of a new Centre for the Study of Public Policy at the University of Strathclyde. The purpose of the Centre is to apply academic methods, techniques and approaches to subjects of concern to decision makers in government, including such issues as devolution, national solvency, and the political and economic difficulties arising from the existence of several overlapping tiers of government, as in the British system today. In 1978 the Centre for Social Policy merged with the Political and Economic Planning Research Institute to form a new Policy Studies Institute.

The ideas and proposals have much in common. They acknowledge that forecasting, objective setting and planning have an important contribution to make to the generation, analysis, selection, implementation and evaluation of government policy. At the same time, they underline in their emphasis upon diversity the fundamental truth that there is no one system of forecasting, objective setting and planning that is right for all central departments, the government as a whole, or for all local authorities. The kind of system adopted should depend upon the task to be undertaken and the policies already in existence. Indeed, this is the main lesson of this survey, which has analysed the different systems of forecasting, objective setting and planning in the Department of Education and Science, in the Ministry of Defence, in central government as a whole (in its system of long-term financial planning, in the work of the Central Policy Review Staff, in the role of special advisers) and in the operation of the education departments in Liverpool, Coventry and Gloucester. We have seen that, in every case, the differences in the systems adopted, and certainly in the way that they have operated, have developed from the different policies that these institutions sought to achieve.

When the need is accepted for completely new plans and policies, they are less likely to result from the output of the planning system alone, than to come from a combination of planning studies, the evaluation of past experience, and outside developments. Within this process, the planners themselves have a crucial role. Naturally enough, such experts as professional planners, social scientists, political advisers, career civil servants and local government officers are interested in and concerned about the policies which their work suggests to them as being correct. They argue for them, as any person of enthusiasm and quality would press for their views. This does not mean that they will sabotage the decisions of elected members, or refuse to carry out instructions. But their role as officials will be more as partners and critics than technicians and passive executants. This naturally influences the whole way policy is worked out and developed and assessed.

The first lesson of the last 10 to 15 years is that the management theorist's view of planning should be supplemented in two ways. First, the policy prescriptions of one group of people must stand analysis and comparison with others. It is therefore valuable to be able to compare the studies produced by one department or authority with those of another, or the studies produced within the government machine with those produced outside it by research institutes or the universities, or to produce studies by co-operative activity, as does the CPRS. Of course, the cost of such richness and diversity can be considerable. And it is sometimes difficult to see the way through the mass of apparently conflicting and contradictory material. More care and co-ordination of policy work in the country at large is obviously required if most of it is not to end up on dusty shelves as unread studies. But in principle the benefits of diversity and a variety of viewpoints are clear and considerable.

The second lesson of this period is that forecasting, objective setting and planning must be susceptible to political control and adjustment in the light of political factors. Indeed, this is not simply a prescription of what ought to happen. Our analysis has shown that it is a description of what actually does happen, since the planning machinery adopted and the way it is operated will be a function of political values and attitudes. What is important is that this should be appreciated, and that planning should be seen as a political and not simply as a technical process. Planning should therefore be done as openly as possible, and forecasts, analysis and policy options should be submitted to the public gaze and public debate. Once again, there is a cost factor. The more public debate and discussion about the work of the planners, the longer it will take to complete, the more resources will be consumed in participation and consideration and the more difficult it will be to make timely decisions. The next challenge for the management theorists is to find how to combine public participation with speed and efficiency.

The paradoxical result of the greater attention to forecasting, objective setting and planning over the last 10 to 15 years has been that, instead of the production of clear, simple technical answers to political problems that some management theorists promised, we have instead an activity that remains highly influenced by political factors, by personal and professional values and attitudes, and which produces not one straightforward answer about how best to proceed, but a plethora of plausible answers that have to be compared and assessed and upon which the final series of judgments must be as political as they have always been in the sphere of public administration. Nevertheless, to the extent that the material upon which the judgment is exercised is now more sophisticated and informed, there is at least a chance that the quality of the decisions taken may result in better administration—especially if we can afford to open the decision making process to a wider public discussion and debate.

CONCLUSIONS AND SUMMARY

(1) The general interest in the study of management over the last 10 to 15 years has encouraged the adoption of systems of forecasting, planning-programming-budgeting systems, output budgeting and the introduction of planning staffs and analytical capabilities in a variety of forms in both central and local government.

(2) There are very few cases where these systems have been as fully developed as their authors proposed, and it is rare to find them remaining in their original form for more than a few years.

(3) This is partly because they are expensive in skilled staff and other resources and, in spite of increases in public sector employment, the means to implement them fully have not been available.

(4) But it is mainly because these systems encapsulate the policies, perceptions, values and attitudes of those who are responsible for setting them up.

(5) In theory, these systems are 'value free', and should be able to accommodate changing events and new policies. But in fact they reflect particular assumptions and policies and, when these change, the mechanics of the system must change as well. If they do not, the system is likely to fall into at least partial disuse.

(6) The greater attention to forecasting, objective setting and planning which has followed the interest in these subjects generated by management theorists has nevertheless been of value to policy makers in central and local government. It has underlined the complexity and difficulty of formulating successful policies; it has emphasized the extent to which policy making requires an accurate understanding of the way that society works, and accurate statistics of social facts and developments. Above all, it has emphasized that successful policy making cannot depend upon hunch, guesswork and prejudice.

(7) This is not to say that attention to forecasting and planning will always produce the right answers. Experience certainly shows that it will not do so; but it should at least produce more rapid and informed assessments of where and why policies are going off course, and so provide the opportunity for more timely adaptation and revision.

(8) These benefits are not purchased without cost. Forecasting, objective setting and planning are expensive in staff, time and money. They produce large quantities of data and information which have to be assembled, analysed and assimilated. They provide ministers, elected members, officials and the public at large with the opportunity to produce a better quality of public administration. But they certainly make public administration more complicated and demanding.

4
Analysis,value and choice

The concern with systems of output budgeting described in the previous chapter led naturally to an interest in how to make decisions. Different courses of action were brought into focus by the new methods of presenting and analysing information, and there was a need to be able to choose between them so as to obtain full value for the resources expended.

Cost-benefit analysis was the main decision making technique available that claimed to be able to value the consequences of different choices. We shall examine this technique below, and assess its strengths and weaknesses in practical application. In addition, many other techniques were available and more were devised. Some were at times employed within the framework of cost-benefit analysis. On other occasions they were applied separately and *ad hoc*.

These techniques can be grouped under three headings: first, techniques of operational research, many of which originally derived from the application of mathematics and natural science to military operations and government work during the Second World War; secondly, improvements in management accounting, mainly devoted to analysing in financial terms the inputs and outputs of administrative processes with a view to comparing costs and seeking the cheapest way of undertaking tasks; thirdly, various techniques concerned with staff selection, training, appraisal and career development. These have their place within the broad heading of value and choice but it will be more convenient to study them separately in the chapter on personnel.

COST-BENEFIT ANALYSIS

If the system of output budgeting described in the previous chapter is to work properly, then programmes of government action undertaken to achieve selected objectives must be the most effective and efficient that can be devised, so that the best value may be obtained for the money and other resources that must be expended. Output budgeting, however, is no more than a method of analysing and displaying information. It does not in itself provide a means for choosing between the various ways in which objectives might be achieved. Techniques are therefore required for evaluating and comparing the various means by which the objectives of public authorities might be attained and cost-benefit analysis has been proposed as a suitable tool.

Cost-benefit analysis, as its name implies, is based on the idea that decisions to proceed with public sector projects should be based on a full analysis of their costs and benefits to society as a whole. This principle is easy to state but hard to put into effect. This can be demonstrated by a simple example. Suppose a public authority is anxious to provide a means for people and goods to cross a river estuary provided the benefits exceed the costs. It has an obvious choice between providing a ferry, building a bridge or boring a tunnel. How can the choice be made between them and how can the authority decide whether to go ahead with even the best of the three? The ferry may cost the least but the tunnel takes most traffic. The tunnel might take five years to build against two for the bridge. Yet the bridge might impede shipping, affect the livelihood of local fishermen and require the destruction of a picturesque church on the riverbank. How are all these factors to be taken into account and the decision taken that will be in the best interests of society as a whole?

Cost-benefit analysis attempts to answer this question by putting a money value on all the costs and benefits arising from the various means of achieving the objective. This requires a careful enumeration not only of direct costs such as construction, maintenance and running, but also of the social costs of the kind mentioned above, which arise when the lives and work of many people are affected by the project. Again, on the benefits side, it is necessary not only to take account of the direct benefits arising from the case of the example quoted—speedier transport across the river estuary—but also of indirect benefits, such as extra jobs created, provided these would not otherwise have come into existence.

It is also necessary to take account of the fact that many of these costs and benefits cannot easily be cast in money terms. There is, for example, no obvious market price for the loss of a picturesque church. Yet some means must be found of putting money values on such items if a comprehensive analysis is to be made. Indeed, cost benefit analysis depends upon the quantifying of what are essentially political, and thus highly variable, values.

Difficulties also arise because costs and benefits fall at different points in time. A large capital project, for example, will have heavy costs during the construction phase with lighter running costs thereafter. The benefits, on the other hand, will probably be small or non-existent during construction but more substantial thereafter. It will therefore be necessary to take account of the time dimension by discounting the flows of costs and benefits to their present value. In the evaluation of investment projects in industry this can often be done by using the interest rate that would have to be paid if money were to be borrowed to finance the project. Thus, if it costs 10 per cent per annum to borrow the money, then the project must earn at least an equivalent return during the course of its life if it is to be worth undertaking. In a similar way, a public project must produce at least as great a dividend as could be obtained from any alternative use of the relevant resources. In our example the bridge, ferry or tunnel should produce at least as great a return to society as it could get by investing the money in, for example, a new airport or new schools.

It will be clear that it is by no means easy to enumerate and to evaluate these streams of costs and benefits or to determine an appropriate rate of discount. Some of these difficulties are described in more detail in Appendix 5, which also describes the elements of discounting and present value calculations. Difficulties also arise because of risk and uncertainty; the further in the future lie the estimates of costs and benefits the greater doubt there must be about their reliability and the wider the range of the possible outcomes. It is necessary to make some allowance in the analysis for these factors, or else to produce a number of analyses, each based on a different view of the risk and uncertainty involved.

Problems also stem from the interdependence between possible programmes. Some projects are mutually exclusive so that the underaking of one rules out the other. For example, if land is used for an airport it cannot be used for a housing estate. Other projects are contingent so that the benefits of one can only be obtained if the other is already undertaken.

In principle, it might be thought possible to apply cost benefit analysis to the entire range of government work so that all projects, whether undertaken by central government, public corporations or local government, could be fully evaluated by cost benefit analysis and ranked in order of attractiveness. But if this ever became technically feasible, there would still be problems. The compilation and administration of the list of projects might well in practice require and promote the further centralization of government power and decision making. This might require so large a bureaucratic machine as to produce serious inefficiency in the conduct of public business, and it might also pose a threat to the democratic process of debate and discussion at local level and in Parliament itself. It is therefore not feasible and has not in fact been attempted.

We shall now consider a variety of attempts that have been made to apply cost benefit analysis to government work so as to reach a view on the strength and weaknesses of this technique in its practical operation.

Examples of cost-benefit studies

One of the first cost-benefit studies was a survey of the M1 motorway project.[1] This was largely experimental and the actual decision to proceed with the motorway was taken before it was finished. But the study was nonetheless interesting since, while the costs of building the motorway could be estimated, the benefits were obviously problematical. Among the benefits included in the study were savings in working time by traffic transferring to the motorway from other roads; in vehicle time through faster journeys; in reduced vehicle fleets; in reduced consumption of fuel, spares and tyres; and in benefits accruing to motorists on other roads which would now be less congested. Putting figures on the savings was not easy. The hourly rates of pay for drivers and passengers could be calculated fairly readily. But estimating the value of the time saved by people like sales representatives and other executives was difficult. Again, there was the problem of estimating the value of leisure time saved through the faster journeys possible on the motorway. Different values (10p, 20p, 30p and 40p per hour) were arbitrarily chosen and the implications of these rates were worked out for the project's rate of return. Another estimate that had to be made was of the new traffic that would be generated by the existence of the motorway. Some traffic would simply switch to the new motorway. But new journeys on the motorway and elsewhere would be generated because of the extra facilities made available. However, while benefits would be enjoyed by this newly generated traffic, they could hardly be valued as highly as the benefits accruing to the traffic which already existed and was prepared to cope with the previous conditions. So the value of the benefits to newly generated traffic was fixed at 50 per cent of the value of the benefits to diverted traffic.

The study concluded that, against construction costs of £23.3 million, the accrued rate of return to diverted traffic alone ranged, with varying speed assumptions, from 3.3 to 4.2 per cent. When account was taken of generated traffic, the rate of return was raised to 3.8 to 4.8 per cent. When leisure-time savings were included, the rates were raised (at 20p per hour) to 5.4 to 7.1 per cent and (at 40p per hour) to 7.0 to 9.4 per cent. In addition, calculations were made of the effect on the economy generally of constructing the motorway. When these were taken into account the rate of return by 1965 rose to 17.6 to 27.3 per cent.

These are impressive returns and might suggest that investment in roads should be greatly enhanced; however, these calculations take no account of the effect of the congestion and other costs arising from travel on busy roads. If road pricing schemes were introduced so as to produce an 'optimal traffic flow' throughout the road system, the likely result would be a fall in traffic since some road users would be unwilling to pay the extra costs of using busy roads and would either not make their journeys or transfer to other means of transport such as railways. It is therefore necessary to consider whether it is right to give full weight to the benefits accruing to those who would not use the new road if they had to pay directly for the costs arising from their journeys. On the other hand, estimating what these costs would be, and working out how they might be charged through such means as excise licences, fuel taxes and road tolls, is by no means straightforward. Figures resulting from such estimates would be unlikely to be more reliable than the estimates of the benefits arising from the construction of new roads.

Another early cost-benefit study was carried out by Professor C. D. Foster and Professor Michael Beesley into the construction of the Victoria Line for London Transport.[2] It was estimated that the new line would be unattractive commercially since it would be unlikely to earn enough from current fares to meet its running costs, depreciation and interest charges. The deficit was put at £2.14 million per year (charging interest at 6 per cent on capital costs) so far as the line itself was concerned, and £3.12 million to London Transport, because of the consequent loss of revenue from other services.

However, Professor Foster and Professor Beesley argued that three other types of benefit should be taken into consideration. First, the traffic diverted to the Victoria Line would produce economies in vehicle operating costs; secondly, traffic not diverted to the Victoria Line and remaining on the surface would benefit from the faster flow and consequent reductions in time and vehicle operating costs; thirdly, newly generated traffic would arise from those who now found it worthwhile to make journeys they would not otherwise have undertaken. The results of the study are shown in Fig. 4.1 and reveal that, assuming a 50-year operating life and a 6 per cent discount rate, the total of benefits less running costs are nearly double the value of the capital expenditure incurred on the line.

While Professor Foster and Professor Beesley carried out an ingenious and valuable study, they did not take into account all the relevant factors, largely because of the difficulty of accommodating them within the calculations. First, they did not undertake a full analysis of all the social consequences of introducing the Victoria Line. To the extent that the construction of the line made living and working in London more attractive it would tend to promote jobs and population. This would be valuable if the objective of government policy was to maintain the level of employment and population of the metropolis; if, on the other hand, its objective was to reduce the number of people living and working in London, and to reduce investment in London's inner city facilities, then the construction on the Victoria Line cannot have been wholly advantageous. Secondly, the Victoria Line calculation, like that for the M1, was undertaken on the basis of current fares and vehicle taxes. Different fares and taxes might have led to a different outcome.

The most ambitious use of cost-benefit techniques in this country was the study of the best site for a third London airport. In February 1968 the government appointed a commission, under the chairmanship of Mr Justice Roskill, 'to inquire into the timing of the need for a four-runway airport to cater for the growth of traffic at existing airports serving the London area, to consider the various alternatives sites and recommend

		Annual amount £m.	Present value at 6% discount £m.
Costs			
(A)	Annual working costs	1.413	16.16
	Benefits		
(B)	Traffic diverted to Victoria Line		
	(1) Underground : time	.378	4.32
	comfort	.347	3.96
	(2) British Railways : time	.205	2.93
	(3) Buses : time	.575	6.58
	(4) Motorists : time	.153	3.25
	cost	.377	8.02
	(5) Pedestrians : time	.020	.28
	Sub-total	2.055	29.34
(C)	Traffic not diverted		
	Sub-total	3.916	44.79
(D)	Generated traffic		
	Sub-total	.822	11.74
	Total benefits		85.87
	Total benefits *less* running costs		69.71
	Value of capital expenditure		38.81

Fig. 4.1 Social benefits from the Victoria Line
Source: C. D. Foster and M. E. Beesley *Estimating the Social Benefit of constructing an Underground Railway in London,* Journal of the Royal Statistical Society, Series A, Vol. 126, Part 1 (1963).

which site should be selected'. The final report was published in January 1971.[3] The Commission held many sessions in public and took views and evidence from a wide variety of people, including experts on noise, the local authorities concerned, the airlines and local residents' pressure groups. The study cost over £1 million and the heart of the Commission's report was a detailed cost-benefit analysis.

The Commission started by considering some 78 sites, reduced this to 29 and finally settled upon four. These were Cublington in Buckinghamshire, Thurleigh in Bedfordshire, Nuthampstead in Hertfordshire, and a coastal site at Foulness in Essex called Maplin. The Commission considered a wide variety of factors affecting the four sites, such as the relative costs of construction, the costs falling on the passengers who would use the airport, costs to provide for air safety, for defence, and the costs falling on local residents who would be affected by such factors as noise. Fig.4.2 sets out the research team's summary of estimates of costs and benefits.

The research team also showed great ingenuity in taking account of some

	Cublington	Foulness	Nuthampstead	Thurleigh
Third London airport construction	184.0	179.0	178.0	166.0
Extension/closure of Luton Airport	-1.3	10.0	-1.3	-1.3
Airport services	74.6	62.9	70.7	67.2
Meteorology	5.0	1.6	3.0	2.0
Airspace movement	960.0	973.0	987.0	972.0
Passenger user costs	887.0	1041.0	868.0	889.0
Freight user costs	13.4	23.1	17.0	13.9
Road capital	7.4	7.4	7.5	2.7
Rail capital	4.4	16.0	8.0	3.8
Air safety	0.5	2.5	0.5	0.5
Defence	66.0	20.0	52.0	73.0
Public scientific establishments	2.0	3.4	11.2	16.6
Private airfields	8.7	3.1	9.8	12.2
Residential conditions (noise, off site)	9.0	3.6	19.0	5.6
Residential conditions (on site)	4.8	0	3.0	2.4
Luton noise costs	0	6.7	0	0
Schools, hospitals and public authority buildings (including noise)	2.5	0.8	4.1	4.9
Agriculture	3.1	4.2	7.2	4.6
Commerce and industry (including noise)	0.6	0.1	1.2	2.0
Recreation (including noise)	6.7	0.3	3.6	3.8
Work and service journeys to airport	26.2	26.5	24.4	25.4

	Cublington	Foulness	Nuthampstead	Thurleigh
Total net costs (discounted to 1975)	2264.6	2385.2	2273.9	2266.3
Total net costs as difference from lowest cost site	0	120.6	9.3	1.7

Fig. 4.2 The third London Airport, summary of best estimates of costs and benefits, £m. 1968 prices, discounted to 1975.
Source: *Commission on the Third London Airport* (HMSO, 1970)

of the factors that were obviously important yet difficult to value in monetary terms. One example was noise, where it was necessary to estimate the amount of noise that would have to be endured by the people living close to the airport. The detailed calculation was extremely complex, but the major elements were as follows. First, it was necessary to estimate the number and noisiness of the aircraft that would be using each site; secondly, a 'noise and nuisance index' (NNI) was calculated as a weighted average of noise intensity and frequency; thirdly, contour lines were drawn around each site showing the areas that would have to endure different noise-levels as measured by the NNI index; fourthly, an attempt was made to determine a money value for noise and nuisance by reference to the average property depreciation in the Gatwick area at the appropriate NNI level. This was based on the argument that the discount revealed by the sale of depreciated property on the market is related to the purchaser's personal valuation of the disadvantages of the noise. This discount varies according to the cost of the houses round Gatwick; rates of depreciation varied between about 30 per cent for the most expensive houses in the noisiest areas to about 10 per cent for the cheapest homes. Fifthly, surveys were made of the number of people expressing degrees of annoyance for each noise and nuisance value. Sixthly, the median or middle score of annoyance was equated with the average property depreciation as calculated above. Seventhly, it was necessary to calculate the 'householders' surplus' which means the amount of money above the market price of property which owners would require to make a willing sale. This surplus derives from such factors as personal liking for a house and its locality, and represents the benefits obtained from living in a particular house over what could be made by selling it on the market. From surveys in areas unaffected by aircraft noise, the research team estimated the average value of householders' surplus at 39 per cent above market values. Putting all these points together the method can be summarized as follows.

> For each NNI level a frequency distribution is formed of annoyance scores, the median of the distribution being taken as equal to the corresponding estimate of property depreciation (D). The result is a distribution of imputed values of noise annoyance (N) among householders within the zone involved. If S is the value of householders' surplus, a household is expected to move if N is greater than S + D. Here S + D is taken as the loss involved. Conversely, if N is less than S + D, a household is expected to stay in the noise affected zone. Here N is taken as the appropriate loss.[4]

This method of valuing noise costs is as arbitrary as it is ingenious. It certainly represents one plausible way in which the effects of noise might be valued. But there is no certainty that people actually do value the costs of noise in this way and, even if they did, implicitly or explicitly, go through such a process, there can be no certainty that the figures used in the calculation, many of which were derived from experience at Gatwick, necessarily applied to all the four sites surveyed by the research team.

As the table above makes clear, the result of the cost-benefit analysis was to favour of the Cublington site. Subsequently, however, the Government concluded that the Commission's recommendation should be rejected in favour of the development of Foulness. Later still, it was decided that the economic situation of the country did not permit the development of any site for a third London airport. This decision was possibly influenced by the development of wide-bodied jet-aircraft, which would enable Heathrow and Gatwick to cater for the likely increase in air traffic for a good deal longer than the Roskill Commission had assumed. This shows how quickly the assumptions of even the most thorough studies can be shown to be wrong. Finally, there is the point that even the detailed analysis made by the Roskill Commission was not comprehensive. The Commission concentrated, as they were asked to do, on recommending a site for a third airport. They were not asked whether the airport would be commercially viable, nor were they asked whether such viability would be maintained if airline operators were asked to pay charges related to the noise and other nuisances of air transport. Similarly no account was taken of the fact that much air travel is subsidized in various ways, very often by governments, including our own. Air fares may therefore fail to reflect the full range of economic costs, and this subsidy may promote extra air journeys. If the Commission had been asked to undertake a wider ranging study of transport pricing problems, and then to enquire into airport demands rather than assumed needs, the final results might have been a better guide to the community's interests. On the other hand, the study would have been even more complicated, more arbitrary assumptions would have had to be made, and the cost and time spent would have been even greater.

It might be tempting to conclude that the third London airport study was a waste of time and money. Common sense suggests that an airport at Foulness would create less of a noise nuisance and involve a smaller interruption to the general social life of the area than would airports at Cublington, Nuthampstead or Thurleigh. Politically, therefore, construction at Foulness would create many fewer problems for the Government and it would have been easy to predict that this site would finally be chosen. It would, however, be wrong to conclude that the analysis was a waste of time. In disclosing that the cost of the most expensive site, Foulness, was only some 5 per cent greater than the cost of the cheapest, Cublington, it did give some idea of the relative economic differences of each site. Furthermore, the analysis was itself a contribution to the political debate. If Foulness was the 'right' decision at the time, then it was much easier for the Government of the day to reach it in the light of the detailed analysis than it would otherwise have been. Without this analysis, the criticisms of the Foulness decision by the airline operators on the grounds of distance from London would have been far greater. And the Government would have come under general attack for making a decision without carrying out anything in the way of full analysis of the problem.

Even more ambitious in principle than the Roskill Commission's investigation of the site for a third London airport were such examples of cost-benefit analysis as various attempts to determine the rate of return to education. There is a *prima facie* case for saying that the community's investment in education by way of providing schools, and universities should be based on assessment of costs and benefits. A study on these lines was undertaken for the Department of Education and Science by Miss Vera Morris and Dr A Ziderman.[5] They sought to estimate the returns to society from the acquisition of different educational qualifications. Their studies were based on surveys of the earnings of people with different qualifications. By comparing these with the costs of providing the education a range of social internal rates of return were calculated. Some of the results are shown in Fig. 4.3.

These social returns were arrived at by comparing the additional income before tax arising from particular qualifications, plus any economic spill-overs which can be identified (such as economic advantages not reflected in earnings) with the full social costs of providing education, i.e., the state expenditure, private fees and income foregone. The table suggests that the highest social rates of return are obtained from technical qualifications and from first degrees. The social value of adding a doctorate to a first degree is very small indeed.

These estimates of social return do not, of course, attempt to value the enhanced enjoyment that the individual may obtain from his higher education. Neither do they measure the general improvement in the quality of social and national life that may come from a higher level of education,

	With no ability adjustment %	With ability adjustment %
'A' Level/Non-qualified	7.6	6.9
ONC/Non-qualified	7.9	7.0
HNC/ONC	>20.0	>20.0
HNC-PQ/HNC	20.0	16.0
First Degree/A-Level	10.0	9.2
Master's/First Degree	1.2	<0.0
Doctorate/First Degree	1.6	<0.0

Fig. 4.3 Estimates of social rates of return to education expressed as incremental comparisons–males 1966–67
Source: V. Morris and A. Ziderman *The Economic Return on Investment in Higher Education in England and Wales* Economic Trends, HMSO, pp. XX-XXXI, (May 1971).

nor the way, for example, that it may promote such social goals as a respect for law and order and an increase in political stability.

The difficulty of undertaking comprehensive cost-benefit analyses has tended to focus attention in recent years on smaller scale studies. One early example was a series of attempts to assess the costs of road accidents. Studies by Mr R.F.F. Dawson, bringing up to date earlier work by Mr D.J. Reynolds and others, have suggested that the cost to the community of road accidents was £246 million in 1965.[6] This figure included a net loss of future output of £24 million, medical treatment at £12 million, damage to property at £164 million, administrative expenses by police and insurance companies at £28 million. Using a discount factor of 6 per cent, the average cost per accident involving injury or death was £360. As the author of the study made clear, this leaves out all the intangible costs of bereavement and suffering. It shows, however, that in purely economic terms there may be limits on what it is worth spending on accident prevention measures. However, this is very much of a blanket result. More detailed analysis of the costs of particular types of accident might suggest that the economic return of accident prevention campaigns could be much greater in some spheres than in others.

COST-EFFECTIVENESS ANALYSIS AND SMALLER SCALE STUDIES

The results of such relatively small scale studies must, of course, be used with care. But they do indicate that future work in the cost-benefit area will probably lie in the detailed investigation of specific and circumscribed questions, particularly in the use of cost-effectiveness analysis. The difference here is that, while cost-benefit analysis is concerned with the monetary value of the costs and benefits of alternative programmes, cost-effectiveness analysis concentrates on the costs associated with various means of reaching a specified objective.

Three kinds of cost-effectiveness studies can be distinguished. First, there are constant-cost studies. These are designed to specify the outputs or results from investing the same amount of resources in different programmes. For example, an estimate might be made of the returns from spending £1 million on extra law and order services in a city by providing more policemen on the beat, or more mobile patrols, or more private alarm systems wired to police stations. Secondly, there are least-cost studies. These are designed to show the least expensive way of achieving some specified objective. Thus, if it is desired to reduce the number of successful burglaries in a city by 20 per cent, a study might be made of whether it is cheaper to try to do this by more policeman on the beat, more patrol cars or more alarm systems or, of course, by some combination of the three. Thirdly, objective level studies show the cost of achieving different levels of performance or output. For example, a study might be made of the costs of trying to cut the number of successful burglaries in a city by, say, 5 per cent, 10 per cent, 15 per cent, or 20 per cent.

This concentration on more modest studies is reflected in recent practice in the field of transport.[7] No attempt is made to use cost-benefit analysis to determine the size of the overall transport budget. This is settled through the work of the Public Expenditure Survey Committee described in a previous chapter. Nor is cost-benefit analysis used for evaluating inter-city rail and bus projects or nationalized freight projects. These are usually susceptible to straightforward financial analysis. But attempts are made to evaluate the average benefits from road improvement schemes, listing such factors as accident savings and time savings. The latter are valued at the cost of employing the kind of traveller concerned including wages, employers' overheads and pension and national insurance contributions. This is based on the assumption that the cost of employing a person must at least equal the value of his output, and that a saving in his time would allow production to be increased by a corresponding amount. Leisure time is valued more cheaply. The figures are based on investigations of how much people are prepared to pay to save time, when alternative means of transport are available. Figures 4.4. and 4.5. set out the data as used in 1975.

	%
Accident savings	20
Vehicle operating cost savings	0
Working time savings:	
Cars	26
Light goods vehicle	11
Heavy goods vehicle	11
Buses	3
Non-working time savings:	
Cars	23
Buses	6

Fig. 4.4 Average benefits from road improvement schemes

Pence per hour (1975)
Working time

(1) Car drivers	331
(2) Car passengers	287
(3) Rail passengers	357
(4) Bus passengers	168
(5) Underground passengers	313
(6) HGV occupants	155
(7) LGV occupants	139
(8) Bus drivers	166
(9) Bus conductors	158

Leisure time

(1) In vehicle time	35
(2) Walk/wait time	70

Fig. 4.5 How time is valued
Source: (Figs. 4.4 and 4.5): *The Economist* 18 December 1976, quoting figures supplied by the Department of the Environment.

Recommendations have also been made for more guarded assessments of schemes for new roads, and for greater publicity for the range of relevant considerations. In 1978, the Advisory Committee on Trunk Road Assessment suggested that changes should be made in the Department of Transport's methods of forecasting the likely growth of road traffic to make them more sensitive to a wider range of factors, and that more attention should be paid and more publicity given to considerations which cannot easily be set out in money values, including the break up of communities and environmental gains and losses.[8] The Committee had been asked to look into this subject following widespread dissatisfaction with plans for road improvements, which had led to many demonstrations and interruptions of public enquiries by people who felt that the Department's calculations were too arbitrary and their approach too inflexible.

OPERATIONAL RESEARCH

Many problems arise in the management of public authorities that cannot easily be tackled by straightforward methods of common sense or everyday experience, but can be more directly approached by the methods of operational research. Operational research is sometimes described as if it were a branch of higher statistics and mathematics, a set of techniques drawn from these disciplines which can be understood only by those who have had a long and elaborate training. It is true that much operational research work consists in applying the methods of mathematics and natural science to management problems; but it is by no means all very difficult to understand and it is wrong to regard operational research as a set of techniques. Operational research is more accurately considered as an approach to solving problems, many of which can be categorized into the following groups.

(*a*) Stockholding problems. Nearly all organizations must hold stocks of various kinds to meet anticipated demands. If stocks are too high, excessive costs are incurred in terms of capital tied up and for storage; if they are too low, work will be interrupted when stocks run out and costs will be incurred. The problem is therefore to determine the level of stocks that will produce an acceptable balance between the costs of stockholding and the costs of being caught short.

(*b*) Allocation problems. These problems arise from the need to distribute available resources between a number of requirements in the most efficient way that will effectively do the job. An example is distributing a limited number of secretaries between a number of senior executives. The problem is to determine the distribution of duties which will reduce to the minimum the amount of time secretaries sit idle and executives are delayed because they cannot get dictated work back when they need it.

(*c*) Queueing problems. An example will illustrate this class of problem. Suppose consideration is being given to the number of telephone lines to be installed in the main office of a local authority. Insufficient lines will mean that many callers will get the engaged signal. If too many are installed, the authority will pay telephone rentals for lines that are seldom used. Some idleness and waste will certainly result. The question to answer is how much can be tolerated. The problem is then to work out the requisite number of lines to be installed.

(*d*) Sequencing or control problems. These problems are concerned with planning, scheduling and controlling scarce resources of time, staff and money, as in planning a construction project so that the different materials and different kinds of skilled craftsmen arrive on the site in good time for their part in the construction. This may involve working out the 'critical path' through the project, which is the sequence of activities that must be completed on time if the project as a whole is not to be delayed. These critical activities can then be distinguished from those with slack time, where some delay can be tolerated without holding up the entire project. Further examples are given in chapter 7 on audit, review and control.

(*e*) Route selection problems. These problems require the finding of the best route or path for the flow of resources necessary to undertake an activity. For example, an organization may have staff in a number of separate buildings. Letters and memoranda must pass between them, and the problem is to find the most efficient route for the delivery vans. This will be the route that meets the prescribed frequency of delivery with the minimum cost in vehicle time and expense.

(*f*) Search problems. One example is that of designing a procedure for tracking down submarines in a wide stretch of ocean. How can the ships and aircraft carrying the radar scanners be deployed so as to maximize their chances of discovering the submarines?

(g) Information problems. These problems range from how best to file information so that it can be rapidly found when needed to deciding what information is needed if correct or, at least, the best possible decisions are to be taken about the development of the economy. The common theme in all such problems is the determination of the data necessary to take the relevant decisions, and how it can be obtained at the desired levels of accuracy at the most reasonable cost.

(h) Replacement problems. An example which illustrates the nature of this class of problem is that of the frequency with which machines and facilities should be replaced. If they are replaced only when they irretrievably break down, costly delays may occur; but blanket replacement of all machines at specified intervals may be very costly. A detailed example of this kind of problem is given below.

(j) Competitive problems. There are many occasions when public authorities have to estimate the behaviour of other groups of people and base their courses of action on these assessments. Examples include the deployment of police resources so as to catch the maximum number of criminals, and the determination of the range of sea, land and air forces most likely to deter and deal effectively with a potential aggressor. Competitive problems are difficult to analyse, since the actions of the competitors are usually based on their assessments of the countervailing action that will be taken against them. Furthermore, the competitors have to decide what their aim is to be—a reasonable success rate in all likely circumstances, or maximum success in the most likely circumstances at the expense, say, of almost complete failure if the less likely possibilities should in fact eventuate.

It is not possible or relevant here to give detailed solutions to all these kinds of problems. As a simple example of operational research in action, let us take the problem that might arise in a prison protected by a perimeter fence that is floodlit by a special type of lighting device.[9] The maximum life of this device is two weeks, and there are three chances in ten that it will fail at the end of the first week. One hundred devices are required, which cost £2 each for individual replacement and £1 each for group replacement. Is it best to replace all devices every week, every other week, every third week or individually when they fail?

This problem can be tackled on the following lines.

(a) If all the devices are replaced every week, the total cost weekly will be £100.

(b) If the devices are replaced every two weeks, the cost incurred in a fortnight is £100 for the group replacement and £60 for the replacement of the thirty devices which will have to be replaced individually at the end of the first week. This gives a total cost of £160 and a weekly cost of £80.

(c) If the devices are replaced every three weeks, the cost will be £100 for the group replacement, plus £60 for the thirty devices that will fail at the end of the first week, £140 for the 70 devices that will fail at the end of the second week, and £18 for the nine devices out of the batch of 30 replacements put in at the end of the first week that will have failed at the end of the second week. This gives a total cost of £318 and an average cost of £106 per week.

(d) If the devices are replaced individually when they expire, the average cost per week can be found by calculating the average number of devices that will need to be replaced individually each week. The average life is

1 week $\times$ 0.3 = 0.3
2 weeks $\times$ 0.7 = 1.4

Average life   1.7 weeks

Therefore 59 devices (100 ÷ 1.7) fail per week on average and the cost of replacing them is £118 per week.

The average cost of each policy is (a) £100 per week, (b) £80 per week, (c) £106 per week, (d) £118 per week. It therefore follows that the cheapest policy is the second, i.e., group replacement every two weeks and individual replacements in between.

This simple example of the application of operational research illustrates two features: the application of mathematical concepts, here the idea of probability; and the use of simple calculations. Not all applications of operational research are as straightforward as this one, but many are less complicated than is commonly supposed.

Examples of operational research in central and local government

One example of operational research in central government is the study that was undertaken to determine the number of berths that would be needed at Peterhead Harbour in north-east Scotland to cope with tankers bringing fuel to a new power station due to become fully operational in 1980, and to ship out various chemicals to be produced at new plants to be erected to process the by-products of North Sea gas.[10] Account had also to be taken of traffic serving North Sea oil rigs and of the local fishing fleet which needed priority in the harbour each morning in order to send its catch to the fish markets.

Chaos and delay would result from insufficient berths, whereas over-provision would lead to idle facilities and waste of resources. This was a clear example of a queuing problem as described above, and was tackled accordingly by the operational research team responsible. The team investigated the servicing of the tankers under four headings:

(a) The 'arrival window' for access to a berth. It is difficult to estimate exactly when ships will arrive in harbour, especially if they have travelled a long way. It is therefore prudent to leave a certain leeway for late or early arrival and to allocate access to a berth for longer than it takes to turn the ship round.

(b) The amount of time each type of tanker would need to occupy a berth.

(c) The amount of time that the available number of berths would consequently be occupied.

(d) The time to clear tanker backlogs of various sizes when the harbour is closed for various periods of bad weather in winter.

The operational research team had to consider the implications of several traffic patterns under each of these headings and of the probability of each pattern occurring. On this basis they made an estimate of the most reasonable number of berths to construct for the tankers. The team were not thereby claiming that there would never be an empty berth or a queue of ships, but they hoped to reduce these events to a minimum. The quality of the team's recommendations obviously depended upon the accuracy of their initial information about the oil needs of the power stations, the outputs of the chemical factories and the size of the tankers. If any of this data turns out to be wider of the mark than the team have allowed for in their studies, then the value of their recommendations will be reduced. Indeed, this points to one of the major difficulties about operational research studies; however sophisticated the analysis, the value of the results will depend upon the accuracy of the forecasts contained in the initial information. In a swiftly changing world such forecasts often need revision.

Another good example can be taken from the work of the Metropolitan Police Management Services Department.[11] In the early 1970s the Metropolitan Police owned some 4500 flats, maisonettes and houses. Although the number of empty quarters was rising, the queue of police families waiting to get into a married quarter was not diminishing. The operational research team discovered that this was because those who were allocating the quarters did not have all the relevant information to discharge their responsibilities. Changes were accordingly made in the organization of the work and in the flow and distribution of information. The team also developed a mathematical relationship between the rate at which accommodation was vacated, the time spent in maintenance and administration, and the rate of allocation. It was possible to determine from this relationship the minimum numbers of flats, maisonettes and houses that were needed to keep the queue of applicants at a reasonable level. It was also possible to determine the effect of increasing maintenance expenditure upon the time spent in getting accommodation ready and thereby estimate the cost of reducing the length of the queue without increasing the total stock of police accommodation.

This was a simple example of how mathematical relationships could be specified between activities and applied to management problems. As with our other examples, there was no question of the operational research study 'solving' the problem. Indeed, in this case, as in most management problems, there was no single solution. Operational research may be able to indicate various courses of action and the costs and benefits of each one. It is then for management to take the decisions, but they are able to do so on the basis of better information than would otherwise have been available.

In the sphere of local government, the organization of school transport presents a series of routing problems. The Local Government Operational Research Unit has designed a series of computer programmes to help education authorities organize their school transport services. The programmes produce sets of routes that either use the minimum possible number of vehicles or minimize the total cost of the service. The programmes allow special features to be studied, such as the effect of staggering school hours and transferring children between specially hired and scheduled buses at points along the route.[12]

The Unit has also devised a set of computer programmes called TRANSEPT which includes a comprehensive representation of the essential details of a bus system. This enables bus operators to feed in data concerning their system and their ideas for change and to extract predictions from the computer that are helpful in designing new and improved schemes of bus operation.

Useful work is also being done to assist local authorities to make the best plans for disposing of waste. Details of the problems naturally vary between authorities. But the approach devised by the Unit is the same in all cases. First, estimates are made of the amount of refuse likely to be produced over the next 30 years in the area for which the authority is responsible. Secondly, assessments are made of the amount of tipping space that is likely to become available during the same period, itemising the different sites suitable for different kinds of waste. Thirdly, the cost can be worked out of various arrangements for distributing the waste likely to be generated between the facilities estimated to be available. These arrangements cover different systems of disposal, such as controlled tipping, different types of treatment and the haulage of waste to distant sites.

The Unit also tries to help authorities monitor their purchasing activities. Local authorities buy large quantities of supplies of all kinds, and they must try to buy at economical prices. The Unit is considering making regular surveys of prices paid by local authorities for their goods. Under the scheme, a range of authorities would provide lists of prices paid for representative samples of goods and services. These lists would be drawn up every six months and sets of price indices for different goods and different methods of purchasing would be calculated. Authorities could use these indices for comparing what they have paid with average prices, and for judging the effectiveness of different kinds of purchasing organization. The lists would also be helpful to authorities engaged in changing from one set of purchasing arrangements to another. Such changes are usually difficult to evaluate as prices alter during the changeover. The use of the indices would enable the effect of price changes to be removed from the data, and the true cost implications of the changed arrangements would be available for analysis by the purchasing staff.

The provision of timely and relevant financial information has been usefully tackled by operational research in central and local government. One example is the introduction of a new financial information system into central government for the 1977–78 financial year. There are basically four systems for estimating the annual expenditure within the purview of central government, running at £35,000 million in 1977. First, a system of strategic expenditure control based on the rolling programmes of public expenditure at constant prices produced by the Public Expenditure Survey Committee, and published after ministerial approval in annual White Papers. Secondly, a system based on cash estimates and flows in line with parliamentary estimates and accounts. Thirdly, a monetary system covering other cash flows and the results of public expenditure in terms of the financial transactions involved, including public sector borrowing. And fourthly, a macro-economic assessment system, calculated at constant prices and designed to forecast the national income and its components.

It is difficult to understand the interconnection between these systems, and difficult to get them to bear on the central problem of estimating government expenditure at a time of high inflation and economic difficulty. High rates of inflation encourage overspending, and it is difficult to determine whether this extra expenditure is entirely inflationary or if it masks an increase in the volume of expenditure. Economic difficulties often work for underspending, as when expenditure on major projects is delayed because of failure to complete them on time. These different forces have often invalidated government expenditure forecasts, and led to a general feeling that 'public expenditure is out of control'.

A joint Treasury and Civil Service Department project team was therefore set up to look into the problem in October 1974.[13] It consisted of operational research scientists, management accountants, outside management consultants, computer specialists and others concerned with government expenditure control. The team undertook a wide-ranging survey, including detailed discussions with spending departments, an analysis of prospective developments in computer technology that might help to provide an improved system of expenditure control and an investigation of expenditure control practices in business and commerce.

The major recommendations of the project team were as follows. First, the expected 'path' of expenditure through the year should be estimated by using 'profiles' of expenditure showing the quarterly or monthly pattern of spending estimated in advance; secondly, quicker and more frequent figures of actual expenditure should be provided; thirdly, regular returns comparing actual expenditure with the 'profiles' should be submitted during the course of the year, explaining the reasons for any differences and projecting their consequences forward; fourthly, expenditure should be analysed into the volume of expenditure at the prices used for the public expenditure survey, and price changes since then, thus making it possible to use a single flow of figures to monitor progress in both cash and constant price terms.

The team then divided into two sections. The first section was responsible for designing and implementing the changes necessary within the Treasury to put these recommendations into effect. The second section was concerned with implementation within departments, and with carrying out a pilot study of the new system within a limited area of Home Office expenditure.

As a result of all this work, it was possible to introduce the new system for the financial year 1977–78. The system should enable the new arrangements for cash limits described in the previous chapter to operate as effectively as possible, and should improve the quality of the Government's financial work generally. Changes will no doubt be necessary with experience, but the work of the team has already demonstrated the value of the operational research approach in making a clear analysis of the task to be undertaken and of the best means of discharging it. The study has also shown the value of including experts from several disciplines within the project team and of discussing the study carefully with all those in the Treasury and other departments who would be affected by it. In this way, the system was specifically designed to cater for the needs of those who would have to work it, and was not imposed upon them with insufficient consultation. Further, a reasonable time was allowed to test the system, including a pilot study, before the full arrangements were put into effect. All these are important points for all operational research projects.

MANAGEMENT ACCOUNTING

Accounting in central and local government is traditionally concerned with the accurate recording of receipts and payments. This is the basis of the vote accounting system of central government. This system is of great value in ensuring that money is spent for the purposes it was voted. But it does not supply all the information necessary to ensure that government programmes are planned and carried out effectively and efficiently. Management accountants can often supply the financial information necessary to do this. In this way, management accounting can make a contribution to analysis, value and choice, as described in this chapter, and to the control of managerial operations as described in chapter 7. In particular, management accountants can often supplement the vote accounts with:

(*a*) Financial accounts. These accounts may be drawn up in whatever form is most appropriate for the objectives and structure of an organization. They summarize its operations in financial terms, and facilitate the preparation of profit and loss accounts, income and expenditure statements, and balance sheets recording the assets and liabilities of the organization and the changes that have taken place in them and in how they are financed in the immediately preceeding financial period.

(*b*) Cost accounts. These provide information about the operation of particular departments or sections of an organization and their activities, outputs and services.

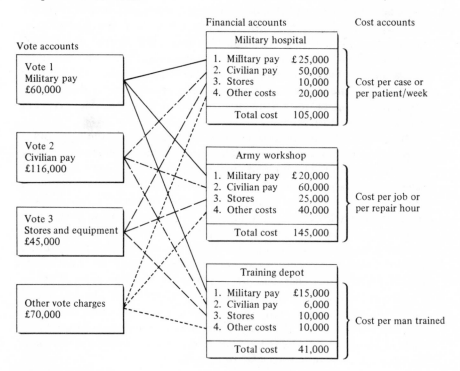

Fig. 4.6
Source: *Management Accounting in the Civil Service* Civil Service Department, (HMSO, London 1976).

For example, Fig. 4.6 shows how some of the vote accounts of the Army Department of the Ministry of Defence can be split between the different activities to which they relate and the relevant financial and cost accounts determined.

Figure 4.7 shows how the three systems of vote accounting, financial accounts and cost accounts yield different information about a few simple transactions.

WIDER ISSUES

In principle, therefore, output budgeting, cost-benefit analysis, operational research and management accounting provide a set of techniques by which government authorities can accurately determine the costs and benefits of their present and proposed activities. In practice, however, we have seen that this is not feasible. The examples we have examined show that it is not possible to enumerate with certainty the costs and benefits of the various different ways of seeking the various objectives that might be selected and, even if it were, there is no necessarily correct rate of discount for reducing these streams and costs and benefits to a present value. Furthermore, when working out the best way of undertaking various projects, neither everyday experience nor operational research points unerringly to the most efficient and effective method of proceeding. This means that, even if all costs and benefits could be enumerated, and a discount rate selected with certainty, we should not always know that we have necessarily costed and selected the most appropriate projects and, without being certain which these projects were, we cannot be certain that the objectives to which they relate are necessarily the most beneficial.

But although the use of these techniques cannot indicate the right course with certainty, their employment can remind us that decisions will usually be better taken if they are based on a detailed enumeration of the various relevant factors rather than hunch, intuition and the accommodation of immediate pressures. We have also seen that cost-benefit analysis and operational research may not be very helpful in tackling large-scale problems, such as the optimum size of public sector expenditure, or the balance between education, health and defence, or in assessing the future behaviour of a potential aggressor, or in estimating the number of manufacturing jobs that will be available in London in 1990, or in suggesting the best ways of revitalizing some of our major cities. They are, however, more helpful with more modest problems, such as a cost-effectiveness analysis of the cheapest way of undertaking a specific military task, or an operational research study to determine the best size of vehicle fleet for the tasks of a particular organization.

Finally, if these techniques are to produce their full value they must be properly understood by a wide range of public officials and by elected representatives. This does not mean that all civil servants, local govern-

	Vote accounting £	Financial accounting £	Cost accounting Product A £	Cost accounting Product B £
1 Payment for materials	100,000	100,000		
Increase in creditors: Closing £20,000 Opening £15,000		5,000		
Expenditure on materials		105,000		
Usage of stocks from previous years purchases Opening stocks: £60,000 Closing stocks: £50,000		10,000		
2 Material usage	120,000	115,000	75,000	40,000
3 Payment of wages	80,000	120,000	70,000	50,000
4 Payments for other items		80,000	55,000	25,000
Decrease in work in progress		5,000	3,000	2,000
5 Total spent	300,000	320,000	203,000	117,000
6 Expenditure on products sold			203,000	117,000
7 Receipts from purchasers of products	350,000	350,000		
8 Increase in debtors		2,000		
9 Total receipts	350,000	352,000		
10 Total sales			245,000	107,000
11 Apparent profit (Item 9–Item 5)	50,000			
12 Actual profit (Item 10–Item 6)		32,000	42,000	
13 Actual loss (Item 9–Item 10)				10,000
14 Expenditure on products sold (Item 6 above)			203,000	117,000
15 Quantity sold			1,000	21,400
16 Average unit cost of product			203	5.47
17 Selling price			245	5.00

Fig. 4.7 Simplified example illustrating different treatments in vote, financial and cost accounts
Source: *Management Accounting in the Civil Service* Civil Service Department HMSO, (1976).

ment officers, councillors and ministers need courses in cost-benefit analysis and operational research. But they do need to know the outline of these subjects and officials need to be able to present the assumptions and results of such studies intelligibly to each other and to elected representatives. Furthermore, and most importantly, the elected representatives need to be able to make these assumptions and results plain in wider political debate and discussion. If democracy is to work effectively, the electorate must be reasonably well informed. This not only entails providing information but also providing it in a readily understandable form and with a clear relevance to the issues under debate.

CONCLUSIONS AND SUMMARY

(1) This chapter has considered three sets of techniques for achieving value for money in public administration: cost-benefit analysis, operational research, and management accounting.

(2) Cost-benefit analysis complements output budgeting, described in the previous chapter, by attempting to provide a means of assessing the costs and benefits to society as a whole of the various projects that might be undertaken to achieve the objectives of central government departments and local authorities. Cost-benefit analysis attempts to enumerate and calculate all the direct and indirect costs and benefits arising from possible projects, expressing them in monetary terms if at all possible, and discounting them to a particular value in time. Case studies of the M1 motorway project, the proposed third London Airport and of attempts to assess the benefits of educational expenditure, showed the difficulties of doing this satisfactorily. The more modest and self contained cost-effectiveness studies of the kind also discussed in the chapter are more likely to be valuable in practice than such broad surveys. However, even the broad surveys can be valuable in bringing out the range of factors relevant to decisions. Many of these factors could easily be forgotten and overlooked in less thorough approaches to decision making.

(3) Cost-benefit analysis therefore requires a variety of means for calculating the most effective and efficient ways of carrying out the various projects that might be undertaken to achieve the various possible goals. Sometimes these calculations are straightforward, and can be based on everyday knowledge and experience. At other times they can be more swiftly undertaken by using methods derived from mathematics and natural science. Operational research is the name customarily given to the selection and application of mathematical and scientific methods to management problems. In this chapter we distinguished for convenience nine broad types of problems; *viz.,* the determination of stocks, the allocation of resources, queueing, sequencing and control, routing, searching, replacement, competitive problems and problems of providing accurate and timely information. The detailed examples made clear that, as

with cost-benefit analysis, operational research is usually more successful in helping to solve narrowly drawn problems than in dealing with wider issues or those depending on speculative assessments of future events and human behaviour.

(4) Management accounting complements both cost-benefit analysis and operational research by providing where appropriate the financial information necessary to evaluate costs and benefits and the alternative courses of action within operational research studies.

(5) It is wrong to regard cost-benefit analysis and operational research as complex techniques beyond the understanding of ordinary people and accessible only to specialists. Some aspects are complicated. But the general principles and even many of the details are straightforward. Officials and elected members need to be able to communicate and discuss with each other the assumptions and results of applying cost-benefit analysis and using operational research. It is also necessary to communicate such information in as readily understandable form as possible to the electorate as a whole and particularly to those who may be affected by decisions based on the use of such techniques. Democracy works effectively only if the electorate is reasonably well informed. The challenge of communicating complex information to people with little relevant training or time to spare to understand it is one of the major problems of modern government.

5
Organization

The increasing interest and concern for management in central and local government over the last 10–15 years had had important implications for organization. Many changes have been introduced during this period, and they naturally cannot all be explained as a response to an increasing interest ·in the theory and practice of management. Nevertheless, this concern has been manifest in at least the following three main ways.

First, the interest in goals, purposes and objectives that we have described in previous chapters has led to attempts to reshape organizations to make them cohere more closely with the purposes and policies that they are designed to achieve. Secondly, the belief that the disciplines of natural and social science have a contribution to make to the generation and administration of policy has led to new forms of organization designed to bring specialists closer to policy making, instead of confining them to advisory roles and to the execution of specialist, scientific and engineering services. Thirdly, the idea that organizations consist of formal hierarchies of officials whose interests are confined to the discharge of their formal, legal and other responsibilities as listed in Acts of Parliament, organization manuals, organization charts and so forth, has yielded ground to the idea that organizations should also be looked upon as social groups or systems whose members consist of interdependent individuals in action and reaction with each other and with the social and political environment in which the organization operates.

This idea has led to an interest in less formal groupings and organizational arrangements, and to looser systems for co-operative activity. The assumption is that such systems will encourage the release of interests and talents that may be stifled by more formal arrangements.

We have already described in earlier chapters the background to the first two of these trends. The background to the third is described below.

THE ORGANIZATION AS A SYSTEM

The idea of an organization as a system can be explained as follows. Any system must be in continual interaction with its environment. A biological system, like a human being or other animal, takes inputs from its environment such as sights, sounds and food, transforms them by physiological and psychological processes, and produces such outputs as actions of various kinds. The object of this transformation must at least be the survival of the system, i.e. that the animal shall continue to live, and at most that it shall attain further goals, which for the human animal may be described as 'satisfaction', 'welfare' or 'happiness'.

The same line of thought can be applied to organizations. The inputs of a local authority, for example, might be taken to be staff and other resources, demands for certain services, and information of various kinds. The outputs might be rules and regulations, services to the community, and wages and other benefits to its staff. The outputs must be in reasonable accord with the inputs: thus if the wages paid and conditions offered do not satisfy the staff they will leave; if the rules and regulations and benefits do not meet to a substantial degree the demands placed upon the organization it will have to produce new programmes, or it will be abolished or amalgamated. As the environment changes, so will the organization's inputs—staff are recruited with new values and attitudes, demands are made for new programmes. And as the inputs change so must the outputs. The organization seeks to maintain its equilibrium in a changing environment. This can be outlined in Fig. 5.1 showing the organization as a system.

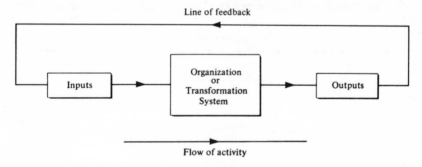

Fig. 5.1

The organization or transformation system is often described as a socio-technical system. By this it is meant that the oganization will have the following elements or sub-systems:

(*a*) *Technical.* The organization will employ certain machines and technologies to carry out its task. In an industrial organization these will include factory machines. In a public organization such as a local authority they are such machines as typewriters, photocopying machines, telephones and such technologies as the system of filing and paper work. The idea is that these machines and technologies determine to a considerable extent the way work is done and the relationships between people.

(*b*) *Psycho-social.* The goals, values, aspirations and modes of behaviour of the members of the organization will also determine the way work is done and the relationships between people. If an organization is staffed by people of modest ambition, respectful of authority, interested in detail, formally polite, it will work in a different way from one which is staffed by buccaneering entrepreneurs.

(*c*) *Structural.* The organization will have to put machines and technologies together with people in order to get work done or, in the language of systems, in order to process inputs into outputs. The structural sub-system is concerned with the ways in which tasks are divided between operating units and with their co-ordination. The formal expression of the structural element of an organization is the organization chart. Differences in structure will have a crucial effect on the way an organization works and the relationships between people. For example, a local authority department concerned with social services could organize itself on functional lines, e.g. one division for each kind of service; on geographical lines; or in terms of client group, e.g. one division for children, one for problem families, one for the old, and so on. Whichever was adopted would affect very considerably the way the department worked.

The socio-technical system can be shown in short-hand form as in Fig. 5.2.

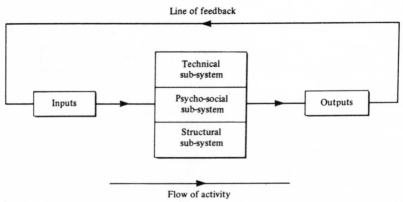

Fig. 5.2.

Specialists in such techniques as organization and methods have paid particular attention to the structural sub-system in their work, the behavioural scientist has emphasized the psycho-social sub-system, while those concerned with management science and operational research have been largely concerned with the technical sub-system. Those who look on organizations as systems claim to have united the three sub-systems and to study the organization as a whole.

It is also useful to look at organizations in terms of three levels—the technical or production level, the organizational level and the institutional or community level.

(a) The production level. This is concerned with the actual task to be done. In a social services department, for example the task might be the payment of a certain benefit. The emphasis at the technical level will be on finding ways to do this at least cost, on the measurement of results, and on efficiency generally. On the whole, the time horizon is the short run.

(b) The organizational level. This is concerned with the co-ordination and integration of the technical work of the organization. Its viewpoint is therefore political in the most general sense and it is concerned with mediation and compromise between the various constituents of the organization in order that the whole enterprise should work well. Its time horizon is compounded of both the short and the long run.

(c) The institutional level. Here the task is to deal with uncertainty and to show how the organization will develop in its environment. The skills include the exercise of judgment and negotiation. The time-scale tends to be long.

These ideas are shown in Fig. 5.3.

Level	Task	Time scale	Approach
Production	Specific operations	Short	Costing and measuring
Organizational	Co-ordination of specific operations	Short/long	Mediation and compromise
Institutional	Selection of operations in light of changing environment	Long	Forecasting and negotiating

Fig. 5.3 *The Organization as a System of Levels*

The above paragraphs give a brief guide to the main ideas and concepts used by those who describe an organization as a system. And the practical value of the 'systems' approach can be illustrated by two interesting pieces of work. The first dealt with the effect of different technical processes. Professor Joan Woodward and some of her colleagues made a study of firms in south-east Essex.[1] To summarize the results, they found that the main determinant of the structure of the firms was the kind of activity and technology with which they were concerned. Putting the matter at its simplest, it was found that small- and medium-sized firms engaged in traditional activities such as printing and tailoring tended to be organized in a simple hierarchy with an organization chart of the usual pyramid shape, (see Fig. 5.4). But organizations concerned with mass production had a very different organizational chart—a pyramid that was elongated at the base, reflecting, of course, that in the manufacture, e.g. of motor-cars, many thousands of employees must work at the basic process while relatively small numbers are required for middle and top management (see Fig. 5.5).

Fig. 5.4

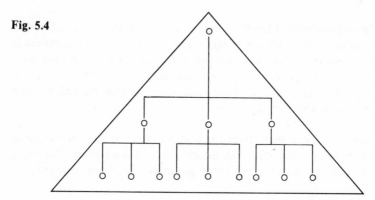

The third kind of firm investigated was concerned with such processes as oil refining and the manufacture of chemicals (see Fig. 5.6). Here the management structure was diamond-shaped, reflecting the fact that only a few employees were required to service the plant and maintain it, there was a relatively large group of middle managers, scientists, accountants, economists and the like, and only a small group of top managers were needed. Problems tended to flow from the structure of the firm; for example, the relatively large group of highly-educated middle managers had relatively restricted outlets to the top.

Another important survey dealt with the effect of the environment. Here a study was made, by Mr T. Burns and Mr G.M. Stalker, of the management of a series of electronic firms.[2] In this environment, commercial success depended upon developing and manufacturing a component

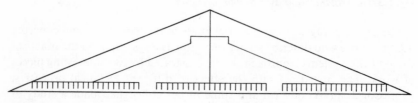

Fig. 5.5

quickly and getting it on to the market fast. It was found that the firms which embodied the traditional organizational structure, with hierarchies and formal methods of business, tended to be slower off the mark and less profitable than those firms which were organized in less formal terms, where there was more lateral communication and where talented individuals were allowed much more initiative. The authors drew a distinction between 'mechanistic' organization, as they called the former, and 'organic' as they called the latter. The conclusion to be drawn from their work is not, of course, that one kind of organization is necessarily better than another. It is that the organization to be selected ought, to a considerable extent, to depend on the environment within which it is operating.

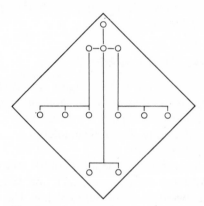

Fig. 5.6

Although the work of Professor Woodward and Mr Burns and Mr Stalker was based on industrial experience, its influence has spread to the public services. At the same time, it has to be recognized that their ideas do not yield any direct guidance about how to change organizational arrangements. It is not possible to transmute general ideas about organizations into specific organizational schemes. The gap between the general and the abstract on the one hand, and the particular and the concrete on the other, is too wide for this to be accomplished. Furthermore, the detailed arrangements of one organization cannot be reproduced exactly in another.

The influence of organizational ideas and specific case studies is therefore of a more general kind. They yield insights and promote speculations which influence ministers, councillors and officials and predispose them to one kind of change rather than another. But such predispositions are mediated by reflection upon practical experience and by the exigences and constraints of the current situation. So that the action that is finally taken, and the result that is achieved, is due only in a measure to ideas and insights derived from management theories and accounts of what others have done. This is so even where the claim is made that new arrangements are the direct result of applying a management theory or of seeking to reproduce the form and structure of another organization. In practice, such a claim will be an exaggeration for the reasons described above.

It follows that the influence of the idea that organizations are to be conceived as systems and of the work of writers like Professor Woodward, Mr Burns and Mr Stalker has been of a diffuse character. It has been manifest in a greater willingness to introduce organizational variety and to admit that different tasks, technologies and people will need different organizational arrangements. It has also helped to promote less formal organizational arrangements, and the crossing of administrative boundaries through the formation of teams and groups to accomplish *ad hoc* tasks. And it has encouraged the view that the links between organizations and the social environment in which they operate are important and need not always be on strictly formal lines.

ORGANIZATIONAL DEVELOPMENT

The three ideas described above—that organizations should cohere with their members' objectives, that scientific and other experts should be brought close to policy making, and that organizations should be viewed as systems—have contributed to the following developments, although they are not the sole causes of them.

First, in central government, these ideas contributed to the decisions to introduce a series of large departments, each one designed to undertake responsibility for a specific area of national life. The idea in the White Paper of 1970 on the reorganization of central government[3] was that each of these departments should have a clearly defined role for a major sector of government activity. This would provide a coherent basis for a range of associated programmes to carry out central government responsibilities as endorsed by Parliament in such fields as the environment, trade and industry, and health and social security.

Secondly, within these organizations, attempts were made to provide special arrangements for those parts of the organization whose activities had affinities with those of a commercial or industrial concern. The idea was that where part of a government department was concerned with manufacture, or with the purchase of goods and the provision of services, there would be advantages in reducing the amount of detailed financial and political control and substituting new arrangements which, while safeguarding taxpayers' money and ultimate ministerial responsibility to Parliament, were more appropriate to a body with affinities to a business corporation. In some cases, this led to 'hiving off' what had once been parts of government departments, as when the Manpower Services Commission was split from the Department of Employment by the Employment and Training Act 1973 and took over responsibility for employment services through the Employment Services Agency, and for industrial training through the Training Services Agency. In other cases, it led to the setting up of partly independent organizations within government departments, as when the Procurement Executive was set up within the Ministry of Defence in 1971 to be responsible for the purchase of aircraft, ships, tanks, guns, stores and equipment generally for the Armed Services. Another organizational device was the trading fund, introduced, for example for the Royal Ordnance Factories, whereby they are required to conduct their manufacturing activities on a business-like basis.

Thirdly, the greater attention to shaping organizations to meet their tasks led to an increasing concern with management services work, and an increase in the number of specialist departments and divisions concerned with such activities as operational research, statistical services, personnel management, and organizational reviews. In the past, work study and organization and methods were the techniques most usually employed in organizational reviews. They concentrated detailed attention upon the work discharged by individual officials and sections, the number of officers required to conduct particular activities, the redesign of office procedures and layouts, and similar activities. Such reviews now often include the employment of other techniques, such as the application of operational research to questions of organization. Wider management reviews, which concentrate on the efficiency and effectiveness of an organization as a whole, have also become more common in the last decade. These usually start with a specification of the general goals and objectives of the organization, and then proceed to examine how far the shape of the organization helps or hinders their achievement.

Fourthly, it was hoped that management theory might contribute to the more productive employment of computers in the public service. The early results of using these machines had generally been disappointing, since they had nearly all cost more than expected, taken longer to get into service, and performed less well than had been hoped. Management expertise has therefore been increasingly applied to planning for the introduction of computers and more account has been taken in recent years of the organizational as against the technical implications of using these machines.

Finally, the last few years have seen a greater willingness to experiment with new organizational forms. Planning units have already been studied in chapter 3. Other devices include project teams to take responsibility for the design, development and execution of a particular project. Examples include the project teams in the Ministry of Defence for the Polaris submarines and Tornado aircraft. These teams usually include members drawn from the regular hierarchies of scientific, engineering, financial and contracting staffs and have both the knowledge and the powers to take the decisions in their areas relevant to the project. In this way, faster progress can often be achieved with major and relatively self-contained projects.

Project teams can, however, lead to problems. If the staff of a department is divided entirely into project teams, it is difficult to provide for the division of inevitably limited resources among what can become warring project teams. And some projects may be too small to warrant a full time team. In these circumstances, traditional forms of hierarchical organization are usually still favoured, though even here there have been changes and 'mixed' hierarchies containing members with different skills have been introduced in some parts of some organizations in place of the traditional pattern of separate hierarchies of financial, legal, engineering, contracting and other staffs. Other devices, including 'matrix management', which is described below, have also been tried, with the aim of combining the benefits to be gained from associating experts together in specialist departments and divisions with those to be reaped from committing them to interdisciplinary activities.

These points can best be illustrated by looking at detailed examples. As explained above, none of these examples can represent more than the general influence of management theories and ideas. But such examples illustrate the wide variety of organizations in central and local government that have felt this influence, and provide some evidence about the practical implications of management ideas. The following examples have therefore been chosen in order to illustrate, in different ways, the results of attempts to apply the management ideas and theories described above within central and local government.

The Treasury

In 1975 a management review of the Treasury was undertaken covering the whole range of its work. This review was part of a programme of management reviews of government departments which has been in progress during the last five years, and has included the Home Office, Welsh Office, Inland Revenue, Customs and Excise, Civil Service Department and the Ministry of Defence as well as the Treasury.[4] The reviews are undertaken for the minister of the department concerned and are carried out under the supervision of a steering committee chaired by the permanent secretary (who is the chief official) of the department, with representation from the Civil Service Department. The report is submitted to the departmental minister and to the minister responsible for the day to day work of the Civil Service Department, currently the Lord Privy Seal.

A review team is appointed to work under the direction of the steering committee and is usually led by a senior officer in the department under review. The team includes other staff from the department, and from the Civil Service Department's Management Services Division. The object of these management reviews is to assist top management to improve the effectiveness and efficiency of the departments' organization and management. Particular attention is paid to the organizational arrangements at the top of the department for the analysis and review of policies and for allocating resources. The reviews therefore concentrate on the organization for planning and resource allocation, and on the supporting systems for planning and controlling financially and manpower resources. The emphasis is on the procedures used rather than the analysis of particular problems.

As a result of the management review, the Treasury was restructured into four sectors, each concerned with a major area of Treasury work. The Domestic Economy Sector is concerned with fiscal, monetary and counter inflation policies, and with the Treasury's contribution to the Government's industrial strategy for the greater productivity and efficiency of British industry, including control of public expenditure on industry and agriculture. The Public Services Sector is responsible for controlling aggregate public expenditure, and for the new devices in this area which we have studied in earlier chapters, including cash limits and the financial information system. The third sector is Overseas Finance. It is responsible for the balance of payments, the management of the currency reserve, international monetary questions, overseas aid and the Treasury's concern with European Community questions. The fourth sector is the Chief Economic Adviser's, which is responsible for specialized economic analysis including economic forecasts and the use of the macro-economic model. It is important to note that the Chief Economic Adviser's sector ranks alongside the other three. This brings the Treasury's chief scientific officer into the centre of Treasury policy making.

Other parts of the Treasury are outside these sectors, including the establishments division, which is responsible for questions of personnel management; the information division, responsible for dealings with the press and media; and the Central Unit. The Central Unit is responsible for the co-ordination of policy advice across the whole department, and for designing major new initiatives in economic management. It is responsible for the management of the annual budget and for similar packages of economic measures.

The main problem in running the Treasury is to unify and co-ordinate the various interests and concerns which are represented within its structure; for example, there may be occasions when the Public Services Sector proposes an expansion of public expenditure while the Overseas Finance Sector has to point out that this may have damaging effects on the international standing of the currency. How can these differences be properly examined and recommendations made to ministers? In the past, the co-ordination would have been mainly accomplished by the preparation of written memoranda by the officials responsible for the various questions. These would have passed up separate hierarchies until reaching the most senior levels, including the permanent secretary. After talking the matter over with his senior colleagues, the permanent secretary might well have tried to sum up the matter and make a recommendation in a minute addressed to the Chancellor of the Exchequer.

This process tends to filter away differences of view and some of the relevant considerations. The Treasury is therefore now concerned to conduct its affairs so that the full range of possibilities and opinions is considered at the time the decision is made. A number of devices are used to bring this about. Some are of long standing, such as the practice of moving staff between divisions so that, as officials' careers develop, they will have had practical experience of domestic as well as overseas questions. In recent years, this has been taken further by the device of posting some economists away from the Chief Economic Adviser's Sector into divisions in the other sectors. This process of 'bedding-out' is designed to make sure that technical economic advice is available within the responsible divisions, and can be taken into account in the earliest stages of policy making.

Another important device is the policy co-ordinating committee, which meets weekly under the chairmanship of the permanent secretary. Papers for this committee are produced in the light of meetings under the chairmanship of the head of the Central Unit. The Central Unit thereby takes account of views of junior and middle levels throughout the department and brings them to the attention of the policy co-ordinating committee which contains the most senior officials in the Treasury.

The policy co-ordinating committee accordingly tries to secure that all possible views are taken into account in the examination of Treasury problems. Sometimes it is possible for an agreed course of action to be determined by discussion in committee. At other times it is the practice of the permanent secretary to put a minute to the Chancellor elaborating the problem and setting out the various considerations and differences in view, naming those who take each position. In this way, the full range of views is put before the Chancellor of the Exchequer and his ministerial colleagues. The process has been described in the following terms.

'The PCC is a two stage process, with unbridled discussion and everybody saying what he likes. But when it gets to the crunch you have in effect weighted voting. The second permanent secretaries and deputy secretaries are there because they are presumed to have better overall judgement than the line men. There is an absolutely binding convention which has never been breached that argument is free up to the time the Chancellor makes up his mind, then all the energy goes into securing what the Chancellor wants.'

Another description of the process is

It's the old civil service consensus technique—never stop trying to agree. It's our job to minimize differences; you can call it a fix but I regard it as what we are paid for. It is our task to make collective responsibility work. If we didn't, there would be chaos or we would have to turn into politicos. That would maximize differences all right.[5]

The work of the policy co-ordinating committee may well lead to sets of alternative policy options being put before the Chancellor, which he may put to his Cabinet colleagues. Ministers can then reach their decisions, either at the meetings held each fortnight of the Cabinet's Economic Strategy Committee, which is chaired by the Prime Minister, or at a meeting of the full Cabinet itself.

Other important features of the Treasury's current methods of work include the formation of *ad hoc* teams, often involving staff from the Inland Revenue and the Bank of England, to look into particular problems and difficulties. There is also a joint Treasury and Civil Service Department operational research unit. Economic forecasting includes the use of a computer model. Although its predictions of the British economy have been correct to within margins of 2–4 per cent in such areas as the size of gross domestic product, the level of exports, imports and investment, the Treasury does not rely upon the computer to reach its judgements about the correct actions to take. Instead, computer forecasts are seen as providing general guidance and as potential safeguards against eccentric and idiosyncratic decisions. Attempts are made to bring new ideas to the Treasury by posting officials between the Treasury, other departments and organizations in the private sector and also, so far as the economists are concerned, by trying to take a number of staff on short-term secondment from universities. The theoretical knowledge available within the Treasury is thereby continually refurbished. This would not be possible if all the economists worked the whole of their official lives within Whitehall.

In these ways, the Treasury exemplifies some of the points we have stressed. The present structure is the result of a full-scale management review of the department, rather than piecemeal adjustment to changing circumstances. The structure is designed to cohere with the major purposes of the Treasury's work in the fields of the domestic economy, overseas economic relations and the control of public expenditure. The economic adviser ranks as a second permanent secretary. He is at the second highest official level in the Treasury, and his sector is equal with the others. Specialist and expert advice is thereby brought to the heart of the policy making process. Many *ad hoc* teams and working groups, including people from both inside and outside the Treasury, have been set up to look at problems. In this way, informal and short-term organizational arrangements are made to deal with specific problems. Finally efforts are made to try to ensure that, while the variety of advice and views on a particular question is brought down to manageable size, there is no question of eliminating all differences of view. Ministers are presented with much more than an anodyne analysis of the situation that points to only one solution. Instead, efforts are made to bring the full range of relevant considerations to the highest level and, where necessary, to put a range of options before ministers together with an analysis of the advantages and disadvantages of each one. In this way, ministers are helped to see problems in the round, and to be aware of the various ways in which they can be tackled, and the pros and cons of each one.

In spite of the reorganization of 1975, debate still continues about the right organization for economic management. It has been suggested, for example, that there is a case for a department of budget and manpower, modelled on United States experience, and combining control over public spending and public manpower. This might be done by uniting the public services sector of the Treasury with the Civil Service Department, and putting them under the control of a powerful Cabinet minister. This would concentrate responsibility for efficient manpower and efficient financial management in one department, leaving to a separate department the responsibility for economic policy as a whole.

This is, of course, not so much a debate about the division of the Treasury as such, as about the organization of what might be called the 'centre' of government, namely the Treasury, the Civil Service Department, the Cabinet Office, the Prime Minister's office and the Central Policy Review Staff.[6] There is a variety of ways of organizing these central responsibilities. Originally, when government work was less extensive and simpler in nature, most of the activities conducted by these bodies were, to the extent that they were conducted at all, the responsibility of the Treasury. Between 1964 and 1969 however, there was a Department of Economic Affairs which was primarily responsible for economic policy. But this division was not a success. Some critics allege that this was because the Treasury was determined that its monopoly of economic power should not be broken. But others claim that the failure lay in a false distinction and that, for example, no real line can be drawn between public expenditure policy and the analysis of particular expenditure programmes. It is said that public spending cannot be settled by an annual economic judgement, after which the only task is to maintain that level of expenditure. There is and must be a continuous dialogue and discussion between Treasury expenditure divisions, the spending departments and those parts of the Treasury concerned with the Government's economic strategy. It is claimed that there would be little advantage in turning the dialogue between spending departments and the Treasury into a three-sided dialogue between the spending departments, a department of budget and manpower and an economic policy department.

This debate is unlikely finally to be resolved. Argument is certain to persist about the best way of distributing these important responsibilities. The study of management, and the attempts we have described to apply some of the ideas have made a useful contribution. But they have not provided a final answer to the question of how best to organize the Treasury and the other central responsibilities of government.

The CPRS review of overseas representation

One example of the concern with objectives, goals and purposes in the review of organizational arrangements, is provided by the review of overseas representation completed by the Central Policy Review Staff in 1977.

In January 1976 the Foreign and Commonwealth Secretary asked the Head of the CPRS

> to review the nature and extent of our overseas interests and requirements and in the light of that review to make recommendations on the most suitable, effective and economic means of representing and promoting those interests both at home and overseas. The Review will embrace all aspects of the work of overseas representation, including political, economic, commercial, consular and immigration activities, whether these tasks are performed by members of Her Majesty's Diplomatic Service, by members of the Home Civil Service, by members of the Armed Forces or by other agencies financially supported by Her Majesty's Government.

In the past, the starting point of such a review might have been a consideration of the organization of the Foreign and Commonwealth Office and the other departments concerned with overseas representation, together with a review of organization overseas, that is to say of British Embassies and High Commissions, and of the Diplomatic Service. In this case, however, the reviewing teams began by specifying the country's objectives overseas. They described them in the following terms.

'The UK seems to us to have four main objectives overseas:

(*a*) to ensure its external security;

(*b*) to promote its economic and social wellbeing;

(*c*) to honour certain commitments or obligations (e.g. to the dependent territories or to individual citizens of its own or other countries);

(*d*) to work for a peaceful and just world.

These four objectives interact and overlap. For instance the UK's economic and social wellbeing is to some extent dependent upon the achievement of a peaceful and just world.'[7]

The team went on to consider the various functions which together make up overseas representation, and the extent to which they contribute to one or more of the four objectives. They identified 14 separate functions: economic, social and environmental work; export services; foreign policy work (i.e. work connected with international political situations and activities in which the United Kingdom is an active participant); defence work; consular services; control of entry into the United Kingdom (i.e. immigration and visa work); the administration of overseas aid; educational and cultural work; external broadcasting; information work; political work (i.e. the conduct of day to day bilateral political relations and the political analysis of overseas countries); communications; entertainment; accommodation and other administration overseas.

The team then considered whether the distribution of resources between these functions reflected their relevant importance and effectiveness. Economic work and export services, which the team considered to be the most important functions, accounted for some 31 per cent of total net expenditure compared with only 10 per cent for foreign policy and defence work. The team thought that this was right. Where they believed the distribution of resources to be wrong was in educational and cultural work, external broadcasting and information work, which accounted for 30 per cent of total net expenditure. The team believed that this was unjustifiably high, given the relevance of these functions to the country's overseas objectives.

The team turned from their assessment of the relevant importance and effectiveness of the functions, to considering how each is at present carried out. They thought that some procedures were unduly complicated, e.g. control of entry and consular services; in others there was duplication and there were some examples of badly defined roles and responsibilities, as in aid administration. They also believed that in some areas work was being done to an unjustifiably high standard, e.g. foreign policy work; and there were other cases where work now done by staff resident overseas could be better done in the United Kingdom or by visitors from London.

Finally, the reviewing team considered the implications of their findings for organization and staffing. They thought it would be possible to close some 20 diplomatic missions and about 35 subordinate posts. On the whole they believed that the scope for reduction was greatest in the countries of the developed world, because overseas representation by resident missions could do less to protect and advance United Kingdom interests than it could do in communist or third world countries.

As for organization in the United Kingdom, the team recommended that the division of responsibilities between government departments in London should be broadly maintained, but that changes should be introduced to ensure that full weight was given to the interests of home departments in making and carrying out overseas policies. They therefore proposed that machinery should be established in the Cabinet Office to co-ordinate departments' interests in the United Kingdom's bilateral relations, and that posts overseas should no longer be controlled and directed by the Foreign and Commonwealth Office alone. They also proposed two options in the field of educational work. The first 'for which we think there is much to be said' was to abolish the British Council and other agencies in this field and distribute their functions between the Ministry of Overseas Development, the Department of Education and Science and a new recruitment and placement agency. The second would be to retain the British Council and transfer most of the smaller agencies' functions to it.

As for staffing, the team suggested three options:

(a) more interchange between the Home Civil Service and the Diplomatic Service;

(b) the creation of a specialist export promotion service and a specialist aid administration service within the Home Civil Service;

(c) the merger of the Home Civil Service and the Diplomatic Service and the creation within the combined Service of a Foreign Service Group which would staff most of the jobs in the United Kingdom and overseas in economic work, export promotion, foreign policy, consular work, aid administration, information, political work, communications, and the administration of posts.

The team indicated that their preference was for the third option.

Our main interest in this report concerns the way the review was carried out and who undertook it. The review started with a survey of objectives and then went on to consider functions, and concluded with a review of organization and staffing. The review was undertaken by a specially designated group from within the Central Policy Review Staff. Working under the Head of the Central Policy Review Staff was a group of seven consisting of four civil servants, and three members, much of whose main experience had laid in university teaching and research: Mr J. Odling Smee, an economist; Dr Tessa Blackstone, a sociologist and Miss K. Mortimer, whose previous jobs had included international economic work. The review reflected the wide range of interests of its members. Perhaps naturally, in view of its composition, it paid less attention to the more specialist aspects of diplomatic work, such as the detailed reporting on political, social and economic developments that has traditionally formed most of the day-to-day work of the diplomat overseas. Such reporting and the range of official contacts upon which it is founded may sometimes appear of marginal value, as it did to the team. On the other hand, this work can be valuable. For example, it can help in providing early warning of political upheavals that may menace the safety of British nationals and their interests, and may provide the foundation for negotiations to preserve the rights of those in danger. However, as the team point out, a balance has to be struck. There is certainly a limit to the volume of resources that can be expended on these purposes.

The work of organization and methods

A good example of an organization and methods study is the investigation made recently into the centralization of government training centre stores in Northern Ireland.[8] This showed that much useful work can still be accomplished by traditional management services techniques.

Northern Ireland has for many years had a higher rate of unemployment than other parts of the country and, as one method of encouraging outside industrial investment, the Government has been concerned to improve the number of skilled work people in Northern Ireland through the establishment and operation of government training centres. The first was established near Belfast in 1945 and, by 1976, there were 12 in operation at various locations throughout the province with a total training staff of about 450 instructors. They provided 1700 training places for first-year apprentices and 1050 places for adult trainees.

The supply organization for the centres comprised a central purchasing branch employing 60 staff; a central holding store with four staff; and a store in each centre employing a total of nearly 68 staff. The annual value of the purchases was approximately £1.3 million. The purchasing branch was responsible for buying all stores except those costing up to £10 per item which were purchased by the local centres.

This decentralized system appeared to have the advantages of flexibility and quick decision making. In fact, however, it meant that a large part of time of the instructing staff at the government training centres was devoted to work connected with stores. Tests made by the organization and methods team showed that up to 30 per cent of management time was involved in stores supervision and checking at the expense of training work. An organization and methods study was therefore commissioned into the advantages and disadvantages of centralized storekeeping. As a first step, a simulation exercise was held in three centres. Instructors were asked to order supplies in weekly batches only, for delivery on a specific day each week, and to forecast two weeks in advance when ordering. It was laid down that all orders and requests for stores should be authorized by chief instructors and should normally be collected once a week by stores staff. In addition, on the weekly delivery date, stores were to be delivered to instructors by stores staff and items to be returned to the stores were to be collected at the same time.

After an initial few weeks, when a number of problems were identified and resolved, the exercise ran smoothly. The introduction of a weekly ordering cycle and the separation of the stores from the instructors had little effect on training. By the end of the exercise the training centre managers agreed that the only important factor in the stores service was reliability; not location or frequency of delivery. As a result of the simulation exercise, the government training centres decided to go over to centralized storekeeping. The central purchasing branch was accordingly reorganized and a new system of documentation was introduced to minimize the work involved in ordering stores. All unnecessary transcription and recording was eliminated and stockholdings on the shop floor were kept to a minimum. The new arrangements were implemented over nine months.

This study showed how a straightforward study of organizational arrangements and working procedures can suggest improvements that should provide as good or better service than before at a lower cost in future. But what is particularly important is the approach taken in the organization and methods study. It was based on full discussion with those who worked the present system; the preparation of provisional proposals;

tests on a pilot basis; the adjustment of the proposals in the light of this experience; and their subsequent introduction over a phased period. These are the necessary conditions of success in this kind of work.

Matrix organization

A useful example of the matrix type of organization can be taken from the field of management services itself. As we have noted above, there is a range of specialisms which contribute to the work of management services, including operational research, organization and methods and work study. There is naturally a risk that the enthusiasm of individual specialists may encourage compartmentalism and a belief that most problems can be tackled with one set of techniques. However, problems increasingly require teams drawn from more than one specialism. Appropriate organizational arrangements and management methods are therefore needed.

Figure 5.7, prepared by Mr J. N. Archer who has been in charge of management services (MS) work in the Civil Service Department, illustrates a type of matrix organization that might be introduced into a management services department to enable the various management

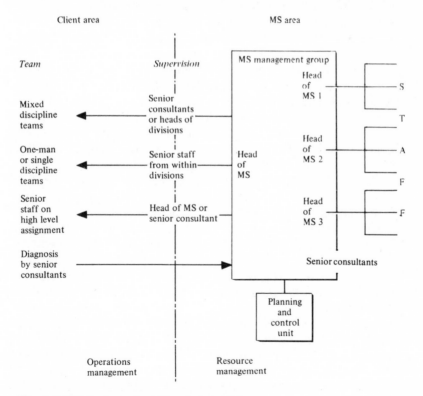

Fig. 5.7 MS Review : An MS unit in action

services experts to preserve and develop their own expertise, and to collaborate together in carefully devised teams related to particular problems.[9]

Mr Archer describes the working of the matrix organization in the following terms.

The Resource Management side of the diagram on the right corresponds with the traditional scalar organizational chart. It provides for organization in specialist groups: MS1 might be General MS or O and M; MS2 might be Computers; MS3 might be OR. Senior consultants would be senior and experienced staff available to lead teams on complex assignments or to carry out preliminary surveys of problem areas in order to decide what is needed. 'Operations Management' on the left of the diagram indicates different ways in which MS resources may be deployed on client problems. These include mixed discipline teams which may be supervised by Senior Consultants or Heads of Divisions, single discipline assignments of the more traditional kind supervised by senior staff drawn from specialist divisions, teams of senior staff on high-level assignments which may be supervised on a part-time basis by the Head of MS or by a Senior Consultant and preliminary survey and diagnostic work often carried out by Senior Consultants.

The concept of a Senior Consultant at or about Assistant Secretary level and able to devote his whole time to assignment work is a new one in Civil Service MS. It parallels developments in management consultancy where the trend is towards the greater full-time involvement of senior staff in assignments. In the past, heads of MS divisions have carried out some assignment work which called for participation at that level; but this has been increasingly difficult as growing demands of this kind and more rapid development of specialisms and numbers engaged on them have exerted rival pulls. I have frequently experienced the difficulty of combining major assignments with running a large and busy MS division: something, usually divisional management, suffers.

It is, of course, vital to provide a link between Resource Management and Operations Management. This is the role of the MS Management Group—the nerve centre of the whole operation. This is in effect a management board chaired by the Head of MS with Heads of the functional Divisions and the Senior Consultants as members. It considers requests for substantial assignments, allocates work to Divisions or mixed teams, appoints responsible team leaders, surveys progress against assignment programmes, and generally keeps watch on the whole MS operation and its priorities. It is served by a planning and control unit which ensures that new work and any reports it requests are submitted to it and also keeps watch on staff resources and career development generally, though heads of functional divisions have a responsibility for this also. By making the heads of specialist divisions

members of such a management group, the tendency towards compartmentalism is countered. And with progress on major assignments being
regularly monitored by the most senior people in the organization, there
is an incentive for assignment teams to perform well and complete work
on time.[10]

Other examples of matrix organizations are given below in the section on
interdepartmental groups of officials in local government.

'Hiving off'

The development of public authorities providing goods and services has led
to increasing interest in the possibility of adopting a 'commercial approach'
to the provision and administration of at least some of these services. The
Fulton Report in particular saw advantages in such an approach in
appropriate circumstances and believed that there was considerable scope
for 'hiving off' executive activities to semi-independent public agencies
and, even where executive work could not be hived off, the Committee
proposed that it should be carried out wherever practicable within units of
accountable management. By accountable management the Committee
meant 'holding individuals and units responsible for performance measured as objectively as possible. Its achievement depends upon identifying
or establishing accountable units within government departments—units
where output can be measured against costs or other criteria, and where
individuals can be held personally responsible for their performance.[11]
They accordingly proposed that 'the manager of each command should be
given clear cut responsibilities and commensurate authority and should be
held accountable for performance against budgets, standards of achievement and other tests'.[12]

In addition to the impetus provided by the Fulton Committee's recommendations, in June 1970 the Government appointed a team of businessmen to advise it on the possibility of applying ideas and concepts derived
from business experience to the work of central government. This team was
led by Sir Richard Meyjes of the Shell International Petroleum Company.

However, while some bodies have been hived off as the Manpower
Services Commission, controlling the Employment Services Agency, and
the Training Services Agency, was hived off from the Department of
Employment, the scope for introducing this new system has been less than
expected. The reasons for this include the reluctance of ministers to lose
control over the relevant spending programmes, and thus the opportunity
to reduce or expand the level of expenditure for political reasons. There is
also a ministerial reluctance to lose control over major individual projects,
which may well be of public and political interest, such as the environmental aspects of public works projects, and the international and employment
implications of major technological projects. There is also the point that a

hived-off body should earn revenue if at all possible, and ultimately become self-supporting. Otherwise, hiving off is likely to be a matter of form rather than substance.

The emphasis therefore turned to developing accountable management in government through departmental agencies, which have been defined by the Civil Service Department as follows.

A departmental agency is an organizational entity under its own executive head, either part of a government department or a corporate body within the departmental framework, acting at the direction of a Minister who is answerable to Parliament for its activities and staffed by civil servants (as at present defined) but distinguished from the conventional pattern of departmental organization by having its own executive and accounting officer, and by a large degree of freedom in staff management.[13]

One such agency is the Property Services Agency, set up in September 1972 to discharge a wide range of responsibilities formerly carried out by the Ministry of Public Building and Works. Its tasks include the provision of equipment for and the maintenance of government buildings and installations for government departments and the Armed Services; for the management of most of the government's land and property at home and overseas; and for the design, purchase, installation and maintenance of a wide range of office, domestic, laboratory and museum furnishing and equipment.

The Property Services Agency was established with a board comprising the chief executive, Mr J.G. Cuckney, a former merchant banker, the deputy chief executives, a principal establishments officer (responsible for personnel matters), a principal finance officer, other senior managers and two outside members from the private sector. This board was designed to operate on the lines of the parent board of a holding company, and the deputy chief executives had their own boards acting in the manner of boards of operating or trading companies. Mr Cuckney described this scheme of management as follows:

Board papers and minutes receive a wide circulation down to Assistant Secretary level or its equivalent at Headquarters and to all Directors of Regions at home and overseas. This has resulted in anticipatory action being taken 'down the line', it acts as a cohesive factor in a large and geographically widespread organization, it has a valuable educative effect, widening management horizons especially at DCE Board level, where we have a 'cross-posting' of directors who serve on other Boards to those which they functionally belong.[14]

Other important aspects of the Property Services Agency's management system included the definition of aims and objectives for the key levels of command. The four deputy chief executives thereby had a framework for a system of annual reports. These reports had two functions; to survey the previous year and indicate the progress achieved in meeting the objectives, and to set objectives for the coming year and make forecasts of developments. A computer based staff costing system was also introduced to provide general information by categories of work and by units of command on the cost of civil engineering projects. The system also enabled comparisons to be made between the agency's costs and those of private consultants' scale fees.

A Property Review and Development Group was set up within the agency to make a selective review of government lands and property so as to determine whether they were being most effectively employed. In the absence of market forces, these government assets might be under-used and the purpose of the review was to see whether they might be employed more productively. A special system of professional and technical audit was introduced in addition to the accounts and finance audit. The object was to provide a substitute for the pressures exerted by market forces in the private sector, and so help the agency to judge whether it was providing services in the most effective and economical fashion to an inevitably captive set of government clients who could not, for the most part, place their business with outside firms but were obliged to deal with the government agency specially set up for their needs.

A second departmental agency was the Procurement Executive, introduced into the Ministry of Defence in 1971 following the report of a Committee under the chairmanship of Sir Derek Rayner, one of Sir Richard Meyjes's businessmen.[15] This committee recommended:

(a) a single procurement organization should be established headed by a Chief Executive responsible to the Defence Secretary and combining the responsibilities of the Ministry of Defence and the Ministry of Aviation Supply;

(b) responsibility for civil aerospace should be transferred to the Department of Trade and Industry;

(c) responsibility for the Atomic Weapons Research Establishment at Aldermaston should be transferred to the Ministry of Defence.

The idea behind this departmental agency was that, while the problems arising in defence procurement cannot be dealt with entirely on commercial lines, it should be possible to develop an organization and a career structure that would concentrate on meeting the Services' requirements for all kinds of equipment in much the same way that Sir Derek Rayner's firm, Marks and Spencer Ltd, tried to meet the requirements of its customers for high quality goods at the lowest price possible. The essence of the relationship with the Ministry of Defence was that the Procurement Executive would advise on the cost and feasibility of Service equipment plans and would then, when they were approved, turn them into hardware at the lowest price possible. But it would not be concerned with the requirement itself. This should be for the Ministry of Defence to determine, in the light of its appreciation of defence, political and economic factors. The Procurement Executive, just like Marks and Spencer, would seek to supply what the customer wanted, and not tell him what he ought to want. The Rayner Committee commented on the fact that Marks and Spencer took more trouble over the quality of men's shirts than some manufacturers seemed to take over equipment on which a man's life might depend. They believed that the Procurement Executive would be able to improve the relationship between customers and suppliers to their mutual benefit.

Over the years since its introduction, the relationship between the Procurement Executive and the Ministry of Defence has grown closer. In 1971 there were systems controllers for sea, land and air projects and for guided weapons. Originally these controllers were accounting officers to Parliament for their own votes. Since then, the chief executive, now retitled the Chief of Defence Procurement, has become accounting officer for all these votes as well as for the research and development establishments. The trend since 1971 has been to strengthen the links with the rest of the Ministry of Defence. A separate Procurement Executive personnel organization no longer exists and there is complete interchangeability of staff between the Executive and the Ministry of Defence. The Ministry of Defence's main financial organization now embraces the Procurement Executive's finance staff, and there is one principal finance officer for the whole of the Ministry, who also sits on the Procurement Executive management board.

Perhaps the commercial approach is most clearly exemplified in the arrangements set out in the Government Trading Fund Act 1973. The purpose of this Act is to enable certain services to be financed by a trading fund instead of by annual votes and appropriations. The Act named five organizations as candidates for trading fund status: the Royal Mint, the Royal Ordnance Factories, Her Majesty's Stationery Office, the Supplies Division of the Property Services Agency and the Royal Dockyards. So far, only the first four have been established as Trading Funds.[16]

Under this system, trading fund status establishes organizations on a commercial basis. Instead of receiving funds voted annually by Parliament, the organization is given an allocation of public dividend capital from the Consolidated Fund. This is made up to the level of capital needed for operations by loans from the National Loans Fund and the organization is then expected to sell its goods and services at a realistic price in order to meet all out-goings properly chargeable to the revenue account and to achieve any further financial objectives which the Treasury may lay down after consultation with the responsible minister, and subject to parliamentary approval. The basic idea is that public dividend capital is analogous to the capital base that might be provided by shareholders' capital in a commercial concern. Thus the Royal Ordnance Factories have £35 million of public dividend capital and they are expected to pay 10 per cent annum on it to the Consolidated Fund, after they have met their outgoings, provided for depreciation, and paid interest on their loans from the National Loans Fund.

The Royal Ordnance Factories came into operation as a trading fund on 1 July 1974. Most of the Royal Ordnance Factories' work consists of manufacturing guns, ammunition, tanks and armoured vehicles for the Army, but an increasing amount is sold overseas and the whole operation is conducted on factory lines. Under present arrangements, the managing director of the Royal Ordnance Factories is the accounting officer for the trading fund and has a direct responsibility to Parliament, but he also has responsibilities within the Ministry of Defence. The Minister of State for Defence is chairman of the Royal Ordnance Factories management board, which comprises representatives from the Ministry and from industry, as well as the managing director and senior staff of the Royal Ordnance Factories.

Furthermore, the Royal Ordnance Factories organization operates within the framework of the Ministry of Defence and looks for guidance from its specialist branches—scientific, technical and financial—as necessary. There is considerable interchange of staff between the Royal Ordnance Factories and the Ministry of Defence and, because of the necessarily close relationship between the Royal Ordnance Factories and the Ministry, it is not always possible for the Ministry to treat the Factories as an independent commercial concern. They look for more guidance and more preferential treatment from the Ministry of Defence than a commercial concern would do; and at the same time the Ministry of Defence is more concerned with the detailed operation of the Factories than if it was dealing with a fully commercial enterprise.

The employment of computers

The application of computers within central and local government has enabled tasks to be undertaken which could not have been carried out manually without enormous expense. It has also offered excellent scope for the application of management ideas.[17] Management theory emphasizes the importance of determining objectives, considering alternative ways of achieving them, choosing the best way in accordance with selected criteria, designing organizational machinery for the implementation of the selected solution, and reviewing the results achieved against the objectives sought. All these points should be taken into account in the feasibility studies that should precede the installation of computers and they are relevant to the evaluation of computers once installed.

In fact, in the early days of computer installation, these ideas were seldom fully appreciated. Few of those responsible for early computer installations asked 'how could the computer contribute to the objectives of the organization?'. Far too many simply asked 'what existing work can be handed over to computers?'. There was a similar concentration on the hardware of computers, that is to say, on the machines themselves, and far too little attention was paid to the software, by which is meant the systems analysis and programming that are essential for an effective computer installation. Systems analysis is the study of the way information flows within an organization and how improvements can be made in its structure and the use of information. Programming is the conversion of the systems analysis into the detailed working instructions for the computer. Programming can be complicated and time consuming; for example, the computer programme for an organization's payroll may well contain 10,000 separate steps. It may take a long time to work out a programme of this kind, and it is scarcely surprising that mistakes are made, sometimes through simple human errors by the programmers and sometimes because of incorrect solutions to the logical difficulties presented in the construction of the programme. Over the years, banks of computer programmes have been assembled which may enable an organization to take over existing programmes and so avoid, either in whole or part, the costs and delays of constructing its own programmes.

Many senior managers in both central and local government believed that computers would produce substantial and early savings in clerical costs and they were disappointed to find that it often took a long time to bring a computer into full use, that it often performed less well than had been hoped, and that it was sometimes necessary to redesign the whole system in the light of experience. Exaggerated expectations about the benefits of computers in the public service have tended to be succeeded by exaggerated pessimism; some now talk as if they believe that computers are large and costly toys that benefit their manufacturers far more than their purchasers. This is, perhaps, a natural reaction to the disappointments of unrealistic hopes.

Turning now to an analysis of the detailed lessons of computer application in central and local government, the following major points stand out. First, computers have so far been mainly installed within the existing management and organizational structures of the public services. It has been rare for changes to be made in the powers and duties of central government departments and local authorities in order to make better use of computing facilities. Computing facilities have usually been fitted in to existing organizational structures, even where changes might have enabled better use to be made of the computers. Of course, it would be wrong for the computer tail to wag the organizational dog. There have, however, been some cases where computer technology has influenced the distribution of powers and responsibilities, as where computer technology paved the way to the transfer from local government to central government of the responsibility for licensing road vehicles and collecting the associated duty.

Consortia have also been formed in the computer field, either for sharing facilities or for exchanging ideas and information; one early example was the consortium formed between 1956 and 1957 by five London boroughs for payroll services, accounting and rating, and there have been further examples in later years. In addition, the Local Authorities Management Services and Computer Committee (LAMSAC) was set up by the local authority associations and the Greater London Council in 1968 to provide comprehensive arrangements for the exchange of information about the use and development of computers in local government. LAMSAC has encouraged authorities to exchange information and join together in the use of computers wherever possible. It has helped to set up study groups and working parties to document standard applications and has promoted co-operation between local authorities and other bodies, including nationalized industries and central government departments. In addition to a central staff, LAMSAC has a number of advisory officers and has established regional groups of computer users with the aim of propagating information about management services techniques and the use of computers widely throughout the country and particularly to smaller authorities. Although LAMSAC is an advisory body, without executive authority, it has been valuable in spreading knowledge about computer use throughout local government and exchanging information between central government and local authorities.

While the use of computers has seldom led to the redistribution of powers and duties between organizations, it has certainly had an effect upon the internal arrangements of many organizations. In particular it has tended to make for increasing centralization; for example, the command and control computer and communication systems employed by some police forces enable all available resources to be deployed from a central point. Thus if a serious crime occurs in one part of a city, resources from a number of police divisions can be sent quickly to the scene of the crime from a central headquarters. The arrival of computers has also encouraged an increase in the number and size of management services departments, and skills and ideas learnt in computer applications have tended to be applied more widely throughout organizations employing computers. Systems analysts and programmers have become increasingly important members of the staff of central and local government authorities. But their employment brings problems—the need for them has been so great that salaries have been high and promotion has been rapid. This has caused a measure of jealousy among other staffs, and problems about the career development of computer specialists since, apart from outlets into management services, there are few immediately obvious openings into higher management. Thus young men and women, used to regular advancement, may find their progress brought to a sudden halt in middle life.

The rapid increase in the use of computers can be seen from Figs. 5.8 and 5.9 illustrating their use in central government.

Figure 5.9 shows that computers have been used for an increasingly wide variety of purposes over the years. Computers were first introduced to save costs in clerical operations but, as we have seen, this has seldom happened in the manner expected. Nevertheless dividends have been gained, very often in the ability to undertake more complicated work. Computers are also helping to provide better information for management. One difficulty here is that senior managers in central and local government do not always have a clear idea of what information they would really like; they tend to ask for more data than they can use, and so computers very often provide large numbers of printouts which are never fully used. It is therefore necessary to assess what information senior managers really need, and can use, and to design a management information system accordingly.

Another important contribution computers can make is to produce control information more quickly than manual methods, such as rapid printouts of an organization's stocks or levels of cash. The tightness of control that such information can provide can sometimes make a substantial contribution to the capital outlay on the computer itself. Computers can also help to increase productivity, as in better production planning in those areas of government work producing goods and services, and they help to give improved services to consumers by providing quicker payments of social benefits. Computers can also be used for such planning work as the Treasury's economic model; for scientific work in the design of the Concorde and other aircraft; and in many other areas where advanced scientific work requires complex and rapid calculations if it is to be fruitfully conducted.

1964–69	20	1973	16
1970	6	1974	9
1971	12	1975	29
1972	21	1976	22

Fig. 5.8 Computers for administrative and general purposes installed in central government before 31 December 1976 (total numbers each year).

The future will almost certainly see the wider use of computers, particularly as the new techniques of microprocessing develop and provide systems with greater potential and flexibility. It is not clear what the impact of this new technology will be; there will certainly be scope for handling more information, analysing and processing it in new ways, and perhaps for staff reductions or redeployment within the public service. Whether the effects will be evolutionary or revolutionary remains to be seen. But two points must be remembered in any expansion. First, experience suggests that the following should be borne in mind when considering the installation and control of computers:

(a) A careful long-term plan should be prepared.

(b) Tenders should be sought from a number of different manufacturers (which may raise awkward political problems where one manufacturer is

Acceptance date	Department	Location	Main uses
December 1964	Export Credit Guarantee Dept.	London	Statistics and Accounts
April 1966	Ministry of Defence	Liverpool	Bill paying
February 1967	Ministry of Defence	Glascoed	Stock Control, costing and payroll
February/May 1969	DHSS	Newcastle	Pension payments, pay and statistics, family allowances
August 1970	Ministry of Defence	Worthy Down	Records and pay of Army personnel
March 1971	Inland Revenue	Liverpool	PAYE collection and accounting, etc.
March 1972	Department of the Environment	Hemel Hempstead	Road accident statistics
July 1972	Home Office	Hendon	Police Records
August 1972	Ministry of Defence	Ensleigh	Naval victualling and stock control
August 1972	Customs and Excise	Southend	Value Added Tax
December 1972	Department of Transport	Swansea	Vehicle registration and licensing, driver licensing
January 1973	Home Office and Metropolitan Police	London	Pay and statistics; traffic tickets; prison records
May 1973	Civil Service Department	Chessington	Civil Service personnel information retrieval and statistics (PRISM)
October 1973	Cabinet Office/ Treasury	London	Econometric modelling, statistical research and progress development
September 1975	Ordance Survey	Southampton	Administration and cartographic work
April 1976	Ministry of Agriculture, Fisheries & Food	Guildford	Subsidy payments, payroll, statistics
August 1976	General Register Office (Scotland)	Edinburgh	Population statistics
September 1976	British Museum	London	Data collection and cataloguing
October 1976	Royal Mint	Glamorgan	Metal accounts; payroll; sales invoices and payments; general accounting, mail order fulfilment

Fig. 5.9 Computers for administrative and general purposes installed in central government before 31 December 1976 (selected examples).
Source: *Supplement to Management Services in Government,* Vol. 32, No. 2 (May 1977).

British and receives government aid and others are foreign companies even though manufacturing in the United Kingdom).

(c) At least two and sometimes more years should be allowed for the implementation of anything but the smallest computer projects.

(d) It is usually best to select the manager of a computer project from among those already possessing management experience rather than from those whose experience is exclusively technical.

(e) Costs will probably be at least twice the estimates of the computer staff and even more than twice those of the computer manufacturer.

(f) All managers who will be concerned with the computer should attend courses on computer systems and analysis, and they need to be involved in the preparatory stages of the project. Indeed, education about the potentialities and operation of computers is a continuing need. It is therefore helpful to exchange staff so far as possible between the computer side of an organization and other work, although care must be taken to preserve the required reservoirs of specialist computer knowledge.

Secondly, as noted above, account must be taken of the political implications of computer projects. The ability to manufacture computers is often taken as an index of a country's prestige and governments often subsidize their own country's firms and direct government orders to them. Again, the influence of politics can sometimes be seen in the way the computer schemes are abandoned or changed when political policies alter. It often takes several years to introduce a new computer scheme. There may be a change in the political complexion of the government or the controlling party in a local authority during the planning of a new scheme, and changes may be ordered to accord with new political priorities, thus leading to a fair amount of nugatory work. Finally, computers have an important role in a representative democracy since they allow government schemes to take account of a wide variety of different circumstances among their citizens and so, hopefully, to produce government services more finely tuned to the needs of individual services.

Some of these points can be illustrated from the computer statistics of the Department of Health and Social Security. Between 1968 and 1977 the number of data processing staff rose from 355 to 1133, and is likely to increase even further. One reason is the many changes in the plans for new pension arrangements, as Mr Crossman's scheme was succeeded by Sir Keith Joseph's which, in its turn, was succeeded by Mrs Barbara Castle's scheme. This has now been modified. The pensions and national insurance records of the United Kingdom now contain some 43 million personal accounts with 11 billion characters on computer tape. It is expected that by 1980 there will be 45 million accounts and 21 billion characters; and in 1990 the forecast is for 47 million accounts and 33 billion characters. Figures of this kind suggest that computers are likely to play an increasing role in the public services of this country[18]

Problems of decentralization and administrative boundaries

We noted above the management theorist's interest in the distribution of functions between different organizational levels and the attempt to differentiate between tasks appropriate to different levels. This classic problem of decentralization is of continuing interest and concern in the organization of public services. The costs of failing to solve it are clear to see in the many examples of overcentralized organizations, where too many decisions are reserved for top levels, and in the many ill-co-ordinated organizations, where the lower levels are allowed to go their own way to the detriment of achieving the organization's general objectives. Yet while it is fairly simple to detect failures to decentralize satisfactorily, it is by no means easy to determine what powers and duties should be allocated to each organizational level or, indeed, to determine what levels there should be. The truth is that government work is so varied and so many tasks are intertwined with each other that straightforward prescription is impossible.

This can be seen by considering the arrangements for providing welfare services in the United Kingdom. In principle, there should be a reasonably clear distinction between the technical business of providing the services to patients and others in need; the organizational task of arranging, co-ordinating and integrating this technical work; and the institutional task of developing the general level of welfare provision. This was recognized by the establishment in 1968 of a unified Department of Health and Social Security to be responsible at central government level for most of the public welfare services. Yet the detailed arrangements reveal an extensive range of organizations and levels. There are in fact three main kinds of services to be considered. First, the provision of financial benefits such as old age pensions and assistance to widows and children in need. Secondly, the health services provided by family doctors, dentists and other professions in surgeries, hospitals and elsewhere. And thirdly, the personal social services, such as homes for orphaned children or those taken into care for other reasons, and facilities for the care of old people and the disabled.

These three services are currently provided by three different systems. The financial benefits are provided by the Department of Health and Social Security, which has a large organization for maintaining comprehensive records of the insurance premiums paid by every member of the working population, and a network of local offices concerned to apply the complicated rules relating to financial assistance to the individual cases coming before them. Benefits are paid in accordance with rules laid down in Acts of Parliament, but these have to be supplemented by extensive codes of administrative practice in order to cover the great variety of cases that come before the officials of the Department. There are opportunities for appeal to independent commissioners as well, of course, as opportunities to raise points with the Secretary of State, his ministers and in Parliament.

The health services are provided by the National Health Service which is organized through a series of regional health authorities, of which there are 14 in England; area health authorities, of which there are 90 in England; and district health authorities. This is a complex system, which is designed to preserve a considerable measure of independence for the medical professions. Detailed arrangements exist at a variety of levels to preserve the standing and status of the various medical professions, so that the individual relationship between the medical practitioner and his patients can be preserved. And, in order to do this in a way that is acceptable to the medical profession, the relationship with the Health Service is by contract rather than salary.

The personal social services are provided by local authorities in their usual way. That is to say, there is a committee of elected members responsible for personal social services and a chief officer and appropriate staff and facilities at the various levels and of the various kinds necessary to carry out the statutory duties to provide services for children in care, disabled people and for others in need.

To describe this system in a nutshell it might be said that the social security services are provided and controlled by the Secretary of State for Social Services and his Department; the National Health Service is planned and monitored by and receives its financial allocations from the Secretary of State, but is administered by the Regional Health Authorities and subsidiary bodies, including the professional elements of the system; and, thirdly, the local authority services are provided with central financial assistance, and carried out within the overall guidance of the Secretary of State, but in accordance with the usual arrangements for the working of local authorities.[19]

Are these arrangements sensible? Do they provide the right distribution of power and authority so that the higher levels of the system are able to concentrate on policy and the allocation of resources; the middle levels on the general administration and co-ordination of the services in their areas; and the local levels on the detailed, effective and humane treatment of the individuals who come to the services in need of assistance? In short, do the management theorist's concepts indicated earlier in this chapter have a ready and sensible application in the arrangements for the welfare services?

So far as the administration of benefits is concerned, the task is relatively self-contained and it is possible to provide a network of offices to pay benefits efficiently and politely to those who seek assistance. Difficulties nevertheless arise and problems occur in individual cases. Administrative systems seldom have sufficient elasticity in their rules to deal satisfactorily with all cases. There will also be times when staff deal rudely or unkindly with individual applicants; and times when applicants cheat and assault the staff! There is also the problem that there are never enough resources to provide benefits on the scale that applicants would find ideal. But within these more or less inevitable limits, to which continuing attention must be paid in the search for improvement, arrangements for the administration of social benefits would appear to provide for a sensible division of powers between organizational levels and the possibility of making sensible links where necessary with the personal social services provided by local authorities. In sum, therefore, the distribution of work between the levels concerned promotes the achievement of the organization's goals.

Yet problems remain and may well become more difficult. For example, between 1966 and 1976 the number of staff working on supplementary benefits in local offices rose by 140 per cent from 12,500 to 30,000. The management increased faster than the staff, since it constituted 4.5 per cent of the work force in 1966 and 5.3 per cent 10 years later. The need for more managers is partly a consequence of increasing work and the need to manage larger and amalgamated offices. But it arises also from the greater complexity of the regulations. As the system grows and develops, the number of variants for which it has to cope increases, and the number of appeals heard by tribunals against the decisions of the Department's officials is growing—it rose 320 per cent in the 10 years to 1976. This creates more higher level work. Again, the number of benefits has increased as the politicians have extended the range of social security. In 1966 the departments that preceded the Department of Health and Social Security managed 11 main benefits; now the total is 19, including special Old People's pensions, Family Incomes Supplement and Mobility Allowances, and there are also special payments like the £10 Christmas bonuses in 1972, 1973, 1974 and the butter and beef tokens that have been issued in recent years to old people.[20] It is therefore reasonable to suppose that the present distributions of powers and activities between the different levels of the social security system will need to be adjusted in the future to take account of the results of recent trends, which are likely to continue into the future.

So far as the health service is concerned, the problems are even greater. A balance has to be struck, and reflected in the powers and duties of the various levels in the service, between the inevitable limitations in funds—since there is no limit to what might be spent on medical care—the requirements of different patterns of health care—the longer patients stay in hospital, the less resources there will be for other forms of treatment—and the need to provide a good standard of service as judged by the medical professions and as perceived by the patients. Do present arrangements enable a fair balance to be struck? Mr R.G.S. Brown, who has made a detailed study of welfare administration, suggests a generally favourable answer—

> ...except at the boundary where medical care shades into social care, the job of assessing and as far as possible meeting the local needs of a community is a distinctive one requiring local knowledge as well as

distinctive professional skills. Both are built into the structure at area and regional levels in a way that should balance without any bias against either patient or professional staff. If an acceptable balance is not reached locally, a higher authority can step in in its monitoring role. Both consumer and professional interest groups operate at national level and enjoy frequent opportunities to persuade the Secretary of State to limit in their favour the discretion of lower-tier authorities. The lower-tier authorities have an incentive to make the budget stretch as far as possible and their responsibilities are wide enough to avoid any temptation to secure sub-rational economies by shunting costs to other public bodies. They have no incentive to keep down the total cost of the service they provide and indeed every incentive to try to have it increased, but their efforts to do so are countered by the rigid control of budgetary allocations from the centre.[21]

This complex arrangement of checks and balances is bound to prompt the question whether all the levels in the system are really necessary. Could as good a service be provided by local hospitals and health service professionals without the whole range of districts, areas, regions and central authorities? The system may work, as Mr Brown shows that it does, but could a simpler pattern produce as good or better results? Management theory raises these questions, but cannot provide the answers by itself since many political and medical considerations are involved on which management theory cannot speak directly. However, there is currently a Royal Commission on the National Health Service and evidence submitted to it both by McKinseys, the firm of management consultants who helped to design the present structure in 1974, and by the Society of Civil and Public Servants, a trade union with members in the Department of Health and Social Security, calls for a reduction in the number of levels in the Health Service by the removal of the Regional Health Authorities.

The personal social services need to be provided in a way that takes account of local needs and requirements. Giving responsibility for them to local government is an obvious way of doing this. But their work has more in common with the National Health Service than with the rest of the work of local authorities and, in times of financial restriction, they may become one of the Cinderallas of local government.

There is an institutional incentive to avoid burdening [the local rates] ...unduly with the cost of home help and residential care for the elderly and mentally handicapped, for whom the nationally financed NHS offers alternative means of care. The overlap element is much more significant, as a proportion of total budget, for the social service departments than for the health authorities. This 'sub-rational' option is much more likely to be taken up if local authorities go in for more corporate planning...and try seriously to work out priorities over local services as a whole. In sum, the wisdom of entrusting social services to local authorities becomes debatable given the interdependence of these services with parts of the NHS ....[22]

In this instance, therefore, the way that powers and duties are allocated between levels and organizations can hinder the achievement of the goals of each one of them.

It will be clear from this account that, in a complex field like the provision of welfare services, there is no straightforward way of deciding upon the distribution of powers and responsibilities between organizations and the various levels within them. As noted earlier in this chapter, the general principles suggested by the study of management may be useful as pointers and indicators. But they do not provide clear guidance on what should be done for the best.

Local government

Local government in England and Wales was reorganized in 1974. Messrs R.O. Greenwood, M.A. Lomer, C.R. Hinings and S. Ranson of the Institute of Local Government Studies of the University of Birmingham carried out a study, published in 1975, of 70 per cent of the new authorities to see what organizational systems had been introduced following the changes.[23] The research team returned to take stock of progress and surveyed 27 of the local authorities that had been considered in their wider survey. This survey, which was published in 1977, was organized around the concepts of differentiation and integration, which the team defined as follows. 'Differentiation refers to the division of labour within the authority expressed as a number of organizational parts. Integration refers to those devices, such as policy committees and central departments, intended to counter-balance the division of labour and unify the authority.'[24]

In carrying out the survey, the authors sought to include a representative cross section of local authorities as below:

Type of Authority	Number of Authorities
Metropolitan County	3
County	8
Metropolitan District	8
Shire District	8
	27

The authors noted that the major influence upon the working of local authorities in the last few years has been economic retrenchment. Reorganization was implicitly based on the belief that there would be opportunities for local authorities to develop their services and that the necessary resources would be made available. Unfortunately, the economic difficulties of the country have confounded this assumption; instead, local authorities have had to put much of their energies into retrenchment and economy.

As noted in chapter 2, the main thrust of the report on *The New Local Authorities: Management and Structure* (the Bains report) was in favour of an integrated approach to the planning and provision of services by local authorities. This was in contrast to their provision by departments individually responsible for planning and carrying out their own services subject, of course, to a minimum co-ordination in the areas of finance and certain common services, such as personnel management. To study how far the organizational changes proposed in the Bains report have been carried out, we will examine the development of:

(*a*) the post of chief executive,

(*b*) the chief officers' management team,

(*c*) interdepartmental working groups of officials,

(*d*) committees of elected members and relationships between elected members and officials,

drawing largely on material in the Institute's study previously cited.

(*a*) The post of chief executive

So far as the chief executive is concerned, the Bains report gave an ambiguous definition of what was required. The report said that:

> the Chief Executive is the head of the council's paid service and shall have authority over all other officers so far as this is necessary for the efficient management and execution of the Council's function.

But this was qualified by the statement that:

> the range of issues and problems facing any local authority is too numerous and varied for the Chief Executive to grasp in detail, and Heads of Departments must therefore retain the responsibility for the effective and efficient running of the services for which their departments are responsible. This means that the Chief Executive must act primarily as the leader of a team of chief officers.

In practice, three types of chief officer have emerged. First, there is the chief executive who continues to act as *primus inter pares* among the chief officers. He may well retain the term Clerk or Town Clerk in his title and he usually retains control over a department on the grounds that this is the best way to exercise his influence over the range of council business. He will usually seek to avoid imposing his personality and his views, believing that each of the senior officers should manage their own affairs. He is unlikely to attend the meetings of the policy and resources committee, and his relationship with its chairman may well be occasional and informal. This kind of chief executive is typical of the smaller shire district. By and large, he continues to carry out his job very much as he used to do before reorganization.

The second kind of executive is described in the research as 'the administrative co-ordinator'. His formal title is often 'chief executive officer' and his department will usually be run by a second in command so that he can build up an executive office, often based on close links with the treasurer. He will usually see his managerial role as securing efficient housekeeping and management of the council's functions, rather than helping to formulate and carrying out a corporate plan. He will tend to have formal and regular relations and meetings with the political leaders, and he will probably spend a good deal of time on external relations, particularly in dealings between the county and the district. This kind of chief officer is typically found in the shire county and the larger shire districts.

The third kind of chief officer is described by the authors of the report as 'a policy maker and director'. This chief executive officer is usually to be found in metropolitan authorities. Like the administrative co-ordinator, he too will probably have given up effective control of running a department, but will seek to develop his position by formulating new links through special relations with key central functions such as personnel and corporate planning. His personal assistant will often have a defined and important role in the working of the authority. The 'policy maker' will usually see his role as guiding, shaping and carrying out a policy of corporate management and planning, and political relationships will usually involve regular meetings with the party leadership both formal and informal in nature, and may include taking part in political group meetings. External relations will also be important, involving negotiations with county and central government.

The post of chief executive officer has therefore developed in a variety of ways. The different kinds of role that have developed depend to a fair extent upon the kind of authority in which the officer is working and the sorts of problems and scale of work with which he has to contend. It appears that, in urban areas, where the idea of a plan for the development of the community as a whole possibly carries a more immediate significance and appeal, chief executives tend to develop on the lines recommended in the Bains report. The political pressure for this kind of policy tends to be greater in urban areas and the opportunities afforded by elected members may well provide scope for a chief executive to develop his role in this way. Professor J.D. Stewart has put the matter in the following words; 'in one way or another, political and economic pressures will resolve the authority issues at present left ambiguous in the chief executive role. The middle ground of consensus will then be abandoned for the clearer definitions of responsibility. If that cannot be achieved, then the role will be abandoned'.[25]

(b) The chief officers' management team
Two kinds of chief officers' management team have developed. First,

there is what might be called the 'administrative management team', which tends to go with the clerk or administrative co-ordinator type of chief executive, and to be found in the shire counties and smaller county districts. This management team is typically conceived as mainly responsible for monitoring and co-ordinating the work of the administrative machine. Policy is seen as the responsibility of the heads of departments and agendas usually consist of matters of administrative detail. The reports presented are usually over the signature of the chief officer concerned, and the team operates more like a meeting of the heads of operating companies rather than a cabinet or policy forming board. Power frequently devolves upon the treasurer since he is concerned with finance, the major resource in which all officers are interested and concerned.

The second kind of team is more in line with the Bains conception of a board or team with a corporate identity and a positive role to play in the corporate management of the authority. This kind of team tends to be associated with the policy making and directing type of chief executive and is mainly found in the metropolitan authorities. Although their agendas are usually concerned with detailed matters, the team often makes a more definite attempt to consider policy issues. This kind of team can provoke tension and resistance on the part of those chief officers who resent what they regard as its interference in their affairs, and it may require a chief executive with a strong personality with political support, and possibly working with an 'inner cabinet' of senior officials, for the team to develop. Here again, Professor J.D. Stewart has made a pertinent comment; 'management teams should consider a drastic pruning of the agenda, less frequent formal meetings of the full team, more emphasis on the consideration of key issues, on the responsibility of chief officers to raise issues, with a review procedure underpinning it. And the review procedure should centre on the use of resources and on key problems. The local authority needs corporate management. It cannot afford a parody'.[26]

(c) Interdepartmental working groups of officials

Although the Bains report did not consider the role of interdisciplinary and interdepartmental working groups of officials in great detail, it could well be argued that corporate management requires some form of matrix organization at the middle levels for its effective operation. If a local authority is to achieve proper co-ordination in devising and implementing plans and programmes for the authority as a whole, then co-ordination must not only come from the formal structure of authority but also through the operation of a lateral structure of interdisciplinary working groups and project teams.

All the 27 authorities investigated in this study showed examples of interdepartmental working groups. There tended to be less of them in the smaller authorities so that, for example, the smaller shire districts had five or six groups on average, whereas the larger authorities reported about 10 to 15. One Metropolitan district had as many as 37. These interdepartmental groups frequently comprise about six or seven second and third tier officers. The role of the group is usually defined as fact finding or policy formulation or monitoring the implementation of policies or the allocation of resources. It is seldom that one of these groups is explicitly charged with decision making. The groups are occasionally the responsibility of a particular department; more frequently they are responsible to the chief officers' management team.

In the smaller authorities, mainly the shire districts, the teams most usually found are 'programme area teams'. The idea is illustrated by one authority quoted in the research report. 'We have an overall system of programme area teams—housing, environmental health, development services (planning and highways), recreation and amenities. Alongside each programme committee there is a team of second, third and fourth tier officers with all departments represented on every programme group (i.e. a programme area team of six members). Each programme area team is chaired by a deputy or third tier officer from the department basically responsible for operating the programme and all the groups are serviced by the secretary's department. Their role is to make reports to the chief

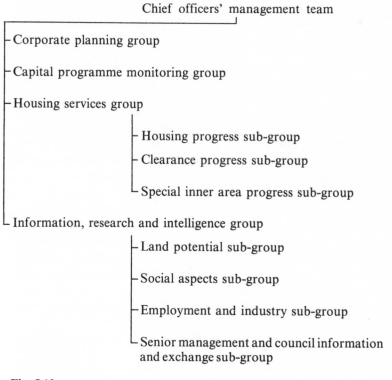

Chief officers' management team

├─ Corporate planning group

├─ Capital programme monitoring group

├─ Housing services group

    ├─ Housing progress sub-group

    ├─ Clearance progress sub-group

    └─ Special inner area progress sub-group

└─ Information, research and intelligence group

    ├─ Land potential sub-group

    ├─ Social aspects sub-group

    ├─ Employment and industry sub-group

    └─ Senior management and council information and exchange sub-group

Fig. 5.10

officers' management team on the forward plans for the programme area and then monitor their implementation. They are also beginning the task of producing position statements'.[27]

In those authorities where the chief executive is an administrative co-ordinator, typically the shire counties, there are fewer examples of programme area teams. But interdisciplinary groups frequently exist and their tasks tend to be concerned with monitoring scarce resources. Thus groups may be set up for resource allocation generally, or more specific groups may exist to monitor particular resources such as land, manpower and capital. These authorities may also have interdisciplinary working groups considering such subjects as information collection and processing, and many authorities use interdepartmental groups to study information and research needs as well as the non-financial use of the computer.

Some authorities, typically the metropolitan districts, have a more comprehensive framework of groups, including programme area groups and resource and co-ordination groups together with groups focusing on corporate policy as such. This leads to a wide variety of groups with very different kinds of activities and responsibilities. The research study quotes one authority with a complex structure including the working groups shown in Fig. 5.10.[28]

The corporate planning group is chaired by the chief executive and is responsible for keeping the machinery and other arrangements for corporate planning under review, and for considering the documentation required, including the form of the community plan, the need for position statements and the form and presentation of the budget. It is also responsible for considering the relationship between the authority and other public bodies, including local authorities, central government departments and business firms. The capital programme monitoring group is charged with preparing a long-term capital programme for the authority, which is to include not only the expenditure figures but also the details of the projects, the objectives they are designed to achieve, and the revenue consequences. The housing programme area group is charged with formulating general policies for the authority in the light of the central government's policy direction. This is largely complete and implementation and monitoring is the prime task now. This is mainly carried out by the sub-groups. The information, research and intelligence group is responsible for assessing the authority's needs for management information; the sub-groups are considering particular areas. For example, the computer sub-group is examining the scope for using the computer for new, non-financial, tasks; and the social aspects group is considering cultural, recreational and welfare requirements. The idea is that the structure of groups should change with the requirements of the authority's work.

Another metropolitan authority—a county council—has a different form of organization.[29] There is a chief officers' management team consisting of the executive heads of most of the council's departments. It excludes the chief environmental officer, the chief inspector for consumer protection and the chief officer for recreation, culture and leisure. It includes the heads of two of the services which are virtually *ad hoc* bodies under the general control of the council—police and passenger transport. While the work of the management team is buttressed by regular meetings of all chief officers, the composition of the management team reflects the county council's major areas of activity—planning, highways and transport.

Below the management team there is a clear division between 'programme area teams' and 'functional groups'. Programme area teams are interdepartmental groups of officers based on broad areas of activity, such as transport and the physical environment. They are responsible for examining alternative policies and programmes for achieving the authority's objectives and reporting their conclusions for consideration by elected members. Functional groups are interdepartmental groups of officers concerned with the co-ordination and development of technical or professional activities covering more than one department, such as financial and manpower procedures, research and information, and purchasing. Details are set out in Fig. 5.11.

(*d*) Committees of elected members and relationships between elected members and officials

Finally, there is the important area of relationships between elected members and officers. There is no doubt that the main thrust of management thinking has been to underline the contribution that the official can

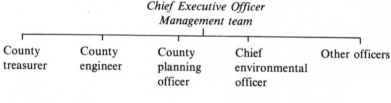

Chief Executive Officer
Management team

| County treasurer | County engineer | County planning officer | Chief environmental officer | Other officers |

Functional groups for

Finance
Manpower
Property
Performance review
Research and information
Computer applications
Structure plan
Project co-ordination
Purchasing
Publicity and public
 participation

Programme area teams

Physical environment
Public safety and protection
Transport
Economic development
Leisure
Social areas

Fig. 5.11

make to the working of local government and to suggest that the official should have a greater role in working out policy options and in their implementation. As a corollary, the councillor's role is seen as primarily concerned with decisions upon issues of broad policy and with their discussion and consideration among the local community at large. In this way, elected members and officials can be seen as specializing in those aspects of the work of a local authority in which each is specially well fitted to make the main contribution.

The result for elected members has been a continuing emphasis on reducing the number of council committees and in developing the ideas outlined in the Bains report for programme area committees and central policy and resource committees. The idea of programme area committees was linked with the idea of programme areas for corporate planning; for example, instead of having separate committees for libraries, recreations, parks and museums, there might be instead a unified leisure and amenities committee. The notion was that, since these services were closely aligned, then it would be right for their policies to be developed together. They should be seen as a co-ordinated whole, and as one aspect of the corporate plan of the authority and its implementation. Central policy committees were based on the idea that programme area committees must be integrated and co-ordinated. There must be a committee where policy decisions between programme areas could be taken, wider priorities set and resources allocated to the various programme areas in accordance with the authority's stated priorities.

To what extent have these ideas worked out in practice? Research has shown that the idea of programme area committees has taken stronger root in some fields of work than others. Programme area committees in the fields of leisure and recreation and public protection are to be found in most of the authorities surveyed, but such committees are rarer in the fields of planning and highways and very rare indeed in such areas as housing and education. Why is this so? Programme committees are generally found in areas which have been the preserve of what are relatively weak departments in local authorities, e.g. the parks as compared with the education department, and in areas which have traditionally been somewhat to the side of the authority's main activities as, for example, the fire service. But where functions have traditionally been exercised by powerful committees and departments, where a lot of money is spent, where there is a high degree of professional expertise among the officers, and a great deal of public interest in the subject, then the traditional organization of council committees and departments tends to be maintained.

One of the major recommendations of the Bains report was that there should be a central co-ordinating policy committee. In all but one of the 27 authorities surveyed in this piece of research, there is a committee of this kind. Most of them are called 'policy and resources' or 'policy' committees which have developed in three different forms. First, there are authorities where the policy and resources committee confines its activities to co-ordinating the work of the other council committees. Secondly, there are authorities where the policy and resource committee has the right to comment on the activities of other committees if they are developing on new and unacceptable lines, and recommendations can be made to the council that the report of the service committee should not be accepted but sent back for further consideration. Thirdly, there is the 'interventionist' policy committee. Here the policy committee will produce its own ideas, comment on proposals from the other committees and generally direct them in their activities. Very often such committees have the power to return reports of other committees before they go to the council and in this sense the policy committee can regularly interpose itself between the service committees and the council as a whole. The research study comments that in many cases special care is taken to select councillors of high quality for service on committees of this kind, and discussions take place between party leaders to try to bring this about.

The usual arrangement in the case of the 'co-ordinating' type of committees is for the service committees to get their policies approved at council level, and the matters are then referred to the policy and resources committee to consider how the requisite resources can be provided. This can easily lead to a concentration upon competition for resources, and in these cases the policy and resources committee can operate rather like an arena for settling committee and departmental bids. The chief executive, treasurer and secretary tend to have very much of a commanding position in the work of such committees compared with that of other officers. The agenda of the policy and resources committee often mainly consists of reports from these three central officers; other chief officers attend to present their professional views and advice. The officers do not attend as members of a management team dealing with general council policy.

So far as the 'commenting' policy committee is concerned, there is a tendency for all the chief officers to attend and to do so increasingly as members of the management team. They may well have discussed the subjects to be considered before the policy committee meets. Nevertheless, since the commenting policy committee is something of a compromise between the 'co-ordinating' and 'interventionist' styles, there can be tensions within the group of chief officers. They may not be clear as to how far they should speak for their own service or programme area committee, and how far they should seek to transcend these considerations and see themselves as members of the management team.

There tend to be two patterns of attendance by officers at meetings of 'interventionist' committees. All the chief officers may attend on a regular basis as members of the chief officers management team, which is here regarded as the officers' equivalent of the policy committee. The alternative practice is for a relatively small group of officers to attend the policy committee. They do not, however, attend as the central officers servicing the 'co-ordinating' style of policy committee. They are present as the senior officers responsible for the resource and planning aspects of the corporate plan and as those who, from their central position in the organization, can see beyond the confines of a single programme area or department.

Finally, it must be recognized that one of the results of local government reorganization has been to strengthen the political impetus within local government. Party politics has always played its part in local government, particularly in urban areas. But local government elections are now increasingly fought on a party basis; more elected members believe their party allegiance to be of prime importance; special arrangements are made to concert a party policy and outlook on issues; and the parties look upon their term of office in the same way that parties at the national level look upon a period of government. That is to say, they not only see it as a period of stewardship but also, funds permitting, as an opportunity to carry out a programme on which they hope to be judged by the local community and re-elected for further office.

In these circumstances, changes have naturally taken place in the relationships between local government officers and elected members. Naturally enough, the formal position remains the same. The officers serve the council, whatever its political complexion, and expect to maintain their standing and status if their political masters change. However, as noted above, the practice has developed in many authorities of regular meetings between the chief officers, particularly the chief executive, and the leaders of the major party. This occasionally takes the form of officials attending party group meetings. But a more usual arrangement is to have regular meetings between leading officials sometimes, though not always, grouped as a chief officers management team, and the chairmen of committees or, informally, with the policy and resources committee. In recent years, the economic climate and the need to make cuts in budgetary allocations has encouraged the formation of a number of joint working groups of elected members and officers, concerned with budget guidelines and financial policy, and there has been an increasing number of meetings between officers and elected members over resource allocation. The incidence of meetings varies between authorities; the research study suggests that quarterly meetings seem to be the average.

The general conclusion that emerges from this piece of research is that management ideas, as set out in the Bains report and other documents, have been important influences upon the structure of elected members' committees; upon the status and roles of officials; and upon working relationships. In particular, the idea of corporate planning, in one form or another, has been taken up by most authorities and attempts have been made to provide the organizational machinery for undertaking it. However, the form that these attempts have taken has varied between authorities and, in practice, the organization adopted and the way that it has developed has tended to depend upon the nature of the authority's problems; the need to make financial savings; the values and attitudes of its officials; and, above all, upon the political consciousness of its elected members.

GENERAL FACTORS

We now turn to some of the general lessons that can be drawn from the examples described above. First, in spite of the increasing concern for and interest in management theory and practice over the last ten to 15 years, it is clear that greater weight is still given to political factors in determining the organization of central government departments and local authorities. Even when claims are made that changes are being introduced for 'management' reasons, it is by no means unusual to find that these changes are subsequently modified for political and policy reasons. For example, the Department of Trade and Industry was set up in 1970 as one of the large scale departments to take responsibility for a major sector of government work. It was stated that the changes of which it had formed a part will 'be longer lasting and will remove the need for continual changes for a considerable period in the future ... the main departmental structures as now outlined are intended and expected to remain valid for a long time to come'.[30] But the Department of Trade and Industry was broken up in less than five years and has by now been divided into four separate departments to indicate the concern of successive governments with four particular problems—the energy crisis; exports; industrial strategy and regeneration; and prices and consumer protection. In the departments of Energy, Trade, Industry, and Prices and Consumer Protection, each 'problem' now has its own government department; though the four departments continue to share certain facilities such as personnel and management services. Again, in local government, while most authorities introduced and have maintained changes inspired by the philosophy of the Bains report, there has been considerable variation in the outcome of their operation. Furthermore, where changes have been seen as disturbing the balance of power and authority between elected members and officials, or have been thought to represent the policy of a particular party, they have often been modified for these reasons.

Secondly, management theory has made little contribution to a number of significant organizational problems, including the relationship between elected members and local government officers and between ministers and civil servants. We have seen the way that changed arrangements for policy analysis and planning have affected this relationship. But management theory has provided little guidance on how the two can best work together. The old idea that elected members decide policy and officials carry it out is as misleading as the more fashionable suggestion that officials determine policy outcomes by slanting their advice to politicians to achieve their own wishes and so act as 'statesmen in disguise'. Yet management theory is strangely silent on how the elected and official elements of public organizations can best co-operate. Management theory has also said little about the crucial problem of how to delegate the maximum authority while preserving the accountability of top management. In a political democracy it is essential that ministers, elected members and senior officials should be capable of being held accountable to the public. If they could be judged by simple criteria—such as return on capital—this might be easily possible. But they must be able to account for a wide range of topics and this makes it difficult to delegate widely and fully within their organization.

Again, management theory has little to say about how organizations can co-operate fruitfully together. A great deal of the work of a public organization consists of dealings with other government organizations; central government departments with each other and with local authorities; hived-off agencies with their parents; and one part of the welfare services with another. How should these relationships be conducted? Should they proceed as if each organization were merely a department of one huge organization—the government as a whole? Or should these organizations conduct their affairs as if they were competitors for resources and clients in the market place? Clearly, both these extremes are wrong. But here again management theory has had little to say. Nor has it made a significant contribution to the crucial debates about devolution, and the various proposals to rearrange government powers between the United Kingdom government and public authorities in Scotland, Wales and Northern Ireland.

Why is this so? The answer probably lies in the fact that management theory mainly evolved from the study of business enterprise, in which it was assumed that everyone, from the Board of Directors to the office boy, had broadly the same kind of interest in the organization—a fact which is certainly not the case in public organizations where the aspirations and perceptions of elected members are very different from those of officials. Similarly, the curious combination of rivalry and co-operation that marks the relationships between public authorities has few parallels in the business world. Competition and co-operation certainly exist in the private sector; but their touchstone is economic and the whole relationship is influenced thereby.

The study of management has accordingly had little to say about the key organizational issues in the public sector described above. It is, of course, part of the argument of this chapter that management theory cannot provide direct guidance upon management practice. But it can provide insights and promote speculation, and induce a greater willingness to change and experiment. Because it has had little to say about the political dimensions of public organization, management theory has failed to respond to this challenge.

Nevertheless, its contribution to organizational change has been significant during the last 10 to 15 years, especially in the committee, officer and departmental structure of local government; in areas where government work has affinities with that of the business world; and in the straightforward change and reorganization of the working levels of government departments and local authorities. In particular, there is a greater consciousness that the nature of the work to be done, and the habits, values, attitudes and past experience of the staff will tend to set limits to the scope and scale of organizational change. The recognition of these constraints is an essential precondition of successful organizational change and, in this sense, the experience of the last 10 to 15 years has been invaluable in providing both central and local government with a greater appreciation of the kind of changes that can be introduced into the organization of public authorities, and an increased understanding of how to make them successfully.

SUMMARY AND CONCLUSIONS

(1) The interest in management thinking over the last 10 to 15 years has had some significant implications for the organization of central government departments and local authorities.

(2) It is naturally not possible to explain all the changes that have taken place as a response to the interest in the theory and practice of management. Nevertheless, three ideas have been particularly important. First, that organizations should be shaped to cohere with their goals and purposes. Secondly, that the disciplines of natural and social science have an important contribution to make to the generation and administration of policy, and that staff with such skills and knowledge should be associated with the central policy making process. Thirdly, that organizations are social groups as well as legal entities and formal hierarchies. Attention should therefore be paid in the design and management of organizations to the informal groups that will certainly grow up within them, and to the values and attitudes of the staff.

(3) These three ideas have been manifest in a number of changes; such as the introduction of large central government departments; the idea of hiving off to separate or to self-contained units those parts of their work of an executive rather than a political character; the introduction of specialist units concerned with management services, operational research, economic analysis; the idea of reviewing organizations as a whole rather than considering aspects of their operation; an interest in and concern for the organizational implications of introducing computers; and the introduction of a greater variety of organizational arrangements including planning teams, project groups and matrix organizations.

(4) We have considered the manifestation of these ideas in a wide range of practical examples in central and local government, including recent changes in the organization of the Tresury; the Central Policy Review Staff's investigation of the arrangements for overseas representation;

organization and methods studies; matrix organizations; recent experience of hiving off executive functions from government departments; problems of decentralization in the welfare services; and experience in local government of the implementation of some of the major ideas of the Bains report on *The New Local Authorities, Management and Structure* including the introduction of chief executives, the chief officer's management team, and interdepartmental working groups.

(5) The general conclusions to be drawn from this survey are as follows; management theory is too general in character to afford precise guidance upon organizational change, and experience in one organization cannot directly be applied in another; the practical assistance that management theory can therefore provide is limited to general insights, the promotion of speculation and examination of current practices, and the realization that useful change is at least possible, even though it is difficult to bring about. Management theory has been valuable in promoting changes in a number of areas of public organizations and in those areas of work which have affinities with business enterprise; but it has proved less valuable, and certainly less durable, when attempts have been made to employ it in politically sensitive areas of government organization.

(6) Indeed, management theory has said relatively little so far about the problems of political organization, as against business organization. Its contributions to change in politically sensitive areas, or even to the analysis of many of the problems, such as the relationships between central and local government, and the form that devolution might take, has therefore been small.

6
Personnel

For the first half of this century central and local government were generally recognized as being in the forefront of the ranks of good employers. They were among the pioneers in providing lifetime careers without fear of dismissal at the whim of the employer. They provided opportunities for promotion, reasonable holidays, and some of the best opportunities for employment open to women. They afforded good pensions, generous sick leave, and some opportunities for training and further education. But since the end of the Second World War there have been doubts and criticisms about the adequacy of personnel management in the public service.

Among the reasons for this have been the following. First, the relative advantages of public sector employment have declined. Its attractions are now matched by those of many private employers, and where private employers have not introduced modern employment practices of their own volition they are increasingly required to do so by law as, for example, in the requirements that women should be under no handicap in their employment and that they should have equal pay with men for equal work. Secondly, the public sector has become very much larger and many of its organizations have increased in size. This has tended to make personnel management remote and impersonal unless compensating steps are taken. Thirdly, the public services now employ very many different kinds of people. As we have seen in previous chapters, the civil service and local government no longer employ mainly clerks, technical specialists and industrial workers, as in the Royal Dockyards and for road repairs. They also employ a full range of social and natural scientists, engineers and other specialists. Nearly all these people want the opportunity to be considered for the highest posts available. Any suspicion that the top jobs are the monopoly or special preserve of particular professional groups is ana-thema to the majority. To the extent that it is difficult to provide equal opportunities for all kinds of staff to be considered for the highest posts, there is a tendency to feel that personnel management is unfair and inequitable. Fourthly, the civil service and local government have been criticized as stuffy and for offering jobs circumscribed by rules, regulations, laws, orders and by the requirements of superior officials, elected members and ministers. The public official is said to be enmeshed in red tape, and his vitality and creativity thereby snuffed out.

It would, of course, be quite wrong to suggest that civil service and local government work is, or has been, uniformly dull. Many men and women have carried out careers as full of excitement and adventure as any available in industry, commerce, in the armed services or overseas. But by and large there has been a feeling that employment in the civil service and local government is duller than it ought to be. Since the end of the Second World War, people have on the whole been better educated than their fathers and grandfathers before them. They are more inclined to question the existing order; they are less inclined to accept instructions as commands. They want reasons for what they are asked to do. They want their work to make sense and to have a purpose they can understand and support. They tend to be less satisfied with the prospect of an entire working lifetime in the contracts department of a Whitehall ministry or in the Borough Treasurer's Department of the local Town Hall. They want at least reasonable opportunities for change, pace, variety and challenge.

Finally, the public services have been in the vanguard of employers in recognizing the place of the unions and working out arrangements for joint consultation with them over a wide range of matters including pay and conditions of service. Indeed, the impact of unions upon the whole range of personnel management matters has been a major factor in central and local government. But in the last few years the unions and their members have become less satisfied than previously. They have been prepared to take industrial action, and they have been willing to criticize the decisions of elected members and ministers about the scale of services provided. Thus certain unions representing civil servants employed in social service departments have opposed cuts in public expenditure not only on the grounds that they may reduce the prospects of their members, but also because of opposition to a reduction in services available to members of the community.

The factors that we have so far distinguished apply to both the Civil Service and local government service. It is important to appreciate, however, that there is a substantial difference between the two. The Civil Service is a unified service. Although its members work for different government departments, they belong to a single Civil Service with common pay scales and conditions of service in all departments.

In local government, on the other hand, there is no single employer. Local government officers work for particular authorities and they are servants of the council. The council delegates responsibility to committees, some of which have a statutory basis of their own, and local government officers accordingly work under the direction of these committees. By and large, local government is more accessible to the local citizen than the day to day work of most civil servants. This is mainly because local government is concerned with supplying services directly affecting a local community. Chief officers such as the director of engineering services and the director of education often become well known in their localities. Many local authorities open at least some of their committee meetings to the public and the press. For these reasons, local government presents a more open face to the community than central government.

Although local government officers work for individual authorities, we can still talk of a local government service. This is partly the consequence of action by central government in prescribing qualifications for certain posts and in regulating superannuation arrangements. But, more importantly, it arises from the activities of professional associations and trade unions in pressing for uniform conditions of service and personnel policies, and from the work of the local authority associations, in introducing a standard pattern of staffing and grading and in promoting joint organizations of staff and authorities at national level as, for example, the Local Government Training Board. The result is that the local government service now offers a uniform system of grading and pay structures which individual local authorities adopt with, of course, some necessary local variations.

The contrast between the Civil Service and local government is perhaps best seen in the different kinds of work that is done. Nearly 40 per cent of local government staff are employed in professional or technical capacities and, if the teachers and policemen were included, this figure would be higher still. On the other hand, only some 25 per cent of central government staff are engaged in work of this kind. This has led to significant differences between the two services.

One of the major criticisms of the Civil Service, for example, is that many senior jobs have usually been held by 'generalists', often men and women with a university degree in an arts subject, recruited on the basis of their intelligence and personality, and engaged mainly in political work from an early age. This tends to lead, according to many commentators and to the Fulton report, to a failure to appreciate the importance of scientific and technical considerations, and a failure to understand how to manage large numbers of staff. There is accordingly held to be a need to supplement the experience of 'generalists' and to give 'specialists' the training and opportunities to compete for senior policy jobs.

In local government, on the other hand, the problem has been the reverse. Chief officers have traditionally been professional officers. They have reached their senior positions in local government on the basis of professional qualifications obtained in youth, together with specialization for many years in a particular aspect of local authority work such as engineering or education. Furthermore, the professionally qualified officer has often been reluctant to transcend his specialism. He has traditionally thought of himself as an engineer or a treasurer or a town clerk and, to the extent he has been concerned with general policy, he has always considered it from the particular viewpoint of his specialist knowledge and experience. In short, general experience covering a wide range of local authority work, and relevant to the responsibilities of, for example, a chief executive, has been hard to come by in local government.

PERSONNEL MANAGEMENT—GENERAL FACTORS

The foregoing problems present a challenge. There is naturally great interest in the extent to which the study of management can suggest solutions. As noted in the previous chapter, it is not possible to derive the answers to the organizational and personnel problems of specific organizations directly from management principles. There are, however, a few general ideas which the study of management suggests are particularly relevant to the personnel problems faced by central and local government.

The first is that personnel should be regarded as a basic resource of the organization to be used as effectively and efficiently as other resources, such as money and land. Secondly, that the effective and efficient use of personnel requires a recognition of human factors and the provision in particular of a pay and grading structure that is recognized as both generally fair and as providing opportunities within which capabilities can develop and the advancement of careers can be achieved. Thirdly, that the provision and management of this structure, and the recruitment, training and development of the staff who work within it, cannot be left to chance and requires specialist personnel management staff and departments. Furthermore, in addition to the contribution made by these specialists in personnel management, it is necessary for everyone responsible for the direction of staff to lead them with perception, humanity and firmness, which entails careful attention to good communication within and between organizations.

Finally, the study of management recognizes that there is no general set of personnel management techniques suitable for all problems, or an ideal pay and grading structure appropriate for all organizations. Neither can it be assumed that all large organizations are dull and dismal and hard to manage, and all small organizations lively, interesting and easy to control. Instead, the study of management suggests, as noted in the previous chapter, that difficulties of personnel management are likely to arise when there are conflicts between technical requirements, the values and attitudes of the staffs, the structures which align people with the tasks they have to undertake, and the environment in which the organization operates. If, for example, new machines are introduced which require overtime working at awkward hours unacceptable to the staff at present pay rates, there is accordingly a conflict between technical requirements and staff values and attitudes. It is the task of personnel management to detect and deal with these conflicts and difficulties and to resolve, or at least accommodate them, so that the organization and its members can proceed as smoothly and as far as possible to the achievement in harmony of their various goals and purposes.

These ideas rest on a great deal of theoretical work. It is not necessary for our purposes to go into this work in detail, but it will be helpful to indicate the main lines of the research which underlies these ideas and which points to the specific developments in personnel management discussed in subsequent sections of this chapter.

RESEARCH AND PERSONNEL MANAGEMENT

The main areas of personnel management research relevant to this chapter concern motivation, leadership and group behaviour.

(I) Motivation

No two people are alike. Everyone needs a certain amount of money but, beyond a basic level of financial reward, research has confirmed that there are wide differences in the factors motivating men and women at work. Some people, of course, are concerned to earn the very highest wages and salaries that they can. Others seem more interested in status and prestige. A third group may value highly the fellowship and comradeship of their colleagues. And others may find their main rewards in their enjoyment of the work itself.

The difficult task which the manager faces is to translate what he knows about needs in general into the specific needs of individual staff and workers and the precise means of meeting them. It is, of course, impossible for the manager to tailor a package of awards precisely corresponding to each individual's needs. But careful attention to this factor can pay dividends; for example the manager who employs numbers of professional workers must recognize their desire for advancement in their professional group. They may be anxious to publish the results of their work in the professional journals. The manager may initially regard this as a waste of time in terms of the immediate job. But if he prevents his staff from undertaking a measure of these activities they are unlikely to be fully motivated.

Again, motivations vary over time. In the past a sufficient motivator might have been the prospect of advancing slowly up the hierarchy in a local government authority, the final objective being to become a chief officer or deputy chief officer in the late fifties. Today such a prospect may be less appealing, and other career patterns and other forms of motivation may become necessary. What people want will vary at different times in their life and a young man with substantial family commitments may be highly motivated by economic measures, whereas the older man without such extensive family requirements may be more interested in other forms of reward.

Students of management have also pointed out that, at one end of the motivational spectrum, are those factors where absence causes dissatisfaction. These are often called the 'hygiene factors'. At the other end of the spectrum are those factors which, if present, can provide a positive force. These are the 'motivational factors'. The hygiene factors include wages, fringe benefits, physical working conditions, sports fields, luncheon arrangements and similar factors. When these matters are properly attended to then dissatisfaction will tend to disappear. But no positive attitude or motivation will result. The hygiene factors are therefore preventive. You avoid trouble by paying attention to them but you do not motivate people to give of their best. The motivational factors include recognition, the opportunity for advancement, potential for personal growth, responsibility and a sense that the job provides the opportunities for self-fulfilment and realization. A manager should not therefore be surprised when his careful attention to the staff dining room produces thanks but no better work from his staff. He must realise that the motivational as well as the hygiene factors need attention.[1]

Some students of management argue further than the extent and degree of motivation is a function of two things; the value of the particular incentive or prize to the individual in question, and his perception of whether or not a given pattern of behaviour will lead to the satisfaction of the need the incentive is designed to satisfy. If the incentive is not valued, or is valued only to a small degree, or if the individual believes that the prize is beyond his reach, then he will not be motivated by it. For example, it seems unlikely that the prospects of earning £15,000–£20,000 a year would be a very great motivating factor so far as social workers are concerned. Again, if we take local government officers as a whole, the fact that a minute proportion of them can earn such salaries places the reward on so remote a plane that few will believe that any endeavours on their part will bring it within their reach. Thus, to offer very large salaries to a tiny minority of people is unlikely to be very much of a motivator in the local government field. On the other hand, we are told that in the world of show business, for example, the fact that only one entertainer in 20,000 makes an income of this kind does not deter large numbers of people from entering the profession; though here we may observe that what seems to motivate them is the desire to be a 'star' for reasons of self-fulfilment rather than the desire to make the large sum of money.

(II) Leadership

How can we translate these insights about motivation into material that can be used by the manager? How, in a word, can he use this knowledge in order to be an effective leader? We know from what has been said so far that effective leadership fosters commitment and involvement on the part of those who are managed and that it must be an activity in which the manager sets the pace, in which he generates enthusiasm, and in which he provides an environment where people's own desires and wishes are met by the achievement of organizational goals.

A manager's approach towards people and their normal reaction to work will very largely condition his general approach to management. In his study of leadership, *The Human Side of Enterprise* Mr Douglas McGregor set out two alternative assumptions which a manager may have about people.[2] He called them theory X and theory Y. The manager who believes in theory X believes that the average person has an inherent dislike for work, and will avoid it if he can. Because of this he believes that people must be controlled, directed, threatened, and punished to get them to give adequate effort towards the achievement of objectives. Furthermore, the average person prefers to be directed, wishes to avoid responsibility and, above all, wants security. The implications of theory X are to lead the manager to a centralized system of organization, in which direction and control is exercised through authority maintained very largely in his own hands. Organizational requirements take precedence over the needs of members, and there is no reason to devote time, effort and money to helping them to realize their full potential. This is because it is believed that individuals of talent and ambition will, themselves, devise the means for their own advancement.

Theory Y, on the other hand, holds that the expenditure of physical and mental effort in work is as natural as play or rest and, depending on the conditions which are under the manager's control, work may be either a source of satisfaction or dissatisfaction. External control and the threat of punishment is not the only means for encouraging good work. Men will exercise self-direction and self-control if they are committed towards the objectives which are placed before them. This commitment is a function of the rewards associated with their achievement and, under proper conditions, people will not only accept but seek responsibility. In carrying out this responsibility they will seek to exercise their imagination, ingenuity and creativity. The implication of theory Y is that it is the task of the manager to create the conditions in which the individuals' various motivating needs can be met and in which they will achieve their own goals by achieving the goals of the enterprise.

It will be apparent from everything that has so far been said that theory Y has the best chance of leading to success for management. It is, however, very helpful for a manager to be able to assess himself, and to realize what kind of managerial leadership he will naturally provide, so that he can try to make any necessary improvement. Drs. Robert Blake and Jane Mouton have suggested a device for describing and assessing different managerial styles, which they call the 'Managerial Grid®'.[3] As will be seen from Fig. 6.1, the purpose of the Grid is to compare management styles in

Fig. 6.1 The Managerial Grid

terms of how each deals with the organizational needs of output and productivity and the human needs for mature and healthy relationships. The horizontal axis of the Grid represents the manager's concern for output while the vertical axis represents his concern for people. Each axis is on a 1–9 scale, indicating that a manager may have varying degrees of concern for either production or people.

For example, the manager with a 9,1 rating has nine degrees of concern for output and only one degree of concern for people. He sees people as tools of production. He tends to run a centralized system; he suppresses conflict by using his own authority; and his idea of motivation is to promote competition among employees in order to get work done. He is shown as the task manager in the diagram.

The converse of the task manager is what might be called the 'country club manager' with a 1,9 rating. This manager has only one degree of concern for output but nine degrees for people. He believes that if people are kept happy and harmony is achieved then a reasonable amount of production will be achieved. In short, people are like children and household pets. If you keep them contented they will do what is required of them. When problems and conflicts arise they can be glossed over or ignored. Managers of this kind are interested in producing compromises between their staff. They look for solutions which represent the lowest common denominator of views. They encourage innovation, but try to sidestep good ideas which might cause difficulties.

The third kind of manager gets a low rating on both scales: 1,1. He believes that the best policy is to make the very minimum movement from his present position. Too much attention to production will cause problems with the staff. Too much attention to the needs of the staff will cause problems with the output. Managers of this kind tend to be extremely remote from their subordinates; indeed, almost completely disinterested in them and their ideas. Furthermore, they never press or push for better output.

The manager with the 5,5 rating is the 'dampened pendulum' manager. He is constantly oscillating between his concern for people and his concern with production. His approach is one of 'live and let live', under which the real issues are muted. Most 'dampened pendulum' managers are basically task managers at heart, but they have learned that you cannot ride roughshod over people, so they have adopted a compromise approach. The point is, however, that by their oscillations they miss the real needs of the situation.

The team manager scores high on both axis: 9,9. He believes that people and production can be integrated. Put another way, he believes that an organization can be created whereby people can best satisfy their needs and objectives by working towards the objectives of the organization. When a problem arises, this manager will meet his staff, present the situation, encourage discussion and get ideas and commitment. He will delegate results and give his people freedom to operate. Where problems of feelings and emotions arise in working relationships the team manager will confront them directly and work out a solution to these differences.

Of course, these particular managers selected for study are men at the extremes of the managerial Grid. Not very many people would come up with these scores: most would be in the position of, e.g., 8,3 or 4,6 managers. In their research the authors of this Grid have found that managers tend to have one dominant style which they use more often than any other. In addition they have noted that many managers have a 'reserve' style, which is adopted if the dominant style does not work in a particular situation. Thus a 9,1 'country club' manager may have a 5,5 'reserve' style. Another research finding is that managers give inadequate descriptions of their own style of management. Usually they describe the way they would like to be, or how they would like to think their superiors and subordinates see them, rather than how they really are.

There are many other analyses of managerial leadership. For example, a distinction is often drawn between the authoritarian leader, who seeks results by order and command; the democratic manager, who seeks results by a process of discussion from which emerges a general consent to a course of action; and the participative leader, who discusses ideas and proposals with his staff but does do so within a setting that is directed to the emergence of clear decisions that will lead to the work being done effectively. The usual result of an analysis on these lines is that participative leadership is obviously the best. Authoritarian leadership can lead to resentment, and to a failure to enlist the enthusiasm and motivation of the staff. And democratic leadership is defective in that it can easily cease to be leadership at all, and become nothing more than the eliciting of compromise proposals from muddied discussion. However, there are times when the two defective forms of leadership can be valuable. For example, the authoritarian mode of leadership is often effective in times of emergency such as military operations, or the organization of rescue operations after fires and other disasters. The special circumstances usually make it acceptable because everybody recognizes that clear leadership and crisply delivered orders are necessary. Similarly, there are times when there is much to be said for the democratic form of leadership, as when, for example, there has been some kind of crisis in the organization and it is necessary to get people talking together and discussing the tasks and work of the organization. But such democratic leadership should only be the precursor to the more appropriate leadership on the participative model.

The general conclusion which emerges from this study of leadership is that the most effective form of leadership will depend on the task to be carried out, the staff available, and the exigencies of the situation. Managers must be alive and receptive to differences in these factors and must model the form of leadership they give on an appreciation of these factors. They must, in short, be flexible in their approach, and remember that the kind of leadership that has been successful once is not likely to be successful on all subsequent occasions. This is an easy trap to fall into. People often remember the jobs they have done well and the times they have been successful, and they think the methods that produced success on one occasion will do so in future. When they try the same methods in new surroundings they often fail, and the conclusion that they often draw is that they must persevere even more strongly with their existing methods rather than make adaptations. Our study of the factors involved in leadership should have made clear that this approach is unlikely to produce good results, and it has also led to the conclusion that the form of leadership most likely to be generally successful is one in which the enthusiasm and motivation of the staff is generated towards the work that has to be done. Too firm and detached a manager may feel that he is doing what is expected of him by keeping people's noses to the grindstone, but the results he gets will be less than effective because of the resentments that he creates. The 'hail-fellow-well-met' type of manager may think that he is doing a good job because of his encouragement and sympathy with the staff, but if the actual results achieved by this approach are poor then it is a fault to be remedied. Participative management demands an equal attention to the work in hand and the staff to carry it out.

(III) Groups

There are two sides to leadership; the leader and the group he manages. The study of how these groups are formed and how they operate is a necessary complement to the managers' knowledge of individuals and their motivation. Formal and informal groups exist in all organizations and are essential to their performance.

Indeed, unless members of the group are co-operating together, it will not be possible for work to be done at all. For example, in a government office dealing with claims for benefit from members of the public it may be necessary for quite a number of people to make their contribution. One person, for example, may assess the benefit due, somebody else may type the cheque, and a third person despatch the envelope. Again, in the planning of development schemes, the skills of engineers, planners, traffic experts and many other specialists have all to be incorporated together to produce a successful outcome. The effective operation of such groups depends upon human factors; it cannot be secured simply by issuing orders and laying down written rules.

The manager in the Civil Service or local government must work within these groups. He must therefore have some understanding of their operation. There are significant advantages in having strong and cohesive groups within an organization. The characteristics of such groups include common ways of behaving, common attitudes and common standards. They may even have their own private slang and, within the group, a variety of roles is likely to emerge, including informal leaders, the office humourist, the lady who always makes the tea and provides sympathy to those in trouble, and so on. The members of groups with considerable cohesiveness will tend to help each other and absenteeism will usually be low. The members will usually work hard and output will be high.

There are, of course, some potential disadvantages to strong and cohesive groups. If the group norms and attitudes lead to the setting of low output targets, then productivity is likely to be disappointing. This may be the case, for example, in groups where the real interest of the members lies outside their work, as for example, in their home or family, or in their impending retirement. Such a group may well have a high degree of cohesion, and may well be a pleasant and apparently helpful set of people. Yet they may set low standards of output, which are often difficult to correct since there will always be plausible excuses as to why so little work has actually been completed. These excuses will be compounded by the supporting statements of the members of the group; thus it will be said, for example, that the members appreciate that they have dealt with relatively few files that day but, on the other hand, one of their number has been unwell and another was called away to the personnel department for some particular task. The manager knows that these excuses do not really explain the low output, but they are sufficiently plausible for it to be difficult for him to make a direct complaint without causing trouble and resentment which may also have a dampening effect on the next day's work.

Another drawback of strong cohesive groups is that if they are based on common professional standards, there may well be a dislike of and contempt for people outside the group. Thus, it is suggested, there may be times when engineers working in local government may come to resent and criticize planners, to the detriment of the work of the local authority as a whole, and similar difficulties may arise with other groups of people.

It is therefore the manager's task to use the groups that will inevitably arise within his organization to produce a good standard of work. This will only be possible if he has an intelligent understanding and an ability to extract from these groups their maximum commitment to the task in hand. How, then, can a manager set about creating the groups that work effectively? To some extent his task will depend on technological factors. If the task demands a series of relatively separate activities as, for example, on a production line where each person makes a separate contribution, and so may get to know only the workers on either side of him, it will be difficult to create a common group feeling. On the other hand, it will be easier to encourage group feeling if the work inevitably throws people together as it may well do, for example, in planning and research, where the members of the research team must necessarily talk and communicate with each other in the determination and execution of the tasks that have been set for them.

However, even where technology is against the evolution of strong and cohesive groups, it is sometimes possible to make changes to encourage them. There has been a good deal of discussion recently of the idea that the arrangements in such mass production activities as the manufacture of cars and other engineering products can be improved if the work is broken down into tasks in which small groups of people can co-operate. Thus, a Swedish motor car manufacturer (the Volvo Company) has engaged in experiments in which workers do a larger range of tasks in co-operation with each other than in the normal production line arrangement, where each person does only one small part of the task. There are, of course, inevitable limits to this process since, if taken to extremes, it can lead to the loss of specialized skills, as would result if each person did more of the job than is really within his competence and skill.

Good communication is another important aspect of group cohesion. A study of a number of hospitals came to the conclusion that the speed of recovery of the patients was to some extent a function of the degree to which the members of the medical staff spoke and communicated with each other. In hospitals where consultants, doctors, matrons, sisters and nurses discussed matters on a reasonably free and easy basis the recovery rate of patients was high and staff turnover was low. The opposite way was true where there were very formal arrangements for communications, where much information was passed by written memoranda, and where people were very conscious of differences in rank and status. The recovery rate tended to be lower in such hospitals, and the happiness and satisfaction of hospital staff was also lower.[4]

The place of work is also relevant. If the members of the group are in the same room it will, by and large, tend to be more cohesive than if it is distributed over several rooms. There are some interesting examples of the importance of work-places. For example, some of the early merchant banks had a 'partners' room'. This meant that all the senior members of the firm sat in the same room. This certainly helped rapid communication, and the growth of understanding among the members. (Cynics, of course, tended to say that the partners' room had its origin in the fact that the members of the bank could not trust each other out of sight!). Another example comes from studies done in offices, where the cohesiveness of staff who could not all work in the same room was much helped by the provision of rest rooms and facilities where they could meet together.

On the other hand, it does not follow that everyone placed in a room will come together to form a cohesive group. Experiments with large open plan offices have not always produced feelings of group cohesiveness among their inhabitants. It has been noticeable, however, that small groups of people have tended to set up their own 'territories' within these large rooms by the strategic siting of filing cabinets, potted plants and other office impedimenta.

Group effectiveness also depends upon what is called, in the literature of management, 'role congruence'. This means that a person should not have a high and responsible position in one respect and a low standing in another. For example, a study was made of a number of restaurants and it was found that the staff did not work together effectively.[5] One of the prime reasons for this was that the cooks, who felt themselves and were generally recognize by the staff to be of relatively high standing, had nonetheless to take orders from the waitresses, who were generally felt to be lower in the social system of the restaurant staff. This conflict of standing was finally resolved by the introduction of automatic ordering processes, so that the cooks knew what the waitresses wanted but were not in the position of having to take instructions from people whom they found it difficult to accept as their superiors.

This may sound a trivial example; much of the framework of human relationships at work and elsewhere is founded on factors which seem to the outsider to be trivial. But many similar examples can be found in public administration as, for example, when the young secretary of a senior officer passes her master's orders on to one of his senior subordinates. The subordinate knows that the secretary is speaking with her master's voice, yet he cannot really get out of his mind the feeling that he is being ordered about by a very junior member of the staff. This kind of situation requires a good deal of tact for which, of course, the best secretaries are renowned. Similarly, relationships can be complicated if the relatively junior man in a central or staff department is in the position of appearing to give instructions to a senior line manager. For example, the line manager may wish to regrade a post and pay one of his people a higher salary. This may be against the policies of the organization, and it may fall to a relatively junior man to tell him so. Here, again, commonsense and tact can overcome the worst of these difficulties, yet the point remains that 'role congruence' has to be carefully considered and fostered to ensure the harmonious working of groups.

Finally, cohesiveness depends upon the relative permanence of groups. It takes time for feelings of sympathy and for knowledge of each other to grow. An effective working group is very different from the casual coming together of a set of people in a railway carriage, a cruise liner or during the summer holidays, when effective discussion and the elements of friendship can be forged in a remarkably short space of time. Yet these groups tend to break up immediately the journey or holiday comes to an end, and the promises to write to each other and to have further contact usually come to nothing. This is partly because insufficient time has elapsed for a real group spirit to develop. It is important for the members of a working group to be together for a reasonably long time, and for the membership to change only slowly. If movement is too fast and turnover too rapid group cohesiveness will suffer.

As far as the management of groups is concerned, experience and research suggests that output tends to be higher when supervisors and managers carry out such tasks as planning the order of work, making sure that supplies are available, training subordinates, and checking and adjusting work while leaving other tasks to members of the group. It may well be that there is an optimum amount of guidance that each particular work group requires for the tasks it has in hand. If less guidance than the optimum is provided, output will tend to fall, just as it will if supervision is too close. It has been suggested, particularly by Professor Elliott Jacques, that the amount of discretion can best be judged in relation to the timespan during which an individual can exercise his own discretion.[6] Those who are able to work for a long time before they need advice will tend to be the most experienced and highly skilled workers or managers.

Professor Jacques suggested, in fact, that the idea of the timespan of discretion might be used as the basis for determining pay. While there is a certain amount of evidence to support the idea that timespan of discretion is a useful explanatory concept in determining the right amount of guidance to give to subordinates, it does not, of course, tell the manager exactly what guidance is right in any particular circumstances. It may be easy enough to determine when the timespan has been exceeded, and disaster has resulted, or if the timespan has been curtailed, and subordinates feel that they are never left alone to complete their work. But determining the precisely correct timespan is not easy. Difficulties are compounded by the fact that managerial guidance is not a straightforward matter. A certain amount of research suggests that work is most effectively carried out when subordinates have continuing access to their manager, not only in the sense of securing his direction and authority but in being able to see him, to talk things over with him, and to secure his approval of what they are doing. Very often subordinates will like to do this, even though they are perfectly capable and happy to take the actual decisions themselves. The position is rather akin to the child's relationship to its mother. A contented child will often play by himself, constructing his own games, and arranging his own toys, but from time to time calling upon his mother to look at what he is doing and to give her approval. It seems that this homely desire for contact and approval may be continued into later life, and into a less juvenile setting, and there is a good deal of evidence that superiors who recognize the desire of their subordinates for discussion and consultation without direct instruction can be among the most effective managers.

The conclusion from this study of groups is that the most effective leaders will in general concentrate their energies upon providing the conditions in which group cohesion can flourish. Recent research has suggested that this can most effectively be done when the manager has a clear idea when to involve the members of his group in his decisions. Decisions about the nature of the task, the order in which operations shall be carried out, and the provision of resources to discharge them are usually best made by the manager himself. The group will usually expect the manager to do these things and will regard it as weakness on his part if he consults them too much. On the other hand, there will be a number of cases where they will expect to make their contribution and will look askance if the manager does not consult them. These include such matters as holiday arrangements, time-keeping, hours of meals and office breaks, and also those parts of the work where the members of the group feel that they have either individually or collectively some special skill. For example, if the work of the group involves dealing with members of the public, and it is the members of the group and not the manager who actually see clients, they will expect their views on how to deal with the public to be considered carefully.

We have talked so far as if the entire task of group leadership concerned what might be 'first line' groups, such as the staff in a local authority who deal with particular cases, or who handle immediate operations. Yet there is, of course, a great deal of group management to be done at higher levels. In any organization of any size a distinction can be drawn between various levels; the level concerned with immediate operations, the level concerned with their co-ordination and control and the level concerned with the setting of general plans and objectives, with relations between the organization and the outside world, and with the major responsibility for reaction to change and for development and progress. Because each level in the organization will have a different task, the kind of managerial responsibility will be different. For example, the second level of managers require less technical expertise than those who head the immediate operational units. But they need to co-ordinate the activities of their different sections, they need to be alive to pressures from within the organization and from outside, and they need to be able to change (or at least propose changes in) the organizational structure to fit new goals and objectives.

One of the particular difficulties faced by the second level manager is communication with those at the lowest level in the hierarchy. The problem is whether he should communicate with them directly, possibly upsetting or undermining the authority of the first line manager, or whether he should proceed through those managers, either leaving them to interpret his instructions or perhaps setting out his requirements in written memoranda or other formal instructions. Again, it is not always easy for the second line manager to get accurate information about what is in progress. This is because of the natural human inclination to give superiors the kind of news we think they wish to hear. It was the practice in certain ancient civilizations to behead the messenger who brought bad news, and there lurks in many people's minds the suspicion that they will be judged by the kind of reports they make, and that bad news will be held against them. The middle or senior manager must therefore guard against the natural human tendency to put forward reports in an optimistic vein.

Probably the most effective way that senior line managers can carry out their work is by their own example and by encouraging the best management practices among their own staff. In this way the senior manager may hope to build and maintain a series of co-operative teams which are well motivated and enthusiastic for the achievement of the common plans and objectives of the organization.

In conclusion, it may help to summarize the major points that research suggests a manager should bear in mind when dealing with groups at work.

(a) He should consider the structure of the groups within the organization and decide if they support or oppose the achievement of the objectives that have been set.

(b) If he reaches the conclusion that the cohesiveness of the groups should be improved, he should consider whether this can be done by such means as altering the organization of the work, improving communications, changing the size and composition of the groups, and changing the time during which the members of the groups remain together.

(c) He should consider his own methods of management to see if he is adopting the right style of leadership—neither too detailed nor too abstract a form of supervision.

(d) He should consider as he moves up the organization how far he should change his methods to fit in with his new position within the organizational framework.

Much of the research in personnel management has tended to confirm obvious and commonsense points. It has seldom produced new and startling truths. Nevertheless, it has encouraged greater self-consciousness and perception about human factors in management and has therefore made a useful contribution.

DEVELOPMENTS IN PERSONNEL MANAGEMENT

We now turn to review some of the developments in personnel management in central and local government that have been influenced by the foregoing research and general factors that we previously distinguished. As in other spheres, the influence is tentative and indirect. Seldom has a deliberate attempt been made to apply a management theory or embody the results of a piece of research into practical arrangements.

Nevertheless, the ideas we have discussed have been manifest in a number of developments in central and local government over the last 10 to 15 years. First, there has been continuing attention to pay and grading structures. As noted above, in local government this has taken the form of developing agreements between unions and local authority associations. In central government, it has taken the form of a modified response to the recommendations of the Fulton Committee that there should be a unified grading structure for the Civil Service as a whole. Secondly, there has been a considerable expansion in the size and expertise of personnel management staffs in central and local government. We shall consider two examples. The first is the Civil Service Department set up by the Government on the recommendation of the Fulton Committee to be responsible for all matters of general personnel management in the Civil Service. The second example is the response to the Bains Report's recommendation that local authorities should pay increasing attention to personnel management and increase the effort they devote to this activity.

Thirdly, the concern with the efficient and effective use of manpower has led to increasing interest in training and in management devices designed to harness the motivation and effort of the staff more effectively to the purposes and goals of the organization. We shall look in particular at the two techniques of management by objectives and of job appraisal reviewing. We shall also look at the comprehensive review of factors affecting job satisfaction in the *Wider Issues Review* which was undertaken by the Civil Service Department and completed in 1975, and the resulting *Guide for New Managers* which was produced in the light of this study as a means of advising managers, particularly at junior levels, on how they could best promote job satisfaction and the efficient use of manpower. We shall also look at the way in which ideas of job satisfaction and enrichment have been applied in the Department of Health and Social Security. The concern with the efficient and effective employment of personnel has also led to increasing recognition of the value of wide experience. Schemes for using consultants and for exchanging staff between the public and private sector have been introduced in the last 10 to 15 years and we shall examine some of the lessons that have been learned.

Finally, we shall consider the participation of workpeople in the policy making functions of the organization in which they are employed. Such participation is clearly in line with those strands of management thinking which point to the advantages for motivation and interest if workpeople have a hand in the policy decisions that affect the organization in which they pass a large part of their daily lives. On the other hand, participation of this kind has to be squared with democratic principles. The prime duty of central and local government organizations is to discharge the decisions of elected members of local authorities and of ministers responsible to Parliament.

The grading structure of the Civil Service

When the Fulton Committee reported in 1968, the Civil Service was divided into 47 general classes, where members were distributed over the entire civil service, and some 1400 departmental classes whose members worked in one department only. Civil servants were recruited on entry into these classes, and their prospects and progress were largely determined by this initial point of entry into the service. Although it was possible for individuals to move from one class to another, the processes were difficult and so only a small proportion ever made the change. The Fulton Committee criticized this structure. It argued that it

prevents the best deployment and use of individual talent. The formal and relatively rigid procedures involved in moving from one class to another place unnecessary barriers in the way of movement of individuals .... It is a major obstacle to the ability of the service to adapt itself to new tasks. Each class tends to regard the posts that its members usually fill as its own preserve, guaranteeing a career structure with a fixed number of posts at various levels. Men and women enter these classes in their youth and form expectations about their prospects to which they cling with increasing tenacity as the years go by. Staff associations naturally tend to serve as the guardians of these territories, and to resist any proposal that seems likely to reduce the number of posts to which they feel their members have a right .... The career opportunities that are thus defined for the different classes vary greatly in their attractiveness and scope, even for people with similar educational qualifications.[7]

The Committee noted that many generalist civil servants, particularly those entering at university level, had extremely diverse careers, moving between financial and staff management work and between one department and another, so that during a 10-year period a man or woman might work in the Department of Education and Science, the Ministry of Defence and the Treasury. The Fulton Committee believed that greater specialization would improve the quality of work and the satisfaction civil servants would obtain from undertaking it. For this reason, they recommended that 'all classes should be abolished and replaced by a single, unified grading structure covering all civil servants from top to bottom in the non-industrial part of the service. The correct grading of each post should be determined by job evaluation'.[8]

On the day that the Fulton Report was published, the Prime Minister announced the Government's decisions. The Government accepted the abolition of classes and said they would enter immediately into consultation with the staff associations with a view to carrying out a thorough going study so that a practical system could be prepared for the implementation of a unified grading structure.[9]

A joint committee of the National Whitley Council, which is the body representing the trade unions and management in the Civil Service, was set up to process the Fulton recommendations accepted by the Government. In the event, a unified grading structure has not been established for the Civil Service. It is interesting to review the periodic reports on the progress of the Fulton Report to see how the efforts to introduce a unified grading structure have developed. In the first report of the Civil Service National Whitley Council on *Developments on Fulton* issued in February 1969, it was said that, as the Fulton Committee itself had agreed, it would not be possible to introduce a unified grading structure overnight.[10] The first priority should be the merger of existing classes, the removal of impediments to movement between classes and the establishment of a common structure for all civil servants at the level of Under Secretary and equivalent grades and above (i.e. for posts paid in 1977 at levels of about £12,000 per annum and above).

The report of the National Whitley Council on *Fulton: a Framework for the Future* in March 1970 still spoke as if the unified grading structure was an aim. It talked of the work in progress and said that 'pending the completion of the long-term study of a unified grading structure, we should simplify the existing grading and pay structure as far as we can, starting with the interim changes that have already been planned for the next couple of years, and developing appropriate groupings in and around the new structures that will emerge from these changes'.[11] By 1972, the idea of a unified grading system had receded into the background. In the National Whitley Council's report *The Shape of the Post-Fulton Civil Service* (March 1972), it was said that 'it has been concluded that, below Under Secretary level, the best course at this juncture would be to pursue the aim of more flexible deployment in the interests of efficiency and staff development by concentrating resources on new arrangements for personnel management and on the development of the category and occupational group system'.[12]

The result of this work has been the evolution of a new system. For all posts at under secretary level and above, there is a unified grading structure throughout the Civil Service. This means that every person, whatever his origin and initial training, is eligible for appointment to all posts. Naturally enough, this does not mean that posts requiring, for example, specialized legal knowledge are likely to be filled by civil servants who started as research scientists. Nonetheless, there are nearly 900 posts in the civil service at under secretary level and above, and nearly 40 per cent of them are now filled by civil servants whose early years of service were spent either wholly or partly in specialist grades.

For appointments to the highest posts, such as the permanent secretaries of departments, there is a committee of permanent secretaries and senior officers, assisted by specialist panels, who advise the Head of the Civil Service on the recommendations to be made to the Prime Minister. This means that the system for considering the whole range of talent is applied in detail to appointments to the very senior posts. It has led, for example, to the appointment as Permanent Secretary of the Department of Education and Science of Sir James Hamilton. He is a civil servant who began his career at the Marine Aircraft Experimental Establishment, and has held a variety of scientific posts, including those of Director of the Anglo/French Combat Aircraft Project in the Ministry of Aviation, and Director General of Concorde at the Ministry of Technology.

Considerable progress has been made since the Fulton Report was published in assimilating classes into larger grading and pay structures. These structures are of two kinds; categories and groups. Categories consist of groups of civil servants, broadly analogous in training and experience, which can easily be compared with people doing comparable work outside the Civil Service. For example, the general category was established in January 1971, the science category in September 1971 and a professional and technical category in January 1972. Other categories include the training category, secretarial category, legal category, social security category for Department of Health and Social Security local officers, data processing category for machine operators, and a police category for the departmental police forces. Within the categories are particular groups. For example, within the general category there is an administration group, which comprises most of the civil servants engaged in general administrative work, and consists of the former clerical, executive and administrative classes. It contains over 270,000 members. The general category also includes the economist group, which was formed from the old economist class and the agricultural economist class and contains some 300 members; the information officer group, containing staff who deal with press relations and information generally; and the librarian and the statistician groups. The idea is that each of these occupational groups should form a unit for recruitment and management purposes. Thus people recruited as economists are to have their postings and careers planned and managed accordingly. But since their work is closely akin to that of general administrators, they form natural members of the same general category.

The National Whitley Council Committee considered whether the general administrators, forming the administration group, should be sub-divided. The Fulton report had recommended that administrators should be divided into two broad groups: the economic and financial, and the social.[13] The Committee carried out a survey of this recommendation and agreed, as stated in their report for March 1970, that there was scope for greater specialization. But it need not start right at the beginning of an officer's career, and they recommended that the best way to proceed would be to consider the work of departments and to distinguish within each one a variety of fields or areas of activity, based on common subject matter, within which a policy of related postings could provide a framework for career development. At the same time, the Committee pointed out that there was a number of functions, such as management services, purchasing, and staff management, which also provided a basis for specialization. They concluded that specialization by function should supplement specialization by departmental sub-field, but that neither should be exclusive, 'there must be enough flexibility to give people from time to time experience of other kinds of work'.[14]

By 1977, some 70 per cent of non-industrial civil servants were included within the system of categories and groups described above. A further 20 per cent are likely to be included within it. The remaining 10 per cent consist, for the most part, of very small classes which cannot easily be assimilated into existing structures. In evidence to the Select Committee on Expenditure in 1976 the Civil Service Department said:

> Progress has been slower than expected, partly because of the intrinsic difficulties of each restructuring task, but also because since 1972 incomes policies have placed restrictions on changes involving pay increases (which most do). Very little can be brought to completion under present conditions. It is not possible in these circumstances to judge how much longer it will take to bring the restructuring programme to a satisfactory conclusion or to attempt to set a target date.[15]

At first sight, this system of categories and groups bears a close resemblance to the system of classes which it has replaced. Yet the present grading system is more flexible than its predecessor. The total number of categories and groups is much smaller than the number of classes. There is a unified structure for the most senior posts. New arrangements have been introduced for reporting on annual performance, for job appraisal reviews and for career interviewing. This means that personnel management departments have greater knowledge of individual capacities and ambitions than was previously available. Manpower planning has been introduced, so that medium- and long-term estimates are available of the Civil Service's requirements for officials with particular skills and of the number of staff that are likely to be available. Accurate knowledge of the age and skill structures of the Civil Service is important. Otherwise, promotion blockages can build up and, conversely, the retirement of a large proportion of particular group of staff in a short period can leave many vacancies unfilled or lead to the promotion of staff barely qualified to fill them.

A computer-based personnel record information system has been developed for all the non-industrial staff of the whole Civil Service based in the United Kingdom. It has been developed from existing computer payroll systems. It contains personal details of all non-industrial civil servants working in the United Kingdom, such as their age, their grade, their education, the jobs they have filled and where they are working now. These personal details are also available as lists of persons with the same attributes. Thus the system can provide lists of all executive officers, of all Home Office staff, and of all staff working in London. It can also provide information about intersections between these lists. Thus it can provide a list of all executive officers working in the Home Office in London. It was, of course, possible to provide information of this kind by manual methods in the past. But the introduction of this computer-based system enables career and manpower planning to proceed much more rapidly and with speedier access to various permutations of information that may be required.

Special efforts have also been made to take account of the particular career needs of various kinds of specialists. For example, a senior professional administrative training scheme was introduced in 1972. Its purpose is to provide opportunities for specialists who show potential for higher management to have an opportunity in policy or management posts in their early thirties, together with a course in management and machinery of government subjects at the Civil Service College. Thus a young statistician or research scientist who seems likely to have the capacity to reach posts at the higher management and policy levels might serve a policy division for two or three years in his or her early thirties. Again, more specialist staff have been appointed to personnel management divisions with the specific responsibility of managing the careers of people of similar background and experience to themselves. Career development panels have been set up for many groups of specialists. These panels are responsible for reviewing the careers and opportunities of particular specialist groups.

Finally, action has been taken to improve the position of specialist groups within the Civil Service. For example, the position of accountants in the civil service was examined by Sir Anthony Burney, a chartered accountant, and Sir Ronald Melville, a permanent secretary, and their report *The Use of Accountants in the Civil Service* was published in 1973.[16] The Government accepted their recommendation that a Government Accountancy Service should be set up, and a former President of the Institute of Chartered Accountants was appointed as head of the profession within the civil service. Investigations have also been made into the scope for increasing the use of accountants and their skills within the Civil Service, giving them opportunities to move into higher positions and providing greater opportunities for training in accountancy within the

Civil Service. Professional accountants within the Civil Service have mainly been employed in technical cost estimation, particularly in the Ministry of Defence. The Burney/Melville report argued that the concepts and ideas employed by accountants had a more general application and that greater effort should be made to secure co-operation between professional accountants within the Civil Service and other staff who could profit by their skills.

It will be clear from this survey that many changes have been introduced into the grading system of the Civil Service since the Fulton Committee reported in 1968. The Committee's main recommendation of a unified grading structure has not, however, been put into effect. The debate will no doubt continue about the need for further progress on these lines. In their report issued in 1977 on *The Civil Service*, the Expenditure Committee of the House of Commons said 'it would not be difficult to extend the open structure downwards to Assistant Secretary (i.e. the next grade down from Under Secretary) and equivalent levels, and we recommend that this should be done as speedily as possible. We realize that it would take much longer to extend the open structure further, below Assistant Secretary, but recommend the Civil Service Department should reactivate its original proposals to do so and begin work on its extension .... '.[17] The Government have agreed to study this proposal.[18]

Recruitment to the Civil Service

The Fulton report underlined the importance of continuing the traditional procedures of open competition, administered by the Civil Service Commission, and designed to ensure that people are not appointed to jobs in the Civil Service for political reasons or for any kind of favouritism. They believed, however, that while preserving its independence from political influence, there would be advantage in incorporating the Civil Service Commission within the new Civil Service Department which they recommended should be set up. They also suggested that the recruitment procedure should be speeded up. Following an investigation by management consultants, which led to the greater employment of computers in recruitment, substantial cuts were made in the time taken to handle cases— up to 30 per cent improvement in some instances—with a 15 per cent reduction in staff.[19]

The Fulton Committee also recommended that departments should be more closely associated with the recruitment process, partly in order to speed it up, and partly to ensure that their own needs were fully represented when new staff were being selected. This recommendation has been accepted in the sense that more staff are now recruited directly by departments, although under standards and by procedures agreed with the Civil Service Commission. The Fulton Committee recommended that, in the selection of graduates for administrative work, preference should be given to those whose university study had been in subjects relevant to the work of the Civil Service. This was rejected by the Government on the grounds that the right course was to select the best people whatever subject they had studied and then to see that, by training and career development, they developed the knowledge necessary to carry out their tasks as well as possible. Research carried out for the Fulton Committee suggested that graduate entrants to the administrative class came predominantly from privileged social and educational backgrounds. They had usually studied arts subjects and graduates of the Universities of Oxford and Cambridge predominated.[20]

Many people believed, although the Fulton Committee did not say this themselves, that such people were likely to be out of tune with the needs of modern society; that they would have insufficient appreciation of the needs of science and technology; that they would not understand enough about the operation of business; that they would be unsympathetic to the needs of those less fortunate than themselves in society; and that either knowingly or unwittingly the kind of advice that they would give to ministers would be heavily weighted in favour of the status quo. They would thus handicap the efforts that might be made by ministers responsible to Parliament to adjust the country's laws and institutions to accord with the needs of the twentieth century.

The Government appointed a committee under Mr J.D.W. Davies, who had been Secretary of the Cambridge University Appointments Board, to examine the selection arrangements for graduate recruitment for administrative work in the light of the Fulton report. The report of the Davies Committee (Cmnd. 4156 of 1969) found no fundamental weaknesses in the system of selection of graduate administrators by the process of extended interview, although they made a number of suggestions for improving the selection and training of assessors' follow up and research. They concluded, however, that there was no evidence of social bias either in the procedures or on the part of assessors, and said that 'the make-up of the entry ... reflects the character of the candidates who choose to compete rather than the choice made by the selectors from within that field'.[21] In other words, if the entry to the Civil Service was socially biased, this was because the competitors as a whole were a socially unrepresentative group.

It is, of course, likely that entrants to the higher grades of both the Civil Service and local government will be socially unrepresentative. Entry to these professions requires a good education, hard work and ambition. These qualities tend to be fostered in families where the parents have these characteristics and, at the same time, have no private means or private businesses with which to endow their own children. Their best means of helping their children financially is to help them to get a good education and the social skills necessary to get a good job. It is therefore likely that civil servants, local government officers, bank managers, insurance officials, executives in large business firms, will be ambitious for their children, see that they obtain a good education and compete for vacancies for high level posts in central and local government, in large public companies, and in higher education.

It should not be assumed, however, that these circumstances necessarily produce biased advice to ministers and elected members. It would, for example, be unreasonable to assume that an individual's views are totally formed by the time that he or she is 21, and that the rest of life brings no variation or modification to them. There is also the point that one of the research investigations commissioned by the Fulton Committee showed that, among members of the administrative class entering the Civil Service in the year 1956, political preferences were distributed over the political spectrum, with more than half voting for the Labour Party.[22]

Nevertheless, changes were made in recruitment and selection procedures. The Fulton Committee recommended that the administrative class should be abolished. As noted above, it was merged with the administrative, executive and clerical classes into the administration group in 1971. New arrangements were introduced for the recruitment of graduates. It was decided to recruit about twice as many graduates each year as previously, which meant a slight lowering of the entry standards, and to give better opportunities for young men and women already in the service to advance on equal terms with the graduate entrant. Arrangements have accordingly been made for graduate and in-service candidates to compete by the same extended interview procedures for appointment as administration trainees. The best of these are selected for promotion to higher executive officer (administration) between two and four years after becoming administration trainees.

The object of this scheme is to select the cadre of young civil servants for rapid advancement on the basis of their performance on the job instead of the standard they reach in their entry tests, and to draw them from a wider group comprising not only direct entrants to the administration trainee grade, who usually come straight from university, but also from those who have been selected for the administration trainee grade from within the civil service. In this way, it is hoped to offset any unfair advantages that might be gained from social and educational background alone.

In spite of these changes, the question of bias in recruitment and selection continues to cause concern, as it is bound to do, in view of the importance of the jobs that will in the future be held by those selected and the anxiety of all groups of staff to be able to compete on equal terms for the best jobs available. In their report on the Civil Service published in 1977, the Expenditure Committee of the House of Commons said that recruitment statistics were not kept in sufficiently detailed a form to be able to refute the charge of bias. They recommended that 'The Civil Service Commission should keep, assess and publish statistics showing the type and class of degree of applicants and recruits, in terms of type of school and university attended, in order to ensure, and to be able to show, that equally able university graduates have equal chances of entering the service'.[23] They also recommended consideration should be given to reducing the proportion of civil servants on final selection boards and that the administration trainee scheme should be dropped. Instead 'graduates with good degrees should still be recruited and given jobs in the service so that their abilities other than solely academic ones can be assessed. They should then compete on even terms with others in the service, graduates and nongraduates, for entry to a new higher management training course'.[24]

The Government have agreed to collect and publish the statistics recommended by the Committee. They will also appoint some part-time Civil Service Commissioners from outside the Civil Service and consult them about widening the membership of selection boards. The administration trainee scheme is also being reassessed.[25]

Whatever the results of the decisions on these recommendations it is likely that debate will continue, especially as it is almost impossible to settle finally the questions of whether bias exists, what can be done about it, and what the real effects of it may be.

Personnel management in the Civil Service

We have drawn attention to the importance of specialized personnel management in the design and operation of a modern pay and grading structure. This was recognized in the Government's acceptance of the Fulton Committee's recommendation that a Civil Service Department should be established for the management of the Civil Service as a whole. Previously, the Treasury had been responsible for the general management of the Civil Service. Many believed that this resulted in personnel management being the mere handmaiden of finance, with the achievement of short-term money savings as the only criterion. These might not be truly economic in the long run. It was also suggested that personnel management was regarded as the less exciting and glamorous side of the Treasury's work, and was less important than trying to understand and control the working of the economy or reviewing the expenditure of government departments. Yet many Treasury civil servants who served in personnel management divisions testify to the challenge and intellectual quality of the work.[26]

The Civil Service Department is currently responsible for three main areas of work. The first is management policy, that is to say, the determination of the categories and occupational groups that make up the structure of the Civil Service, and for policy on recruitment, selection, training, promotion, postings, career management, terms of service, pay and allowances, co-ordination of public sector pension arrangements, catering, welfare and security. Secondly, it is responsible for administrative and managerial efficiency, that is to say, for the development and dissemination of management techniques, for the oversight and general review of the organization of government departments, for the overall review of the machinery of government, and for providing central management services including organization and methods, computers and operational research. It is also responsible for controlling departmental manpower requirements, including both numbers and gradings, and Civil Service administrative costs, such as travel, subsistence, postage and telephones. Thirdly, the Civil Service Department provides common services for a number of departments as, for example, catering and a computerized payroll service. The Civil Service Department is also responsible for the Civil Service College.

The Civil Service Department has a particular responsibility for senior staff. We have already noted the arrangements that were introduced after the Fulton report for advising the Prime Minister on the very highest appointments. These are the responsibility of the Head of the Home Civil Service, who is also the Permanent Secretary of the Civil Service Department. The Civil Service Department is also consulted on the filling of all appointments at under secretary level to ensure common standards are maintained throughout the service, and to discharge a central role in managing and the career development of senior staff. The Civil Service Department maintains a register of all staff at and above the under secretary level, and of staff below this level who appear sufficiently promising for consideration in due course for appointments to this level. Particular attention is paid to career development. For example, it is the practice to try to ensure that all potential candidates for posts at the permanent secretary level and deputy secretary level are given opportunities to work in more than one department.

The management of this senior cadre of personnel is a vital task. Exceptional talent is as scarce in the Civil Service as it is in other walks of life, and departments are always anxious to obtain and develop good people. The Civil Service Department must act as a broker of this talent. It must sometimes encourage departments to take senior staff whom they would not have chosen themselves in the interest of individual career development and of the service as a whole.

The general pattern of relationships between the Civil Service Department and the rest of Whitehall is one of growing self-reliance on the part of the departments. The Civil Service Department sets the policy framework and discharges the particular responsibilities that we have described above. But the great bulk of personnel management work is done by the departments themselves. The main machinery for the interplay between departments and the Civil Service Department is the establishment officers' committee and supporting sub-committees. They meet under Civil Service Department chairmanship and contain the establishment officers (i.e. the chief personnel officers) and other staff from the departments. The committees meet to consider general problems in the field of personnel management, and to agree upon policy and guidelines for their solution.

The Civil Service Department has a special relationship with the Treasury. Initially, the Department consisted mainly of the 'hived-off' personnel management divisions of the Treasury. Under current arrangements, departments send estimates for expenditure on staff to the Treasury, but the Civil Service Department is responsible for decisions concerning the scale of staffing and financial questions involving manpower.

The Civil Service Department is staffed by officials with a wide variety of knowledge and skills. The increasing emphasis during the last 10 years on personnel management has led to an increase in the number of specialists in personnel management including, as noted above, scientists and engineers and other professional staffs concerned with the personnel management of particular specialist groups. The Civil Service Department aims to fill at least 25 per cent of its posts at any one time with staff on secondment from other departments, and thus knowledgeable about their problems.[27]

The Civil Service Department has now existed for 10 years. Has it a permanent place in the Whitehall scene? Now that the work of carrying out those recommendations of the Fulton report which the Government accepted has been largely completed, and further developments are part of the continuing personnel management of the Civil Service, it has been suggested that a separate department is no longer necessary. An alternative arrangement would be for the Treasury to control expenditure on staff, while all the details of personnel management were discharged by the departments. Another possibility, as noted in Chapter 5, would be to amalgamate the public expenditure control divisions of the Treasury with the Civil Service Department on the pattern of the arrangements in the United States. This would entail setting up a new department for economic management. In their report on the Civil Service published in 1977, the Expenditure Committee recommended that 'those parts of the CSD concerned with the control of manpower and the efficiency of the Civil Service should be transferred to the Treasury, the CSD releasing responsibility for personnel, appointments, recruitment, training, pay and pensions'.[28]

It is indeed possible that changes in the central organization of government affecting the Civil Service Department may at some stage be justifiable and right. Whatever these may be, it will be important for the functions now discharged by the Civil Service Department to continue to be undertaken. As we have seen, the personnel management of the Civil Service requires not only the determination of a pay and grading structure but also policies of personnel management to secure its effective and efficient operation, covering questions of economy and resource allocation as well as those of career development and job satisfaction. The detailed work of personnel management day by day can only be carried out by the various departments, and, indeed, within those departments mainly by the operational and line managers themselves. But it is necessary to determine centrally some general policies and guidelines for the Civil Service as a whole.

There should also continue to be a central point with whom the Civil Service unions can deal. The Whitley Council machinery provides a traditional and generally successful method of discussing the views of management and unions at the national and departmental levels. It has been suggested that the inauguration of an independent Civil Service Department provided an opportunity for the public sector unions to increase their influence over personnel management policies in much the same way, it is alleged, as the agricultural industry is supposed to exercise influence over the Ministry of Agriculture, and large industrial firms to exercise influence over the Departments of Trade and Industry. There is, however, no objective test of how much influence is too much. But there can be no doubt of the value of a central forum for discussion between the management of the Civil Service and union representatives.

Personnel management in local government

We now turn to the development of specialized personnel management functions in local government. The Bains report said 'there must be a much greater awareness of the importance of personnel management in Local Government. Manpower is the leading resource of any authority and must be properly deployed. The appointment of the senior officer responsible for personnel management is crucial and must be made at an early date'.[29] Bains also said that the chief personnel officer 'should have access to the chief executive and not be subordinated to the director of administration or any other chief officer'.[30]

This forthright statement was a clear affirmation of the importance of regarding personnel as one of the major resources of local government and seeking its efficient and effective management. To what extent have developments borne it out? Some answers are suggested in the research study on progress since reorganization noted above.[31] The results are broadly as follows.

(a) The position of the personnel department and the access of the chief personnel officer to the chief executive officer.
The research study showed that 10 of the 27 authorities placed the personnel department as part of the chief executive officer's department; in five cases it was part of the secretary's staff; and in 12 it was an independent department. These are small numbers on which to base any generalization. It seems, however, that separate departments are more usually favoured by metropolitan authorities. This may well reflect the fact that metropolitan authorities, possibly because of their larger staff and because the idea of corporate management seems more directly applicable to the problems of urban government, have been generally more inclined to follow the Bains

prescriptions. So far as access to the chief executive is concerned, the study shows that the degree of contact between the chief personnel officer and the chief executive depends less on whether the chief personnel officer is a member of the latter's staff and more on the chief executive's interest in personnel, the personality of the chief personnel officer and the general approach to personnel matters in the authority concerned.

(b) The main functions performed by the personnel management departments.

All the personnel departments included in the study were responsible for the traditional functions of establishments control, encompassing every-day matters of staff administration, conditions of service and, in most cases a watch dog role over claims for new staff and regrading. They also bore responsibility for recruitment and selection. But there were variations. Some personnel departments were concerned simply with advertising the posts and passing replies to the relevant department. In others, personnel staff sat on all interview boards. The general practice, particularly in the larger authorities, was for the personnel department to be responsible for recruiting all junior administrative support staff and allocating them to departments. Above this level, departments generally recruited their own staff.

Most personnel departments also took responsibility for work study and organization and methods, though these activities were usually conducted by separate sections with some autonomy. The general pattern, whether management services was within or without the personnel department, was for departmental chief officers or committees or unions to request an investigation, which was then carried out by management services. In some authorities, however, there were opportunities for management services and work study to initiate assignments, and in some cases it was laid down that departmental requests for extra staff should be investigated by the management services department to determine the justification for the claim and the actual number of staff to be increased. Since reorganization, management services departments have been particularly busy. The amal-gamation of authorities has required the working out of common adminis-trative practices. The construction of these schemes has usually required a good deal of discussion and negotiation, and a trial period before their final implementation, together with adjustments in the light of experience.

Personnel departments also take responsibility for training. Practice and progress has varied. In some of the authorities, the main effort has been devoted to arranging day release and other courses and facilities for staff employed throughout the authority. In other authorities, wider ranging efforts have been made, including running some courses of their own, particularly induction courses for new staff, and making plans for some individual training needs as part of the career development of members of the staff. Progress has been slowed down by the need for economic retrenchment in the 1970s; training budgets are obvious candidates for economy cuts in both central and local government.

Other functions carried out by at least some of the personnel departments included manpower planning and manpower budgeting; that is to say, working out a manpower plan for the authority's future manpower needs over the next few years and producing a financial budget of their implications. Personnel departments have also been concerned with job evaluation, welfare and industrial relations. Indeed, the volume of legislation, including the Employment Protection Act 1975, the Health and Safety at Work Act 1974 and the Sex Discrimination Act 1975, has created a good deal of work in these areas. There is an increasing tendency for the various departments of local authorities to look to the personnel departments to provide a central service of advice on these complex codes.

(c) The organization of the personnel function.

The research study distinguished two main forms of organization. The first is a centralized system, by which all personnel work is conducted by a central personnel department and the other departments of the local authority must liaise with it on all significant matters, subject, usually, to delegation on relatively minor matters. The second is a decentralized system under which there is a division of labour between a central personnel department and the other departments of the local authority. The research study distinguished between 'strong' and 'weak' decentralization, the difference turning on such factors as whether the personnel officer of each department is responsible to the authority's chief personnel officer (strong decentralization) or to his own chief officer (weak decentralization). There is often something of a compromise here, as in the case of the authority which said 'the ideal is that personnel men in the departments are responsible to the departmental chief officer, but accountable to the personnel officer'.[32] Other relevant factors include the ranking of the chief personnel officers in the departments. If they are at fourth or lower tier they will seldom cut a great deal of ice in their own departments.

(d) The committee structure for personnel matters.

The most usual arrangement is for personnel to be a sub-committee of the policy or policy and resources committee. The extent to which the authority's chief personnel officer attends committee meetings depends upon the degree of decentralization. With a centralized system, there is a tendency for the chief personnel officer to attend the discussion of personnel matters at the relevant committees. In a decentralized system, he usually attends only his own committee or the policy and resources committee, where he will generally be responsible for presenting reports about the personnel work of the authority as a whole. It is rare for a personnel officer and his department to have anything to do with management of specialist staff such as teachers.

Summing up, it must be recognized that the personnel management function has not developed the influence that the Bains report suggested that it should. If personnel is to be regarded as one of the major resources of a local authority, then it is important for there to be a developed system of manpower planning and manpower budgeting, together with a system of recruitment, training and career development that enables staff to pass through the grading structure in a way that maximizes their contribution to the work of the authority and promotes their own development. It is, however, relatively rare for authorities to have developed manpower plans and manpower budgets, even though the failure to cater for the manpower implications of schemes of development, such as urban planning and of major road developments, is increasingly recognized as one of the reasons why they so often fail to be completed on time.

The major reason for this failure to develop personnel policies is the traditional attitude of suspicion towards personnel management in local government, where the specialized departments have often regarded anything but the very minimum of central personnel functions as unnecessary obstruction and interference. Yet much the same suspicion applies to the financial function which has, over the years, built up practices and methods which have enabled it to be dovetailed effectively into the working of most local authorities. So there is some reason to believe that personnel will follow finance in the scale of its specialized development as both staff and management appreciate its importance.

Training

One of the prime recommendations of the Fulton Committee which was accepted by the Government right away was the establishment of a Civil Service College. This was formally opened in 1970. The first principal of the college was Mr E. Grebenik, who had previously been professor of social studies at Leeds University. His staff consisted of academics and serving civil servants, and there were directors of studies in economics, in statistics and operational research, in personnel management, in public administration and in social policy and social administration. A number of changes have been made on the basis of experiment and experience. The general pattern now adopted is as follows.[33] First, there are courses, usually of a few days, for senior civil servants to bring them up to date on particular subjects, such as personnel management techniques, problems of running large departments, relationships between ministers and civil servants. These are not so much courses of instruction as seminars designed to spread ideas and promote reflection and reconsideration. They also bring together a wide selection of senior civil servants, and this opportunity of meeting professional colleagues is in itself valuable. Secondly, there is a range of courses mainly for civil servants in the administration group, usually lasting a week or so, and divided under the broad headings of public administration, personnel management, social policy and administration, economics and statistics and operational research. The idea is to introduce staffs to the latest concepts and ideas in these subjects that will be valuable to them in their work. Thirdly, there are courses for specialist civil servants, including an introductory course for graduate specialists to promote their understanding of the British system of government and to improve management capabilities, courses for specialists who have been accepted for the senior professional training scheme, and refresher courses for economists, lawyers, statisticians and other specialists. Fourthly, there are courses for administration trainees and higher executive officers (administration), designed to introduce them to management techniques and the machinery and practice of government. Fifthly, there are courses in management services and accountancy and automatic data processing training for computer staff. Finally, there are courses for departmental tutors and lecturers in techniques of instruction and a number of short courses for staff who work in departments that are too small to have their own training facilities. It must be remembered here that by far the greater amount of civil service training is carried out by the departments themselves. Most large departments have comprehensive training facilities and schools, and provide courses in management and other subjects related in particular, to the needs of their own departments.

Indeed, one of the major decisions to be taken in the organization of the Civil Service training is the split between the courses provided by the college and those by the departments. To help in determining the right balance the college has its own advisory council under the chairmanship of the Permanent Secretary of the Civil Service Department and containing senior civil servants from the Home Civil Service and the Foreign and Commonwealth Office, together with members from the academic and business world, local government and from the national staff side. This committee keeps the balance of work under general review and there is a consultative committee containing a number of principal establishment officers which acts as a medium for the exchange of information and views on college teaching and research between the college and its principal clients. As a result, therefore, the college tends to concentrate on courses where it is useful for the course members to come from a range of departments. During the first years of its existence, the Civil Service College has put increasing emphasis upon designing courses which are relevant to the day to day work of departments. It would, of course, be quite wrong for the college to become too inward looking and cut off from the development of new ideas in social science, management and other subjects of relevance to the work of government. At the same time, the college is increasingly conscious of the importance of rendering those ideas relevant to the day-to-day work of government, and this is the principle which has governed most of the changes which have taken place in its scheme of training over the last few years.

Training in local government is organized on different lines from that of the Civil Service. This is largely a consequence of the fact that the local government service is not a unified service in the same way as the Civil Service. As we have noted above, local government officers are employed by particular authorities. Furthermore, training in local government has been traditionally concerned with acquiring professional and other qualifications by examination.[34]

Three major lines of development contribute to the recent history of local government training. First, the introduction of more qualifications and examinations within the local government service, instead of confining them to officers destined for only the highest posts. Secondly, the provision of facilities for staff to attend courses and to have wider opportunities generally to work for their examinations instead of their having to do all their study in their own time. Finally, it has come to be realized that training is more than passing examinations, however valuable that may be, and opportunities are being extended for guidance and instruction on other relevant matters, including opportunities for qualified staff to bring themselves up to date in their own subjects and in relevant management techniques and practices.

The National Joint Council for Administrative, Professional, Technical and Clerical Staffs has made an important contribution to these developments. The Council was founded in 1943 and has always received full support from local authorities and the trade unions, particularly the National and Local Government Officers Association (NALGO), in pressing for the encouragement and development of staff training. The National Joint Council's scheme of conditions says that 'local authorities should advise their staff on, and encourage them to undertake, approved courses of study and training, as this is in the interests of the service as a whole, of the individual local authority and of the officer concerned'.

In 1946 the Council founded the Local Government Examinations Board. Its main function was to develop and administer a system of examinations for clerical and administrative staffs. In its 22 years of existence until 1968 the Board developed a wide range of examinations, extended its activities into the training of manual workers in local government, and provided an information and advisory service for training.

In 1968, the Board's functions were transferred to the Local Government Training Board. The Local Government Training Board first met in 1967. Its membership consisted of representatives of the employers, nominated mainly by the local authority associations; trade union members from the National and Local Government Officers Association, National Union of Public Employees, Transport and General Workers Union and General and Municipal Workers Union; education members and assessors from central government. In its first bulletin, issued in 1967, the Board described its aim as seeking to increase the efficiency of local government by ensuring that sufficient training of the right type and quality was given to the staff and employees of local authorities at all levels. A system of training levies and training grants was introduced so that the cost of this training should be spread fairly and evenly among all authorities. And the Board urged that the general principles adopted by the industrial training boards should be followed in local government. These principles are first, that each training recommendation should be based on a thorough analysis of the occupation and work involved and should not only lay down a training programme, but also the standards of performance which the training should achieve and the methods by which its effectiveness can be evaluated; that all the education and training necessary for an employee to carry out his job efficiently should as a general rule be given during working hours; that training should not be considered as incidental but as part of the authority's personnel policy; and that the training should be part of a carefully devised training programme with close liaison between authorities and educational institutions.

The Local Government Training Board's bulletin of 1970 stressed the importance of supplementing the traditional concentration on professional examinations. The bulletin pressed the need for 'a wide range of short courses: for example training for management and supervision, specialist and appreciation courses, courses in management services techniques, updating of professional skills, revision courses for examination students and so on'.

The Board has paid particular attention to training in personnel management. It produced a booklet in 1973 called *Personnel Management in the New Authorities*. This set out a comprehensive view of personnel management work for local government. It divided personnel management into three categories of work:

(a) analytic activities; including manpower utilization, records and statistics, job description, job evaluation, manpower planning;

(b) personnel development activities; including recruitment and selection; performance appraisal, training and career development and salary administration;

(c) human relations activities; encompassing communications, industrial relations and organization development.

Two broad kinds of skills were distinguished for the personnel officer: problem solving skills, such as the ability to detect and act upon the strengths, weaknesses, opportunities and threats presented to an organization; and communication and social skills, such as effective speaking and writing, the ability to deal with groups and to help in the resolution of conflict. The board also produced a training package called *Personnel Practice,* containing material such as tutors' notes and exercises, for the use of colleges and individual authorities in running training sessions for new personnel staff.

This was a useful initiative. But the economic retrenchment of the 1970s has slowed down the expansion of training in local government. Future developments may well be on the lines of expanding the scale and scope of professional qualifications, which are likely to include management as well as technical subjects in their curricula, and the use of short courses run by the authorities themselves and by universities, polytechnics and staff associations.

There is no central local government training college corresponding to the Civil Service College. On the other hand, many bodies have provided courses for the training of local government officers, including the Royal Institute of Public Administration, universities and polytechnics, and the Institute of Local Government Studies at Birmingham University. This Institute has also sponsored a great deal of research into the development of local government. Finally, NALGO has a large education department that runs a correspondence institute for assisting local government officers for their preparation for examinations and it also sponsors courses in general management subjects.

Indeed, NALGO has made a unique contribution to local government training. It has argued the case within the national committee machinery for improved training standards and opportunities; it has pressed local authorities to support training with facilities, finance and reasonable opportunities for staff to study and attend courses; it has provided a wide range of lectures, courses, seminars, week-end and summer schools in all aspects of training, both for examinations and for the general improvement of its members' skills and standards. Its courses provide opportunities for local government officers from all over the country to exchange experience and discuss problems of common interest with each other, with members of other public services who attend the courses, and with the tutorial staff, who are drawn from both public service and academic backgrounds.

Summary. The case for training in professional and technical subjects for civil servants and local government officers is not in doubt. Provided the curricula are relevant, the course and other forms of instruction are well conducted, and proper allowance is made for practical as well as theoretical aspects, it is generally accepted that the training of young men and women is valuable for both individuals concerned and the organization employing them. There is, however, more of a question mark over management training. As we have seen in this book, management is a general and disparate subject that cannot be resolved into a series of principles capable of straightforward application. It is difficult to arrange courses in management which are of immediate and obvious relevance to individual jobs. Even when courses are enjoyed by the participants, this may have more to do with the general interest aroused than the immediate relevance of what is taught.

The long-term benefits of management training in promoting improved performance are impossible to disentangle from all the other influences that determine the overall competence and performance of a civil servant or local government officer. Nevertheless, it is important to evaluate as far as possible the costs and benefits of such training. Some assessment can be made by careful surveys of the value of the courses, both at the conclusion of the training and following a reasonable period after the return to work. It is also useful to take the views of those who have attended the courses and their superiors. In this way it should be possible to eliminate the least useful courses.

Cost-effectiveness may also be increased by the careful selection of those who attend general management courses. Individual interests and temperaments vary, and courses that may be valuable to some can easily be a complete waste of time and money to others. Selection of course members is therefore an important constituent of cost-effectiveness.

Management by objectives

Everyone in central and local government today will have heard of management by objectives, even if he has no direct experience of the technique. Indeed, technique may not be the best word, because management by objectives refers to a system of management which can take many different forms in different authorities and organizations, but is marked by an attention to many of the points which have been made in the section on research in this chapter. In essence, these points are that effective work requires the setting of clear objectives; the acceptance and full understanding and, if necessary, the modification of these objectives by all whose efforts are necessary to secure them, i.e. managers and staff at every level; the design and re-organization of authorities and departments so that organizational structures help rather than hinder the achievement of objectives, goals and purposes; the specification of what are called 'key results areas', i.e. those tasks which must necessarily be done on time and in the correct way if the objective is to be secured at all; and finally, a means of determining whether the objectives have been achieved.

Management by objectives therefore fits in with the discussion of corporate planning and PPBS in chapter 3 and with the discussion of audit, control and review in chapter 7. If corporate planning is concerned with the general objectives and goals of the authority, management by objectives is concerned with breaking them down into a series of particular objectives to be undertaken by the various parts of the organization and, within each part, the specification of objectives into increasingly detailed form until the whole task of the organization is resolved into individual objectives for each member of the staff. This does, of course, represent the fullest possible form of management by objectives, and it is not always realistic to expect to see it reproduced in all this detail. There is a detailed example of management by objectives in a local authority architect's department in Appendix 6.

One experiment in management objectives in central government was undertaken in the teachers' pensions branch of the Department of Education and Science.[35] When the idea of introducing management by objectives was raised in 1969, the teachers' pension branch contained 200 staff and was responsible for all aspects of the statutory superannuation scheme for teachers in England and Wales. This included the investigation of service and eligibility for pension; the implications of interchanges between teaching and other kinds of pensionable employment; the purchase of 'added years'; the collection and repayment of superannuation contributions; and the award of age and infirmity pensions and death gratuities. At first sight, this seemed to be the kind of regular and continuing clerical activity that could be improved in performance by the introduction of management by objectives.

After consultation with the Civil Service Department, three management consultants were invited to tender for the job of installing the system, and a steering committee was set up consisting of members of the pension branch, the department's management services unit and the consultants. The staff associations were not members of the steering committee, but were kept informed of its progress.

The consultants carried out a lengthy investigation; seminars were held to introduce staff to the idea of management by objectives; the various teams that made up the branch as a whole were divided into a series of 'effectiveness areas', and attempts were made to set team objectives. Attention was also given to staff training and to the careful explanation and introduction of the system. Meetings were held between all members of the staff and their superiors to determine individual objectives.

A number of difficulties were found in trying to put this scheme into effect. It was easy to set objectives for activities with a 'time' base, such as answering letters or notifying details of pensions. But it was difficult to set objectives where the work involved dealing with complex individual cases and the policy issues arising therefrom. It was also difficult to forecast the flow of work; it was possible to work out the number of teachers going to pension each month, but it was not possible to determine the number who would ask for advice or the kind of questions that they put forward. Again, the rules of the pension scheme were being changed and some staff were being dispersed from London to the provinces at the same time as the scheme for management by objectives was being put into effect. This caused problems.

It was therefore decided to modify the scheme in the light of experience. Working out a full set of objectives for individuals was found to take up too much time, require too much paper work, and to be too inflexible. But three useful results came out of the attempt to apply management by objectives. First, it was decided to continue with the system of team and group meetings, very often setting objectives related to blocks of work immediately in hand. For example, if a new pension regulation came into existence it was sensible to set an objective for its incorporation within the scheme as a whole. Secondly, the attempt to design and operate a scheme of management by objectives led to a greater appreciation of and interest in managerial responsibilities. Those in charge of staff at all levels became more concerned, knowledgeable and skillful at undertaking the managerial aspects of their duties. Thirdly, discussion of objectives and the system of team and group meetings led to generally improved communications, so these meetings have continued to be part of the day-to-day management of the pensions branch.

It is clear from this and other examples that management by objectives seldom works in the way the authors intended. It is rare for a full scale management by objectives scheme to remain in operation, with a full range of documentation, for even a few years. The detailed scheme is usually soon abandoned, and this is especially likely to happen when changes are made in organization or duties which would require the detailed revision of the scheme. This is seldom attempted. Nevertheless, dividends tend to accrue from a greater attention to the purposes of an organization's work, better communications and information, and more discussion and consultation among staff and managers. In this way, management by objectives often makes a useful contribution.

It may well be that management by objectives is an organizational equivalent of toning up and exercizing the human body. Most organizations which try out management by objectives like most people who try out a scheme of physical exercise, are glad that they have undertaken it, find that the results are generally beneficial, although not exactly in the ways they had expected, and moderate the programme after a time, blending it in with their normal life and habits.

Job appraisal reviews

In 1970, the Civil Service started to introduce a system of job appraisal reviews. Their object was to promote better performance and job satisfaction by annual discussions between managers and their staff. The job appraisal review would concentrate on how well and how effectively staff had been working, would analyse what had been achieved over the last year and the difficulties that had been encountered and would make plans for the following year. These would not only cover planned improvements in staff performance but would also set out changes which the management could introduce to improve the performance of the section or branch.

The Civil Service Department undertook a comprehensive system of explanation and discussions with departments and trade unions. The Civil Service College gave instruction to departmental training staff so that they, in their turn, could give their own courses. While in no way replacing regular contact between the manager and his staff, the idea was that the interview would give a clear and identifiable opportunity for the staff to discuss their work. Both interviewer and interviewee were required to prepare carefully for the interview, completing appropriate forms to serve as the basis of discussion. The interviewer was expected to write up the results of the interview, and to make a record of action to be taken. He was expected to make subsequent notes on the progress made.

Job appraisal reviews exclude discussion of career opportunities and promotion possibilities, although they do cover training needs. The idea is to concentrate on performance on the job rather than long-term career possibilities. Since the publication of the Fulton report, personnel departments have been giving increasing attention to career development interviews, particularly for those in the first few years of their service.

There was a certain scepticism when job appraisal reviews were first introduced. It was said that good managers discussed work with the staff anyway, and that job appraisal reviews were therefore unnecessary. It was also suggested that it would in practice be impossible to separate discussions about career prospects and promotion possibilities from discussions of performance. It was claimed that discussions about performance would seldom be conducted frankly. They could easily become sessions of mutual congratulation, in which staff were thanked by the management for their excellent performance, and the management were congratulated by the staff for their excellent leadership. On the other hand, if a real attempt were to be made to investigate and criticize performance, then the staff would be bound to produce alibis. They would say, for example, that they would have done better with superior supporting staff, or if their requests for extra facilities had been granted.

Job appraisal reviews were introduced gradually, each department choosing to adopt what seemed to be the most sensible system for its own needs. After three years experience, the Behavioural Science Research Division of the Civil Service Department carried out a survey in Her Majesty's Stationery Office and the Property Services Agency to see how far job appraisal reviews had met the purposes for which they were introduced.[36] The views of 500 staff in HMSO were taken, covering both appraisers and appraisees, and they were consulted before the introduction of the scheme and when they had had experience of it. In the Property Services Agency, views were sought from over 800 potential appraisees and 200 officers in appraising grades.

A high proportion of appraisees said they were generally in favour of the scheme. The figure was 71 per cent in the Property Services Agency and 70 per cent in HMSO. The appraisers also had a generally favourable opinion, although their figures were not quite as high as those of the appraisees.

The survey showed that job appraisal reviews were better received, and were felt to be most useful, in branches and sections where the managers were keen to introduce them, the staff had been properly briefed, and both sides had received training. Finally, the benefits were felt mainly to come from making both staff and management think more carefully about the work, its purpose and its problems, and from better communications between both sides. In short, the benefits were much the same as had been derived from management by objectives.

Job satisfaction studies

In 1973 there was considerable discontent in the civil service. Strikes took place and received widespread publicity. Following discussions between staff and management, a review was commissioned into the wider issues beyond pay that were causing dissatisfaction. A report was issued in 1975 called *Civil Servants and Change*. It was to serve as a basis of further discussion by staff and management throughout the Civil Service and for consideration and action by departments.

The 'wider issues' review team visited 39 working units, including, for example, the automatic data processing division of the Ministry of Agriculture at Guildford, the Victoria and Albert Museum, the Passport Office, civil servants working with the Army in Northern Ireland, staff at HM Prison Peterhead, the staff of the Inspector of Taxes at Grantham, and the Exports Credit Guarantee Department in the City of London. During each visit the team had discussions with staff representatives; it also attended a number of annual conferences of Civil Service staff associations.

In their report, the team pointed out that 'the cartoon stereotype of a non-industrial civil servant shows a middle-aged man with a bowler hat'.[37] In fact, men outnumber women by only three to two. In the clerical grades, two-thirds of the staff are women. Furthermore, the age structure of the civil service is predominantly young. A third of civil servants were born after the war. The middle generation between 30 and 50 years old, who might be expected to compose half the civil service, account in fact for less than a third. In the Department of Health and Social Security, for example, nearly half of the staff are under 30. In others, the older generation has the majority. Nearly half of the staff of the Ministry of Defence, for example, are over 50. The report points out that the civil service today

is much more widely dispersed through the country, much more involved in local rather than national affairs, and much more diverse in the work it does than is generally supposed—even by many civil servants. It is also, and will increasingly be, a young service. And socially it is much more representative of the working population than it may seem if you look down Whitehall...the Civil Service has changed in character. In many parts of it, the majority do not have traditional white collar attitudes and do not aspire to them.[38]

The results of this comprehensive review were to confirm that pay was the single most important cause of dissatisfaction in the civil service, and that it aggravated other discontents. But the main problem exposed by the wider issues review can be summarized in the following extract from the review team's report.

Although work ought to give people a sense of fulfilment, a good many jobs in the Civil Service can be unrewarding: checking entries on forms or compiling statistical returns can easily become monotonous or seem pointless; interviewing a succession of clients, with complex human problems can wear down the patience and human feeling of the person who does it all day and every day. It is not surprising if those who do these jobs under relentless pressure do not come whistling to work. But the work has to be done; and it has come to be accepted—perhaps too readily—that national schemes of taxation or social security or subsidy have to be run in ways which require large numbers of people to spend their working days in narrowly specialized, repetitive or grinding jobs....

We have met a good many managers in their everyday surroundings during this Review, from the Executive Officer level all the way up to Under Secretary and beyond, and in scientific and professional units as well as in administrative units. A good manager knows that provided he keeps his unit's output up from day-to-day he can to some extent help his staff do a better job in the longer term. He can encourage them; he may be able to move them around; he may be able to anticipate difficulties, explain procedures, and seek out and use their suggestions; he may be able to secure some improvement in their physical working conditions. He can be wise and practical with their personal problems or their development. But he has much else to do too. He may have an exacting personal load of case work; he has to cope with staff turnover, staff shortages and work fluctuations; he has to organize his unit's response to changes in procedural instructions, or to external events (a postmen's strike, the failure of the central heating, or public criticism). Instead of the support and drive of colleagues in a management team he may be rather hazy about what is required of him, and of what can be expected of his subordinates, and of his superiors as managers. He may feel very much at the mercy of outside events or the constraints of the system. Not every manager has the experience, training, information, authority or character to get the best out of his staff. These are all factors over which he has little or no control: they are rather the result of the traditions of the organization, and the cumulative decisions of central and senior management, who are responsible both for broader management systems, and for the development of managers. In practice management systems and styles tend to perpetuate themselves.[39]

Several initiatives were taken following the publication of this report. One of them was the issue in 1975 of a *Guide for New Managers*.[40] This is primarily intended for staff at junior and middle management level when they first take up a post which involves the management of a group of people. The guide sets out straightforward advice on what are distinguished as the four interrelated tasks of planning, organizing, motivating and controlling. The section of this guide dealing with 'Motivating' is reproduced as Appendix 7. Its main message is the importance of good communications and of treating members of the staff as individuals, and of showing an interest in their concerns and welfare while avoiding intrusion into their private lives.

A second example of work undertaken in the context of the wider issues review, and one which is mentioned in the report, concerns an experiment conducted at three local offices of the Department of Health and Social Security. The essence of the experiment was to leave a greater discretion than normally to the staff to see how the work of the office should be conducted. The staff had naturally to work within the confines of the relevant legal and other rules, and to produce good work on time. The results have so far been generally encouraging. Among the new arrangements that have been introduced in the offices where the experiments have taken place are improved procedures for work at the counters, better liaison with local authority social services departments, improved training schemes, and better communications. Managerial staff have been seen more as people of experience to be consulted, to guide their colleagues and to warn about practical snags, instead of authoritarian bosses. It would clearly be wrong to base too many conclusions on isolated experiments in special conditions. But a report on these experiments concluded that:

despite the stresses of social security work, there exists among local office staff at all levels a considerable reservoir of energy, ability, ideas, goodwill and enthusiasm which conventional Civil Service–style management does not adequately tap. The feasibility of tapping it to a greater degree than is usually achieved has been amply demonstrated in these three offices.[41]

The interchange of staff and the use of outside experience

There are benefits to be gained by exchanging staff between employments. Relevant experience gained in one environment can be usefully translated to that of another. The Fulton Committee recommended that efforts should be made to bring more people into the Civil Service in middle life, especially where they had helpful experience in business. It has, of course, always been the practice to recruit local government officers with experience of other authorities, and it is general practice in both central and local government to recruit technical and specialist staff from business, industry and other walks of life including the universities and other parts of the public sector. Again, during and just after the war there was wide-spread recruitment into government service, particularly into departments which expanded a great deal, such as the Ministry of Food and the Ministry of Supply. Many of those who joined the Civil Service during that time stayed and made permanent careers. At least five permanent secretaries came from the ranks of such late entrants, and one of them became the Head of the Home Civil Service.[42]

The Government accepted the Fulton Committee's recommendation that people with relevant outside experience should be encouraged to join the Civil Service, and there are now schemes for late entry into the administration group and to many specialist fields. A number of very senior people have joined the Civil Service direct. For example, Sir Hermann Bondi, the Chief Scientific Adviser at the Ministry of Defence from 1971 to 1977 and subsequently at the Department of Energy, joined the Civil Service at the age of 55 having been Professor of Mathematics at the University of London. Similarly Sir Alan Cottrell, who was also Chief Scientific Adviser at the Ministry of Defence and then became Chief Scientific Adviser to the Government, joined the Civil Service at the age of 52, having been a Professor of Metallurgy at Cambridge University.

Experience can also be tapped in three main ways for shorter periods and assignments. First, by the use of teams of individuals specially recruited. We have already noted the example of the team of businessmen recruited by the Government in 1970, which contributed to such organizational changes as the setting up of the procurement executive. We have also studied the special advisers that have been recruited to assist ministers in recent years. Other examples include the industrial advisers recruited initially into the Department of Economic Affairs but now forming a small team within the Department of Industry. The advisers have business and trade union experience of particular relevance to the work of the Department. They serve for a number of years and then return to their main careers.

Secondly, there are arrangements for the secondment of particular individuals. In 1977 there were over 20 members of the administration group seconded to industry, local authorities and other organizations, and nearly sixty people from industry and other organizations were on secondment to the Civil Service. There is a comparable scheme for scientists and engineers, and over the period 1973-5 there were nearly 30 secondments into the Civil Service and over 20 outside.[43]

These secondments require careful planning. It is important to find individuals both inside and outside the Civil Service who have good career prospects, and who will benefit themselves and both employers from the interchange. There is no point in seeking to exchange experience when the greater part of the time has to be spent in teaching the job to the newcomer. But people of high quality who could benefit most from such exchanges are very often the last ones that organizations believe they can spare. Exchange is probably easier to arrange into rather than out of the Civil Service. There are a number of Civil Service tasks in the fields of assistance to industry, in production management and in personnel management where outside experience is directly relevant and valuable. On the other hand, few organizations in the private sector can make much use of the political, policy and Parliamentary skills possessed by many civil servants. Nevertheless, some scientific and financial knowledge and skills are relevant to private sector work, and those who possess them are often welcomed on secondment.

A number of those who have served on secondment in the Civil Service have recorded their impressions.[44] Generally speaking, they came to the Civil Service expecting to find its members honest but dull, pedantic, rule bound, and unwilling to take risks. In short, they expected to find them worthy rather than inspiring servants of the public good. But in practice they were impressed by the imagination, energy and devotion to work shown by the great majority of the civil servants with whom they came into contact. They generally pay tribute to the high quality of staff work in the Civil Service, and to the orderly and careful preparation of papers for and minutes of Cabinet and other discussions. They draw attention to the civil servant's emphasis on securing agreement and consensus, the concern with public opinion, and the desire to secure co-operation between Civil Service unions and management. The commentators had some reservations as well. They said that many civil servants did not appreciate the nature of management problems, tending to try to tackle them as if they were political, technical or scientific tasks. Thus in a division concerned with securing supplies, the emphasis might be less upon securing value for money and more upon clear and detailed record keeping, so that the departmental auditors and the Exchequer audit department could be readily satisfied. Again, in a division concerned with purchasing aircraft or advanced equipment, the main emphasis might be laid on trying to secure the most up to date pieces of equipment, embodying the latest technical and scientific developments. There might be less concern with securing delivery on price and on time.

Many commentators who have served in the Civil Service emphasize that this balance of priorities is only a matter of emphasis. It is by no means the case that questions of value for money, and delivery on time and cost are universally regarded as unimportant. The real difficulty seems to be that they are regarded as relatively easy tasks, and that the main effort is accordingly devoted to political work and to the solution of scientific problems. This tends to reduce the attention paid to management matters. It is too often assumed that all that is necessary to secure supplies or to purchase equipment is to set up a simple and straightforward system and the results will be achieved. In fact, experience shows that the management of such work requires unremitting attention, close liaison with suppliers and clients, carefully devised systems of control and oversight, and an ability to forsee and head off potential difficulties. All these can present problems as difficult as any that arise in the political and scientific arenas.

The third method of utilizing outside experience is by the employment of management consultants. During the last 10 to 15 years, consultants have been increasingly employed both in central and local government. In the early years, there was a disposition to look upon the consultants as experts who would arrive to apply techniques to government organizations rather like poultices are applied to boils. Having set the organization on a new course, the consultant would move on to new problems. Experience soon revealed, as it has also done in the private sector, that this method of employing consultants is unsatisfactory from every point of view, including that of the consultant.

Instead, in both central and local government, attention is increasingly concerned with the following factors in consultancy investigations. First, care has to be paid to determine the precise nature of the assignment. It is common experience for organizations to confuse the symptoms of their disorders for their true causes. What may seem to be a problem of organization, for example, may turn out to be a problem of personnel management to be overcome by better communication and staff management. Secondly, most investigations by consultants are best undertaken under the aegis of a steering committee or other group comprising members of the organization being investigated as well as the consultants.

Thirdly, it will often be useful for the investigation to be done jointly by consultants and members of the staff of the management services department of the organization concerned. The consultants are usually men or women of wide experience and specialized knowledge of techniques. The members of the organization's staff can complement this knowledge by their particular understanding of how the organization works in practice. Finally, it is important to provide wherever possible for pilot projects, for full discussion of the proposed solution with those who will be affected by its introduction, and by evaluation and adjustment in the light of experience. All these points have already been touched on in earlier chapters.

Over the last 10 to 15 years, experience has suggested that the task of the consultant is less one of correcting mistakes and telling an organization how to improve its performance, and more a question of discussion and investigation with the members of an organization itself, so that they are led themselves to appreciate the need for change and improvement. The eventual outcome of the consultant's work is seen less as a solution imposed from outside, and far more as the answer to difficulties which the members of the organization have themselves resolved with the help of dialogue with the consultants.

The following tables list some of the assignments given by the Civil Service to consultants in 1969 and 1970, and some of those given during 1976. Seventy-nine were commissioned in 1969 and 1970 and 34 in 1976. The earlier assignments were particularly concerned with investigations following Fulton Committee recommendations, as in the studies of the pay and structures of the highest levels of the Civil Service, and the review of recruitment procedures. Investigations into the working of government departments and into schemes for management by objectives were also popular.

By 1976 there was a change of emphasis. There were more studies concerned with the government's relations with business, commerce and other organizations, and less concentration upon the working of the government machine. For example there were studies of the prospects of Greenwell Dry Dock Ltd and of the footwear manufacturing industry. And where studies of the government machine were commissioned, they tended to focus on personnel management.

Participation

Staff participation in policy decisions has been widely discussed during the last few years. As we have seen, good management will always seek to

Department	Nature of assignment	Consultant used
Ministry of Agriculture, Fisheries and Food	Introduction of the principles of Management by Objectives to senior managers in the Regional and Divisional Organization	Urwick Orr & Partners Ltd.
Civil Service Department	A study of the pay and structure at the highest levels in the Civil Service	Associated Industrial Consultants Ltd
Civil Service Department	The translation of the handbook on Statutory Instrument Procedure into algorithmic form	Cambridge Consultants (Training) Ltd
Civil Service Department	Review of recruitment procedures	Cooper Bros. & Co.
Ministry of Defence	To develop a productivity indicator for HM Dockyards	Associated Industrial Consultants Ltd
Department of the Environment	To indicate the advantages of the use of logical trees in the presentation of the effect of social legislation	Cambridge Consultants (Training) Ltd
Department of the Environment	Management accounting for New Towns	Peat, Marwick, Mitchell & Co.
Ordnance Survey	Review of marketing arrangements for Ordnance Survey small-scale maps	Urwick Orr & Partners Ltd.

Fig.6.2   Examples of Assignments Commissioned in 1969/70
Source: Extract from "O & M Bulletin: The Journal of Government Management Services" Vol 26, Number 2, May 1971

ensure that the ideas and views of the staff are properly taken into account. But there has recently been greater interest in special arrangements to secure the participation of staff in policy making. A committee chaired by Lord Bullock on staff participation in policy decisions in industrial companies reported in 1977.[45] The majority of the members proposed that the boards of directors of industrial companies should be composed of an equal number of worker directors and shareholder representatives, together with a third and smaller group from among whom the chairman would be chosen. This group would be elected equally by both worker and shareholder board members. This scheme would apply to the country's leading 600 firms with more than 2000 employees. The arrangements would be introduced in each company if and when one or more of the company's recognized unions, representing at least one-fifth of its employees, asked for the arrangements to be introduced.

Whatever action may be taken on the Bullock report, the question arises as to what should be done in the public sector. Nationalized industries are closest to industrial companies. It might be possible to bring them generally within the arrangements that are finally introduced for private industry. But central and local government are very different. Local authorities are responsible to the local electorate, and government departments directed by ministers are responsible to Parliament. This democratic principle rules out worker participation on equal terms with elected representatives.

Department	Nature of assignment	Consultant used
Cabinet Office	Study of the UK power plant equipment industry	Booz Allen & Hamilton International BV.
Civil Service Department	Job satisfaction studies	Imitax Ltd.
Department of the Environment,	Research project for monitoring development plans for local authorities	Institute for Operational Research
Department of Industry	To examine the prospect of Greenwell Drydocks Ltd.	Touche Ross & Co.
	Studies of footwear manufacturing industry's costs, productivity, design and materials supply	Shoe and Allied Trades Research Association Ltd
Training Services Agency	Women and management	Ashridge Management College

Fig.6.3 Examples of Assignments Commissioned in 1976
Source: Extract from "Management Services in Government" February 1977, Vol. 32, Number 1.

The Greater London Council voted to seek government legislation to allow employees to become non-voting members of local authority committees. In the meantime, before legislation was passed, they planned to invite employees' representatives to speak at committee meetings. The association representing metropolitan authorities supported the GLC's move. But the associations representing other local authorities did not support it. They argued that staff representation on policy making committees is inconsistent with the democratic principles of local government. They believed that other opportunities should be provided for local authority staffs to contribute their views on matters that affect them directly.[46]

The same considerations apply in the Civil Service. Civil Service unions have not asked for direct participation in policy making. For the time being at least, therefore, it seems that the most likely way forward in both central and local government is through increasing consultation between staff and management. Major areas likely to be discussed in the Civil Service include union representation on departmental management reviews, and the inclusion of staff representatives on the boards of such organizations as the Property Services Agency and the Royal Ordnance Factories.[47]

CONCLUSIONS AND SUMMARY

(1) The Fulton Committee's report and the Bains report both emphasized the importance of improving personnel management in central and local government. This reflected a growing interest and concern in this subject over the last 10 to 15 years.

(2) This interest and concern has centred upon a number of general ideas and their development in a variety of practical arrangements. The ideas are that:

(a) personnel should be regarded as a resource which ought to be managed as effectively and efficiently as other resources such as money and land;

(b) the effective and efficient management of personnel requires a pay and grading structure that allows for the recruitment, deployment and development of the full range of talent available to the public service concerned;

(c) the design and operation of such a grading structure requires policies of staff selection, training, promotion, career development, welfare, wage and salary administration and superannuation arrangements. Specialist personnel staffs are required to undertake such work effectively;

(d) the effective and efficient use of staff also requires good leadership by working managers. Such leadership requires the ability to harmonize the goals and aspirations of the staff with those of the organization. Good communications are one of the major keys to success.

(3) In this chapter we have reviewed some of the theories and research that lie behind these ideas. We have also reviewed some of the changes that have been made in personnel management in central and local government to try to give effect to them. We have looked at changes in the pay and grading structure of the Civil Service; and in recruiting; we have examined improvements in the machinery of personnel management through the establishment of the Civil Service Department, and changes in personnel management in local authorities. We have also reviewed developments in training, and in techniques for harmonizing the requirements of the organization with individual aspirations through schemes of management by objectives and by job appraisal reviews. We have looked at schemes for improving job satisfaction, and for interchanging staff and using outside experience. Finally, we have considered a number of ideas for staff participation in policy making both in the Civil Service and in local government.

(4) The general conclusion arising from these studies is that the effectiveness and efficiency of systems and schemes of personnel management depend upon the fairness and equity with which they are designed and administered. But fairness and equity are necessary rather than sufficient conditions. Opportunities must also be provided for the staff to develop and demonstrate their knowledge, commitment and enthusiasm for their work, and thereby make the best contribution they can to the success of the organizations within which they work.

(5) Training schemes, management by objectives, job appraisal reviews, job satisfaction studies, and participative management experiments are some of the vehicles that have been used for the development of these qualities.

(6) Experience suggests that the outward form of these devices is less important than the spirit of interest, commitment and enthusiasm which they can help to generate. They do this mainly by improving communications and securing a better understanding of the respective points of view of the staff and their managers. These improvements tend to last longer than the formal schemes which helped to bring them into existence. These schemes are often substantially modified after a few years of experience, or fall into disuse.

(7) Personnel management is therefore less a matter of imposing systems and using techniques and more the designing of a framework within which individuals can manage themselves in co-operation with their colleagues and their superiors.

(8) This tends to make the manager's life both harder and potentially more successful. It tends to be harder because of the care necessary to design and manage new arrangements and approaches to personnel management. It is potentially more successful because of the new energy and controlled enthusiasm that can result from the successful employment of the new approaches to personnel management.

(9) These approaches offer the prospect of better results for staff, managers and the public at large than the two alternative systems most usually employed—authoritarian management on the one hand and drift on the other.

7
Audit, review and control

The audit, review and control of government activities is of crucial importance in a democracy. Indeed, the central idea of democracy is that the government should be accountable and responsible to the people for the policies adopted and the manner in which they are carried out.

This simple principle has always been difficult to apply. The development of parliamentary democracy and the expansion of government activities at both central and local level has made it even more difficult to make sure that the activities of public servants are made known to and are acceptable to the people at large and, indeed, to give real meaning to the ideas of auditing, reviewing and controlling the work of government departments and local authorities to ensure that they accord with the wishes of the people.

Six different approaches to this problem may be distinguished. They may be described as the political, the legal, the procedural, the organizational, the responsive, and the managerial. We will examine them in turn. But first we must note an important difference in principle between the first five approaches, which have to do with external review, audit and political and democratic supervision, and the sixth approach, which is more concerned with internal control and the monitoring of operations. Both internal and external control are important, but they are not alternatives and must not be confused with each other.

THE POLITICAL APPROACH

Parliament is at the heart of the political approach to audit, control and review. Under the British system of parliamentary democracy, members of Parliament are elected by universal adult suffrage in 635 constituencies to form the House of Commons which, with the House of Lords, constitutes Parliament. The Queen appoints as Prime Minister the leader of the party best able to form a government, who is usually, though not invariably, the leader of the party with most seats in the House of Commons. The Prime Minister chooses his ministerial colleagues, most of whom are appointed to be in charge of government departments and are responsible to Parliament accordingly. Under this system, ministers are responsible individually for the work of their own departments and collectively for the policy of the Government as a whole. The Government must secure parliamentary support for new legislation and for its continuing policies. Ministers can be asked parliamentary questions and be interrogated in debate upon the policies and administration of the Government as a whole and of particular departments. In this way, the members of Parliament, both opposition members and government supporters, have an opportunity to investigate the work of government. And the people at large have an opportunity at least every five years, and more frequently if Parliament is dissolved, to give their verdict on the Government's performance at a general election.

This is no more than a sketch of a changing system, in which pressure groups are tending to play an increasing part through their dealings with ministers and civil servants. Yet Parliamentary discussion, review and control remains of great political importance. It is the basis of the day-to-day working of our democracy. Nevertheless, it does not provide the detailed and continuing analysis of the work of government that is implied by the ideas of audit, control and review. Inevitably, parliamentarians concentrate on particular features of the Government's work; usually, though not invariably, those of immediate political significance and those which catch public interest and attention. These are only a small portion of the Government's activities, and so Parliament cannot provide a comprehensive system of audit, control and review.

Parliament has sought to buttress the opportunities for debate on the floor of the House of Commons by the institution of select committees of members who are able to investigate the work of government in more detail. The best known of these committees is the Public Accounts Committee, which was set up in 1861 to exercise control over the expenditure of public funds. The House of Commons Standing Order 86 lays down that the Committee's function is to examine and report from time to time on 'the accounts showing the appropriation of the sums granted by Parliament to meet public expenditure and such other accounts laid before Parliament as the committee may think fit'. The Committee concentrates upon the expenditure of government departments and certain other bodies. Its prime concern is to ensure that money is spent on the purposes for which it is voted; if £1 million is voted for regional assistance to industry, the Public Accounts Committee will be concerned to see that the money is spent on this purpose and not, shall we say, on overseas aid. The Committee goes beyond its formal remit by making some investigations into the financial administration of departments and makes recommendations to improve their efficiency.

The Committee is aided by the Comptroller and Auditor General. He is in charge of the Exchequer and Audit Department, whose staff have access to the accounts of all government departments. They provide the material upon which the Public Accounts Committee carries out its investigation of the financial administration and interrogates the accounting officers of government departments. The accounting officers are the chief financial officers of the departments. Usually the post is filled by the permanent secretary, who is the chief civil servant of the department.

During the 1960s experiments were made in increasing the number and scope of Parliament's Select Committees. It was argued that foreign legislatures, such as the United States Congress, found the ability of their specialist committees to investigate the detailed work of government departments of great value, and it was suggested that Parliament could strengthen its powers by adopting similar practices. In December 1966 it was announced that Select Committees would be set up on science and technology and on agriculture, and subsequently committees were set up on race relations and immigration, education and science, overseas aid and Scottish affairs. Some of these committees were concerned with particular government functions, such as science and technology. These committees have been more successful on the whole than those which, like agriculture, education, and overseas aid, concentrated on the work of particular departments and have since been discontinued. The existence of a select committee specializing in the affairs of a single department makes the position of the minister more difficult. On the whole, ministers prefer to exercise responsibility to Parliament as a whole and not to be called to account by a small group of members. The same point arises in some measure with the functional committees. They are certainly concerned with the work of specific government departments. But their reports have often been on more general subjects, such as the problems of coloured school leavers, and the relations between immigrants and the police.

However, the most significant select committee from the viewpoint of audit, control and review, is the Expenditure Committee. The Committee was first set up in 1971. Its terms of reference allow it, under Standing Order 87, 'to consider any papers on public expenditure presented to this House and such of the estimates as may seem fit to the committee and in particular to consider how, if at all, the policies implied in the figures of expenditure and in the estimates may be carried out more economically, and to examine the form of the papers and of the estimates presented to this House'. The Committee works through sub-committees on a variety of subjects, such as education and the arts; the environment and Home Office; defence and external affairs; and employment and social services. The Committee hears some evidence in public and frequently appoints specialist advisers to help in its investigations. As its terms of reference imply, the Committee is not concerned with directly investigating the policy of the government. It is concerned with economy. Yet it is often impossible to draw a line between investigating policies and investigating the economy of their administration.

We shall investigate the work of Parliamentary Select Committees by looking in more detail at the Expenditure Committee's report on the Civil Service which was issued in 1977. This and many other reports bring a great deal of information before Parliament and the public at large. Nevertheless, the general difficulties noted above about the audit, controlling and reviewing work of Parliament apply to these committees. Their investigations are inevitably partial and specialized. They cannot cover the whole range of the work of government departments, and they inevitably concentrate on the subjects of interest to the members at the time. They are therefore no substitute for a continuing and comprehensive programme of audit control and review, although they can be extremely useful in highlighting current problems.

So far as local government is concerned, the arrangements for audit, control and review at the political level are naturally different. The elected members are responsible for the administration of the work of the local authority. They are often organized on political lines, and the majority party of the authority usually seeks to carry out a programme of work in line with its political philosophy. It aims to appeal to the electorate on the basis of its performance and by calling upon the general political sympathies and loyalties of its adherents. The whole council takes part in administration, since all elected members have opportunities to serve on committees responsible for policy and administration; though opportunities for policy making are more circumscribed in local government than in central departments.

Because elected members work closely with the officials of local authorities, they tend to have a greater knowledge of the day-to-day work of the authority than members of Parliament obtain of the work of central government departments. In this sense, elected members in local authorities are better able to undertake a continuing role of audit, control and review. Yet the same limitations apply in local authorities. The work of local authorities is detailed and technical. In some cases it is hard for the busy layman to grasp. This means that elected members tend to concentrate on the politically sensitive issues, or matters in which they are particularly interested. They cannot provide a comprehensive system of audit, control and review.

THE LEGAL APPROACH

Gaps in the system of political audit, control and review might in theory be filled by legal remedies. It might appear feasible to provide for audit, review and control by the application of the general principle that public authorities must have legal justification for their activities and that they must carry out these activities in a defined way. If they fail to act within the law, or if they break the procedural rules they are legally obliged to follow, then actions may be brought against them in the courts and grievances redressed.

There are, however, a number of difficulties. First, public authorities have some widely drawn powers. For example, the Crown has powers to conduct negotiations with foreign states and to recognize foreign governments. A citizen might object to the recognition of a new regime. But he would be unable to persuade the courts to review the matter. This is because, in this instance, the Crown would be using powers which derive from the Royal Prerogative. The courts will not inquire into the use of such powers once they have established that they do indeed exist. The citizen could not succeed in his action unless he could prove that ministers had acted corruptly.

Again, various Acts of Parliament lay down the procedures to be followed in certain lines of administration. Some of them grant rights of appeal to the courts. It does not follow, however, that the court will substitute its own judgement for that taken by the properly designated authority so long as it has acted in accordance with the designated rules. Furthermore, where a public authority is required to hold a public hearing or enquiry it by no means follows that the courts will insist that the authority must observe the same procedures as a court of law. Finally, there are limitations on the right of an individual to take action against public authorities on grounds of his general objections to their policies and activities. He has usually to show that he is personally and directly affected by the authority's actions in a closer way than as a member of the general public.

The following quotation indicates the difficulties of using the law as a straightforward method of audit, control and review.

For example, T's licence to sell peanuts in the street is revoked by the local authority. No appeal is provided by statute. T applies to the Divisional Court of the Queen's Bench Division for an order of certiorari to quash the decision on the grounds that the council acted ultra vires and refused to give him a hearing according to natural justice. Revocation of a licence is analytically an administrative act, if a decision whether or not to revoke is discretionary. The courts have sometimes said that certiorari will issue to quash only judicial acts. They have also said many times that an obligation to ensure rules of natural justice arises only where there is a duty to act judicially; and they have quite often held that such a duty does not arise where the competent authority's functions are analytically administrative. But if a court were to conclude that the local authority acted ultra vires, it would make no bones about quashing its decision by certiorari; and if it thought that in fairness to a licensee the authority ought to have given him a proper hearing before taking away his livelihood it would probably hold that the authority was required to 'act judicially' according to natural justice. In the course of the judgement one might even find a dictum that taking away a licence was a 'judicial act'.[1]

This quotation of a hypothetical case illustrates that while judicial remedies are of the greatest importance in defending the rights and liberties of the citizen they do not amount to a general and all-embracing system of audit, control and review for all activities of public authorities. Judicial remedies will provide protection and relief for those directly disadvantaged by acts which are established in the courts as illegal. What is an illegal act may not be always clear until a case has been tested in the courts.

THE PROCEDURAL APPROACH

If detailed procedures were laid down for the activities of public authorities and if checks were made to see that they were observed then, in principle, the work of all public authorities would conform with defined standards. This would amount to a complete system of audit, control and review.

Procedural control systems exist in some areas of government work. For example, there are rules about the way in which government departments must spend the money which Parliament has authorized. The Comptroller and Auditor General is required by law to investigate the accounts of government departments and certain other bodies, and his officials in the Exchequer and Audit Department are required to satisfy themselves

(a) that the money expended has been applied to the purposes for which the grants made by Parliament were intended to provide; (b) that the expenditure conforms to the authority which governs it; (c) that where necessary the expenditure is supported by Treasury authority; (d) that the accounts include no sums other than those that have actually come in course of payment within the financial year concerned; (e) as regards receipts that the sums brought to account are correct.[2]

The most important new procedural controls derive from the institution of a series of commissioners able to investigate certain actions of central government departments, the health service and local authorities, in response to complaints by members of the public that they have been unfairly treated. The Parliamentary Commissioner for Administration was set up in 1967 under the Parliamentary Commissioner Act 1967 to investigate complaints against central government departments. The Commissioner is appointed by the Crown on the advice of the Prime Minister. His status is akin to that of the Comptroller and Auditor General and his salary is charged on the Consolidated Fund rather than of that of any departmental vote. He holds office during good behaviour subject to retiring at 65. He may be removed on addresses from both Houses of Parliament. His duties are to investigate complaints by individuals and corporate bodies except local authorities and other public corporations, who claim to have 'sustained injustice in consequence of maladministration'. He is confined to certain classes of complaints. He cannot, for example, investigate complaints about personnel management in the civil service, or where other remedies are provided, such as reference to the courts or to a special tribunal.

The Commissioner cannot act on his own initiative or be approached directly by a member of the public. The procedure is for a member of public to make a complaint to an MP and for the MP to forward this to the Commissioner. In the development of the Commissioner's work the influence of the practice and procedures of the Comptroller and Auditor General is very evident. Indeed, the first Parliamentary Commissioner, Sir Edward Compton, had previously been the Comptroller and Auditor General. Thus the Parliamentary Commissioner is at pains in his procedures and investigations not only to be fair to the complainant, and to investigate his complaints in full, but also to be fair to the department. He gives the department the opportunity to hear the allegations made against them and make comments. Over the years, the Commissioner has come to ascribe a specific meaning to 'injustice' and 'maladministration'. The former, judging by the decisions, includes hardship and the sense of grievance arising from the way in which individuals are treated by the administration. 'Maladministration' has been shown in cases decided against government departments to include such matters as bias, unfair discrimination, harshness, misleading a member of public as to their rights, failing to notify members of the public of their rights or to explain the reasons for a decision, high-handedness, using powers for incorrect purposes, failing to consider relevant material and taking irrelevant matter into consideration, losing and failing to reply to correspondence, making unreasonable delays in tax refunds and similar examples of where correct and efficient office procedure would have obviated the hardships felt by the members of the public. The Commissioner has been at pains to make clear that maladministration is more than the exercise of discretion in a way that may be unpopular to those who are affected by it. The remedy for those who disagree with the results of properly exercised discretion lies in complaining to the minister and Parliament.[3]

The Health Service Commissioner acts in a generally similar way, although his powers are somewhat wider. He can investigate complaints that individuals have suffered injustice, or hardship, as a result of failure in a service provided by a Health Service Authority, or failure to provide a service which it had a duty to provide, or any other action by a Health Service Authority involving maladministration. And the Commissioner can be approached directly by a member of the public. On the other hand, he is precluded from investigating complaints about the clinical judgements of Health Service staff.

The Local Government Act 1974 provided for the establishment of a body of Commissioners for Local Administration in England and a similar body of Commissioners for Local Administration in Wales. There are similar officials in Scotland and Northern Ireland. The English Commissioners work on a regional basis. The Commissioners work under limitations. They are excluded from investigating complaints in various subjects, including local authority staff matters, crime detection and prevention, and the internal administration of schools and colleges. And they must satisfy themselves that the complainant has first approached the local authority, who must have a reasonable opportunity to reply.

In their report for 1977, the English Commissioners said that during 1976–77 they had completed full investigations into 189 complaints, and found faults in 107 cases.[4] They had also received 2277 complaints, mainly in the fields of planning, housing and education; 1671 were not suitable for investigation, either because they were outside the Commissioners' terms of reference, or because there were no signs of injustice or bad administration. Lady Serota, the Chairman of the Commission, said that 'we cannot investigate council policies just because they are unpopular; our concern is with the manner in which decisions are taken and the way those decisions are taken'. About two-thirds of the complaints were sent back, as they had not been referred to councillors. To the surprise of the Commission, many of them were then dropped. The complaint therefore remaining unsettled, owing to the unwillingness of the complainant to forward his representations to an elected member of the council. The main faults that the Commissioners found were in failures to consult members of the public, failures to take action; failures to keep promises; the giving of incorrect advice and defective administrative procedures. The chairman said 'Ideally each authority should have a clear and well publicized system for handling complaints. The public should have confidence in that system and use it first, knowing that the local ombudsman is available if local action fails'.

The procedural approach to audit, control and review certainly makes a useful contribution and could be developed further. Procedural checks do ensure that many examples of unacceptable action are put right and, perhaps more importantly, the knowledge that such checks exist no doubt helps to keep civil servants and local government officers on their toes, thus deterring further errors. But the number of cases that can be picked up in this way is quite small, and the procedural controls that exist do not bite upon the full range of governmental actions or upon dubious actions which have been carried out according to the rules. Present procedural checks are therefore not comprehensive, and it is difficult to believe that they could be made so without the erection of so complex a set of rules and reviewing bodies that the work of government would be brought almost to a halt.

THE ORGANIZATIONAL APPROACH

Another approach to audit, control and review is to concentrate upon securing good organizations within central government departments and local authorities by requiring the use, for example, of the ideas and techniques discussed in chapters 5 and 6. The idea is that if organizations are soundly conceived and structured, properly staffed, and intelligently managed, then they will, almost by definition, be bound to operate in the public interest. The need for audit, control and review is accordingly diminished by the quality of the machine as originally laid down by those responsible for designing it.

It is true that good organization can reduce the number of mistakes that are made and the volume of public dissatisfaction. But we cannot take organizational promise as necessarily ensuring organizational performance. However good an organization may be, arrangements for the continuing review of its performance are essential.

THE RESPONSIVE APPROACH

A more recent and currently fashionable approach to audit, control and review is to suggest that the decisions of public authorities and their day-to-day work will be improved if members of the public have greater access to the materials on which public servants operate, have wider opportunities to comment before decisions are taken, and have the chance to review programmes of government work during the course of their implementation. 'Open government' is the slogan of this approach and, in the last few years, steps have been taken to allow greater access to the work of government.

In central government, for example, there is the recent practice of issuing 'green papers' on subjects of current concern. The idea is that the 'green paper' provides an opportunity for public debate and discussion on possible ways of tackling a problem and that the government will be able to put forward more definite ideas in the light of this debate, leading, where necessary, to legislative proposals coming before Parliament. Greater attention has also been paid to public relations work at both central and local level, and to inviting members of public to attend more meetings of the full council and sometimes its committees. There is a generally freer and more open attitude than 10 to 15 years ago to providing information to journalists from the press and television, to answering more of their questions, and generally trying to promote an informed debate.

In August 1977, further developments were announced from 10 Downing Street.[5] Additional information is henceforth to be made available to the public by way of more green papers; a newer range of even 'greener' papers, more provisional still in their proposals; and by departments being required to respond 'positively and sympathetically' to specific requests for information from MPs, journalists, the public and research scholars. At the same time, on the Prime Minister's instructions, the Head of the Home Civil Service issued new guidance to departments. Departments will in future have to draw a distinction in their policy analyses between:

(a) the options drawn up for Ministers in the later stages of policy making and their factual bases; and

(b) the advice of civil servants and the view of Ministers upon them.

When the decision has been taken, the first part of the material will be made available to the public. This will not, of course, represent completely 'open' government; the information about options will not be available until after the decision has been taken, and the views of civil servants and ministers on the different options will still not be available.

Another contribution to 'open government' was the series of public meetings planned and carried out by the Secretary of State for Education and Science in 1976 and 1977. These meetings were carefully structured to focus on a variety of educational issues and to give a wide range of those concerned with education, including teachers, parents and pupils, the opportunity to put forward their points of view and to hear those of other interested parties. The meetings captured a lot of attention, and may have had value in demonstrating how difficult it is to secure general agreement on both the nature of and the possible solutions to current problems of educational policy and its implementation.

Another proposal, of a different kind, concerns the 'open government' of schools. A report published in 1977 proposed that teachers should have equal representation with local authorities, parents and community representatives in the governing bodies of state schools, and these bodies should have increased powers over the content and methods of teaching.[6]

These various proposals for providing more information, for encouraging more debate about possible policies, and for associating interested members of the public with the administration of certain public services would have many advantages. They would make government more open and less secretive. On the other hand, there would be problems. Widespread consultation takes time and costs money. It may encourage certain groups to take up entrenched positions. It may cause dissension between the lay public and professional public servants. The suggestions for increasing lay governors' concern for teaching methods has provoked opposition from teachers unions. 'Open government' therefore has costs as well as benefits. The provision of more information and more public participation must therefore be undertaken in ways that promote the orderly conduct of public business. And it would be a mistake to believe that the procedures of 'open government', valuable as they may be, can provide a comprehensive system of audit, control and review for public authorities.

THE MANAGERIAL APPROACH

The managerial approach to audit, review and control takes as its starting point the cycle of managerial activities discussed in chapter 2. This approach conceives management as a series of interdependent activities including the formulation of objectives, the examination of alternative ways of achieving them, and their implementation by programmes of executive action conducted within organizations designed, staffed and directed to the particular tasks in hand. According to this approach, systems of audit, control and review should be directed to assessing the degree to which objectives have been achieved, measuring the extent and causes of any short fall, and guiding management to successful remedial action.

Such a system of audit, control and review has four essential elements. First, the targets and objectives of the organization must be clearly specified in such a way that the degree and quality of their achievement can be measured. This is the crucial feature of a control system, since unless it is clear what the organization is trying to do, there will be no means of deciding whether it has been successful or not.

The second aspect of a control system is a system of reporting. This system must provide useful, practical and timely information, and do so in a form that enables the manager to pinpoint deviations from the planned line of progress. Interpretation and evaluation is the third aspect. The results of the reporting system will give the manager a range of information about his progress. It is important to be able to interpret and evaluate that information.

The final element of control and review is the taking of corrective action. When interpretation and evaluation of the information yielded by the system of reporting shows that the targets and objectives are not being met, then the manager must be armed with the requisite authority to put matters right and to work towards the achievement of his goals. And if this is not possible, then he should use his control system to make clear that the objectives and targets of the organization are unrealistic and require amendment.

(I) The fundamentals of a good control system

It is easy to list these four elements. But if they are to operate successfully, it is necessary to take account of a number of factors.

The first essential of a good control system is that it must be relevant to the needs and nature of the activity to which it relates. This might seem obvious. Yet it is often ignored in both public and private administration. We may take an example from the field of social services. If the object of a particular service is to improve the quality of life of the group of people for whom it is provided, then it will not be enough simply to know that the relevant authority's estimate has been spent on this activity without any over or underspending. We also need to know how far the quality of life of the recipients of the service has been improved. We may find, for example, that the greater share of the expenditure has in fact gone to the better-off, who may need it less than the poor. This may be because those with higher incomes are more adept at explaining their needs, both in writing and in discussion, and this may give them some advantage in securing financial and other forms of aid. The control system must be alive to this kind of point and must be sufficiently sophisticated and sensitive to provide information of this nature.

The second fundamental of a good control system is that it must report deviations from the planned outcome quickly, so that action to remedy the failure can be set promptly in hand. For example, there are many cases where the estimate for a service is likely to be overspent, and the information arrives too late for anything to be done.

The third aspect of a good control system is that it should draw attention to the crucial factors in the administration of a service. These are the factors which are essential to the success of the service as a whole and which, if they go wrong, can ruin the whole scheme. For example, we may take the case of a hypothetical municipal restaurant. The manager of the restaurant has the task of breaking even, including an allowance for return on the capital he employs. How does he check up on his progress? What information does he need to be certain that his efforts are well directed? A considerable range of information will be useful. For example, it will help to know the total number of orders taken at various meal sittings, so that the staff can be most expeditiously deployed in order to cope with peaks of demand without leaving them idle for the less busy parts of the day. Again, it will be important to know the number of meals produced by each chef, and the amount of work got through by each waiter. But the crucial piece of information will be the flow of cash. Unless there is sufficient cash to pay bills and meet the wages the objectives of the enterprise will not be met. It is therefore a prime essential of a control system to provide information on those aspects of an administrative process which are crucial to its success.

The next important characteristic of a good control system is that it should yield objective information. By this we mean that the information should come forward in figures and facts which cannot reasonably be questioned. If the information comes forward as views and opinions, then management will have to interpret it as best it can, and take action on assessments which are inevitably a matter of guesswork to some degree. Take, for example, the monitoring of a civil engineering project. This can be done by taking general opinions on how well the work is going, or by the provision of objective information about the quantity of work done each day, with explanations for variations from the target. The example has only to be cited for it to be clear that the latter system is to be preferred for reliable and timely control.

Next, a good control system must be flexible. By this we mean that the information that it yields must be immune from the influence of extraneous factors which are irrelevant to the purpose in hand. For example, a control system might specify that reports should be made to higher management on engineering jobs which had over-run their estimate by £1000. Such a form of control will be unsound for two reasons: first, a £1000 excess may be a very large proportion of a small job or a very small proportion of a large one. If the same figure is applied to both small and large jobs, then the large jobs may be monitored too closely and the small jobs will probably not be monitored enough. Secondly, at a time of rising prices, a £1000 excess will become progressively less serious. The result of adhering to the £1000 figure will be to draw management's attention to less important questions. In the example chosen a better form of control might be to specify that reference should be made to higher authority when the cost over-run exceeds a specified percentage. A control system designed in this way would apply equally to large and small jobs, and it would be largely immune from the effects of inflation.

Furthermore, a good control system should conform with the organizational pattern of the authority. This means that information should be supplied to those who are capable of using it. For example, a control system might be instituted for the oversight of the construction of houses and flats. The control system might show that the estimate is being exceeded. But this information by itself may be inadequate; we need to know the cause of the excess. Is it, for example, because raw material supplies have increased in price? Or is it because of the unexpectedly low output of certain workers? Or is it because there are defects in the co-ordination of different parts of the job, so that groups of workers are standing idle while supplies are awaited? What is needed is for information to be supplied to the officers who have the responsibility for specified areas of management, and for this information to appear in a form which shows clearly what action needs to be taken.

Another characteristic of a good control system is that the information it provides must be comprehensible to those who have to act upon it. If the manager is a person of restricted education and background knowledge— let us suppose, for example, that he is the foreman of what is basically an industrial process—then his control information will be less than helpful if it is a sophisticated collection of financial and output ratios. The manager may well not understand information presented to him in this way, and so he will tend to disregard it, hoping that the continuation of the good work which brought his original promotion will enable him to meet his present requirements. On the other hand, there are government activities of extreme sophistication, administered by staffs of great technical expertise. These people will be annoyed by, and tend to disregard, a system of reporting which is too juvenile and insufficiently directed to the cause of the difficulties. So, just as managers with little formal education will probably be glad to have control information that is presented in simple terms, the more sophisticated officer must have more sophisticated information. This is not to say, of course, that control information should be needlessly over-elaborate. Even the most sophisticated manager will disregard irrelevant information, however attractively it may be presented.

Another characteristic of a good control system is that it must address itself to causes rather than symptoms. A homely analogy may make the point here. Toothache can be treated by a stiff dose of whisky or a visit to the dentist. The stiff whisky produces immediate results in the alleviation of pain, yet a visit to the dentist is likely to be of more value because it is designed to treat the cause of the discomfort. In the same way, government control systems must yield information about the causes of deviations from plans.

Finally, systems of control must themselves be reviewed. They must not be too elaborate and costly, measured against the results they produce, and they must be adapted to meet any changes that may take place in the work to which they are being applied.

(II) The human elements of management control

Many members of staff are suspicious of systems of control and review. This is largely for historical reasons, and has arisen because management's approach to installing control systems has been far more often based on the authoritarian assumptions of theory X management, that were discussed in chapter 6, than on the belief that people are naturally interested in working hard. As a result, many control systems have been designed and administered in a negative way. They have been used only to exert pressure and discipline, and as a measure of enforcing obedience to externally imposed standards.

This can lead to various unintended consequences. First, there can be antagonism to the controls and dislike of those who administer them. Secondly, the members of staff whose activities are being reviewed set up measures of successful resistance and non-compliance. This occurs at every level. If people feel that the controls threaten their jobs, salaries or standing, then they will either find means of circumventing them or they will ensure that the results they submit will show their performance in a good light. It is not suggested that there is usually a deliberate fraud; it is more a matter of putting the best possible construction on the revealed facts in order to provide an insurance policy against management criticism.

Thirdly, as management learns that its control systems tend to be circumvented, it re-doubles its efforts to survey performance. Close surveillance restricts delegation. This handicaps senior managers and saps the morale and initiative of the staff. These unintended consequences tend to occur where the management emphasizes punishment and discipline as opposed to supporting and helping the staff in meeting standards and objectives; where there is a lack of trust between the management and the staff; and where the results of the control systems are believed to affect unfairly the individual's standing and the progress of his career.

How can these unintended consequences be removed? It must be recognized, of course, that control systems are bound to create some tension within an organization. The foregoing points should not be construed as an apologia for slackness and mismanagement. Indeed, the improvement of performance is the whole purpose of a control system. If the information it produces is hidden, and if awkward problems are smoothed away, then the control system is not working properly. How, then, can the control system be made to yield the relevant information, without appearing to the staff as an unfair threat to them and encouraging them to provide false information to the reviewing system?

The answer to this question has been given in the previous chapter. The manager must communicate, discuss and gain the highest possible commitment among his staff to the goals and objectives of the authority, the department and their individual jobs. Management by objectives can be useful here. The more people are committed to objectives, the better their performance tends to be.

Summary Successful systems of audit, review and control require far more than the competent selection of control techniques. They require a careful and imaginative attention to the attitudes of the staff, and the enlistment of the support of the staff in the purposes of control.

(III) The review of the organization as a whole

From time to time the responsible ministers, elected members or senior officials of a public authority may take the view that there will be advantage in reviewing the operation of the authority as a whole, or some major department within it. How can this best be done? The main point is that such a review is quite different from the system of continuing internal monitoring and control. It must evaluate the whole range of managerial activities and machinery, including those for forecasting, for determining objectives, for specifying problems, for determining and evaluating the solutions to these problems, for selecting the best of them, for securing agreement amongst all those concerned to the relevant course of action, for the execution of work through measures of organization, staffing and direction and for control and review.

There are four main ways by which an examination of this kind can be set in hand. First, it may be entrusted to a single individual. This may be an eminent expert from outside or, perhaps, a senior civil servant or local government officer, often one within a measurable distance of retirement. The advantage of using an individual for this work is that he will invariably have great experience and that, being a single individual, his work can often be done quickly and relatively inexpensively. But the drawback of an individual report is that it may be idiosyncratic, developing hobby-horses nurtured over many years, but never previously given free rein. There is also the point that an officer close to retirement may well wish in such a final report to take a new and unusual line, just to emphasize the fact that he is still capable of fresh and original thought. Very often these ideas are less than fully helpful because they have not been mediated by debate and discussion.

Mention of these difficulties leads to the second possibility, which is an internal committee of officials or elected members. In central government, it is usual to have committees of officials reporting to a single minister or committee of ministers. In local government there tends to be a greater variety of review arrangements. Such a reviewing committee will usually take longer to carry out its remit and it will be more expensive than investigation by an individual. It is likely to avoid eccentric views, since the cut-and-thrust of committee debate will usually have weeded out the more bizarre suggestions. But the drawback of an internal committee will often be that its recommendations represent no more than a compromise between interested parties. For this reason a report by an inside committee, although usually based on considerable knowledge, can often be less helpful than it should be.

Thirdly, it is possible to undertake a review of this kind by the employment of outsiders such as a firm of consultants, or an academic specialist or the granting of a contract to a research organization or to a university. Here the benefits of objectivity are gained, since the reviewers will be unlikely to be *parti pris* to a particular solution. Furthermore, outsiders may be able to contribute the benefits of a wide experience gained from many other assignments. Against these advantages lies the fact that outsiders may not fully understand the special circumstances and characteristics of the authority, and so their recommendations may be based to some degree on ignorance of the true facts This ignorance of the true facts may be compounded by the outsiders' enthusiasm for particular techniques or theories or solutions. This is, of course, always a possible risk with the employment of consultants, or academic specialists, who may have a particular approach to management problems which they recommend to many clients. It would be unfair to make too much of this point, since most consultants and academics are experienced people and do their best to avoid the recommendation of glib and unsatisfactory solutions. The fact remains, however, that an outside specialist often has to make a relatively brief analysis of what can sometimes be a complex managerial situation and he may therefore be inclined to produce his stock recommendations.

A fourth way of making this kind of review is to try to devise a procedure which brings the benefits of both outside and inside experience. A reviewing team or committee involving, possibly, the employment of consultants and other outsiders but carefully devised so that the right blend of internal and external skills is available is often the best way of setting about reviewing a public authority or one of its departments. For example, it may be worth setting up a small steering committee of outsiders and insiders which will decide on a programme of work and give this to study teams whose members are also drawn from both within and without the organization. These study teams might make their reports on particular aspects of management to the reviewing committee as a whole, so that the final report can be based on the consideration of these particular contributions and can serve as a full and fair investigation of the organization as a whole.

EXAMPLES OF AUDIT, REVIEW AND CONTROL

We shall now examine five examples of audit, review and control—managerial control systems, the work of the Expenditure Committee of the House of Commons; internal audit in the Civil Service, the pursuit of efficiency in the Department of Health and Social Security, and monitoring the planning process in local government.

Managerial control systems

The managerial approach to audit, review and control can be applied in a variety of ways. The following examples, many drawn from management accounting, show the wide range:

(*a*) controls may be used to standardize performance in order to increase efficiency and to lower costs. Examples of this type of control include time and motion studies, inspections and written procedures;

(*b*) controls can be instituted to safeguard assets from theft, wastage or misuse. Examples here include the division of responsibilities for the custody and use of an asset, separation of operational and accounting activities, and a developed system of authorization and record-keeping;

(*c*) controls may be used to standardize quality to meet the specifications of senior managers. Examples include inspection and statistical quality controls which analyse a sample of work to guage how far general quality is up to standard;

(*d*) a fourth type of control system is designed to set limits within which delegated authority can be exercised without more senior management approval. Examples here include organization charts and manuals of procedure, policy directives and internal audit. All these help to spell out the limits within which subordinates have a free hand, and in this way they constitute a means of control and review;

(*e*) another type of control system is designed to measure performance on the job. Typical examples of such controls are special reports, statistics of output per hour or per member of staff, and budgets or standard costs which set out the amount of resources expected to be used in a process or activity;

(*f*) controls may be used for planning and programming operations. Such controls include production forecasts, budgets of resources and output, various systems of costing and standards of work measurement;

(g) controls may be instituted to help senior officials to keep an authority's programmes and plans in balance. Examples of such controls include general operating plans, perhaps couched in the form of a system of planning, programming and budgeting, as discussed in chapter 3, together with manuals of policies and instructions and such organizational techniques as reviewing committees and the use of outside consultants;

(h) controls may be used to help to motivate members of an authority's staff to contribute their best efforts. These systems of control may be directed either to punishment for errors or, more fruitfully perhaps, to maintaining and encouraging orderly and disciplined performance by the recognition of achievement by such steps as promotion, awards for suggestions, and by the participation of staff in the formation and discussion of policy insofar as this can be done without trespassing on the proper preserves of the politically elected members.

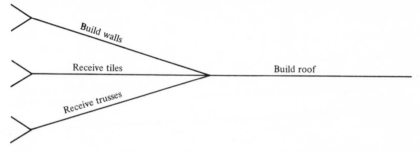

Fig. 7.1

Network analysis is also relevant here, since these methods provide useful means of controlling many types of work. These methods were originally designed to help in the planning and control of civil engineering projects and expensive and complex defence weapon systems such as Polaris submarines. They appear under such names as 'network techniques', 'critical path method', and 'programme evaluation and review technique'. It is not necessary to describe them in detail here. But the principle behind them all is the analysis of a project or piece of work into its component parts and the recording of these details on a network model or diagram which is then used for planning and controlling the interrelated activities in carrying the project to completion. Different versions of these techniques cater for various possibilities, including the analysis of the most optimistic, the most pessimistic and the most likely times of completing each activity; and the relationship between the time taken to complete activities and the costs incurred.

To illustrate the principle by a simple example (see Fig. 7.1) everyone knows that a building cannot be completed until: (a) the walls have been built, and (b) the tiles, and (c) the roof trusses have been delivered to the site. There is a network of activities to be completed, each one dependent upon the completion of one or several others:

Some of these activities take longer than others. Even more important, some *sequences* of activities take longer than other sequences. In fact there is almost certain to be one sequence that determines the completion time of the whole project. It might be the following sequence (Fig. 7.2):

Dig foundations

Lay concrete

Build walls

Build roof

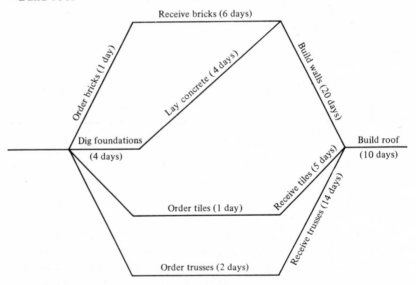

Fig. 7.2

This is known as the critical path because, if the time to complete this sequence could be shortened, the whole project could be completed earlier, while if it took longer, the whole project would be late. All the other activities that do not lie on the critical path can be treated as less urgent—although, of course, if one of them is greatly delayed, this might then lie in the critical path.[7]

This method can be used in a variety of situations. Its advantages include the encouragement it gives managers to make a plan of their activities, because it is impossible to complete such a network without such a plan. Secondly, it encourages planning and control at all levels in the organization, because each member of staff must plan the events for which he is responsible. Thirdly, it concentrates the attention on critical points that may need attention and correction and pinpoints the responsibilities for taking action upon them. Fourthly, by concentrating on the events and processes which are critical to the timely completion of the plan it makes the manager look forward and anticipate problems that may arise.

Network systems do, however, have some drawbacks. They are of little use where a programme is so nebulous that no reasonable schedule of times and events can be prepared, and they are not much use for routine activities which are well understood and where a repetitive sequence of events makes detailed scheduling unnecessary. Finally, the network can be very complicated if many events are involved and in some instances it may be necessary to put the network on a computer. In these and other complex cases the cost of the control system in time, staff and money has to be weighed against the results it produces.

Network analysis in its various forms is therefore not a panacea. Its employment does not guarantee that work is properly controlled and reviewed, but is a useful framework for such activities in many cases.

The Expenditure Committee's report on the Civil Service (1977)

In 1977 the General Sub-Committee of the Expenditure Committee published a report on the Civil Service.[8] The report described a number of areas where the progress made in implementing the Fulton Committee's recommendations had been less than the Committee considered desirable. Some of them have been noted in earlier chapters. But other important points were made.

For example, the Committee endorsed the Fulton Committee's recommendation for the introduction of accountable units whereby the organization of executive work is arranged in separate commands whose managers have clear cut responsibilities and commensurate authority and are held accountable for programmes, budgets and standards of achievement. The Committee said that too few of these units have been introduced in government departments. They suggested two reasons for this. The first is a liking for the status quo and unwillingness to accept change on the part of the Civil Service. The second is the result of the system of parallel hierarchies, whereby responsibilities are often divided between hierarchies of staff responsible for separate aspects of the work, e.g. technical, financial and contractual. The Committee said that this system makes it difficult to set up accountable units. The Committee recommended 'a determined drive to introduce accountable units in all areas of executive work and, where possible, in administrative work' i.e. policy work.[9] The Committee recognized that accountable units must be quite small if they are to be headed by individual officers and work effectively. They recommended that accountable units in government should be scaled down accordingly.

The Committee also noted modifications in the doctrine of ministerial responsibility. Sir John Hunt, the Secretary of the Cabinet, pointed out in his evidence that, in the complex circumstances of modern government, it is unreasonable for ministers to resign if a mistake is made in their departments on subjects of which they knew nothing. 'The concept that because somebody whom the Minister has never heard of, has made a mistake, means that the Minister should resign, is out of date, and rightly so. I think, equally, that a Minister has got a responsibility which he cannot devolve to his permanent secretary, for the efficiency and drive of his department.'[10] The Committee say that it would be right for heads of accountable units to be publicly responsible for their work and publicly accountable for it to such bodies as the Select Committees of the House of Commons.

The Committee also said that if a system of publicly accountable units is to work, then it is necessary to provide adequate information about those parts of the organization to which costs can be precisely allocated and benefits of the work quantified. They said that cost and management accounting is satisfactorily carried out in some departments but not in all. They believed that improvements were necessary to provide the basic information for accountable management to become a reality. The Committee recommended that the accounts presented to Parliament should be related to the work of the accountable units as a means of reinforcing the public and financial accountability of their heads and facilitating Parliamentary control. They recognized, however, that a complete reconstruction of the government accounting system to bring this about would be a major and costly exercise. The Committee also said that Parliamentary scrutiny would be much improved if Parliament were given information which showed the objectives of individual spending programmes and the results of past programmes, and that the Treasury should undertake research into the possibility of introducing such analyses in consultation with the General Sub-Committee of the Expenditure Committee.

The Committee also made recommendations about monitoring efficiency. They recognized that cost comparisons between the public and private sector can be misleading, but they thought that they should be normal practice in whatever areas of the Civil Service they are feasible. They also said that management services should be placed on the same basis as staff inspection of the Civil Service, i.e. that their entry to a particular organization should be compulsory. The Committee accepted, however, that the recommendations of management services units should not be compulsory, and that it should still be for line management to determine the action to be taken upon them.

Finally, there were some general points. The Committee noted that their investigation of the Civil Service was the first that had been undertaken by a select committee of the House of Commons for 104 years, and they recommended that in future the Civil Service should be regularly reviewed by appropriate committees of the House of Commons. Secondly, they recommended that more information about the workings of Government should be disclosed to the House of Commons and to the public at large.

Thirdly, as well as providing a progress report on the Fulton recommendations, the Committee had some new ideas to put forward; for example, they recommended that there should be regular surveys of the possibilities of reducing costs through policy changes. They pointed out that, in such fields as taxation, policy changes can easily build up over time and lead to complicated administrative systems that require many staff to operate. They said that the Inland Revenue was able to suggest policy changes that would save 4500 staff by such means as simplifying the rules relating to building society mortgage interest relief and life assurance relief. They recognized that such changes would be policy decisions that would have to be taken by Ministers. But they said that Parliament should be regularly informed of potential savings that might come from policy changes in order that there might be informed debate and criticism of such measures.

There are interesting parallels here with the 1976 report of the Supplementary Benefits Commission which recommended raising the level of a number of basic allowances and reducing the number of discretionary allowances so as to simplify the process of determining applicants' entitlements.[11] Such changes would, of course, make the allowances somewhat blunter instruments, less finely tuned to individual need. Yet they would save staff, reduce complexity and remove the scope for different treatment of different individuals.

The Committee's report is a good example of the way in which such general investigations can pursue a number of themes. In addition to their concern with efficiency in the Civil Service, it is clear from many of their recommendations that the Committee were also concerned with greater parliamentary control of executive government. In short, they wanted to increase the powers of the House of Commons to be informed about and question the formulation and implementation of policy. This implies a changing balance in the constitution, diminishing the powers of ministers and increasing those of Parliament. Ideas for improving managerial efficiency may therefore have political and constitutional implications. There is no sharp dividing line between politics and administration.

This is clear from the Government's response to the Select Committee's report. Although 31 out of the 54 recommendations were accepted,

The Prime Minister has ruled out any reorganization of central government in the near future. A White Paper, published . . . in reply to a report on the Civil Service from the Commons Select Committee on Expenditure, leaves as they are the size and scope of the Treasury and the Civil Service Department and their respective responsibilities for public spending and manpower. In a document more notable for the changes it rules out than the reforms it proposes, . . . the Cabinet decided to delay a decision on the relationship between government and select committees until the Select Committee on Procedure has reported. But its reservations about a suggestion that select committees should be reorganized, with adequate specialist staff, to monitor the work of individual departments and to consider appropriations in detail are clear from the White Paper's comment that those 'recommendations would involve a fundamental change in our parliamentary system and in the relationship between the Executive and Parliament'.... The White Paper rejects any change in constitutional practice 'which would detract from the principle that the advice tendered to ministers by civil servants should be confidential and objective, or require civil servants rather than ministers, to defend Government policies before parliamentary committees'.[12]

The Government also said that, while they support the Committee's emphasis on accountability and efficiency, they do not believe that accountable units can be introduced as widely as the Committee suggest because the objectives of Government departments are 'complex and interrelated in a way and to an extent which limit the number of tasks to which this approach can be successfully applied'. Finally, the Government said that policy is regularly reviewed. They 'do not believe that there would be much advantage in undertaking a series of regular special surveys (as suggested by the Committee).... There is, however, advantage in reviewing particular areas from time to time'. The issues raised by the Select Committee and the Government's observations upon them are at the heart of modern British government. They are likely to be the subject of continuing debate.

Internal audit

An important aspect of audit, control and review is the oversight of the control arrangements themselves. In 1973 the Civil Service Department published a manual about internal audit within the Civil Service.[13] Following the formula proposed by the Institute of Internal Audit, the Civil Service Department defined it as 'a managerial control which functions by measuring and evaluating the effectiveness of other controls'.

The manual listed four principal functions of internal audit. First, verifying for management that there is an adequate system of internal control within the organization. This verification entails checking that the system is functioning properly, that it is not excessive to requirements and that the accounting records form a reliable basis for the production of the Appropriation White Paper and other accounts including, where appropriate, management and trading accounts. Secondly, internal audit should draw the attention of management to deficiencies in the organization or system of control, instances of duplicated functions, excessive checking, wastage and other inefficiencies, suggesting appropriate remedies and checking later to ensure that the corrective action has been taken. Thirdly, an internal audit should be associated with the development of control systems but it should not be responsible for them. There will normally be a separate source of advice on accounting and information systems. Finally, internal audit may carry out special reviews or assignments on subjects which seem to the internal auditors as worthy of further investigations, or where the management asks for a review to be undertaken. It is part of the duty of internal audit to examine particular areas where their other work and experience lead to the conclusion that additional audit resources are justified. Where general management takes the initiative care is normally taken to establish whether audit skills are essential and to ensure that auditors are not deployed on organization and methods work. Investigations may be mounted because controls have broken down, or simply because an area is due for a more rigorous study in accordance with the audit section's plan. These four broad functions of internal audit apply in principle to both clerical and computer systems, but the extent to which audit can consider individual elements, such as computer efficiency, will depend upon the expertise available. On computerised systems it is vital that internal audit should be closely concerned with the development of new or existing application.

It is important that internal audit and examination should remain distinct from the continuing control system, and that the special reviews undertaken should not impair the auditor's independence. A specimen questionnaire from the booklet is set out at Appendix 8 as an example of the work of the internal auditor.

The pursuit of efficiency in the Department of Health and Social Security

In their evidence to the Expenditure Committee, the Department of Health and Social Security described their arrangements for assessing the efficiency of their system for paying social security benefits through some 600 local offices and some 350 'caller' offices which provide points of contact for the public to the Department.[14] These local offices, with 10 regional offices and central offices for Scotland and Wales, employ 56,000 staff.

It might in theory be possible for the Department to compare their own costs with other organizations at home or abroad. There is, however, no other organization in the United Kingdom which is engaged in the same task, and foreign social security systems are so different that cost comparisons are not helpful. Alternatively, it might be possible to compare the ratios of administrative to benefit expenditures. If, for example, the Department found that the cost of administering a benefit as calculated in this way was rising from year to year this might be *prima facie* evidence of falling efficiency. The snag here is that the rules relating to benefits change frequently, and usually make the work more complicated. This means that administrative costs are bound to rise and any figure of the relationship between administrative and benefit expenditures will be a misleading guide to the efficiency of the local offices' operation.

The Department therefore seeks to measure efficiency in several other ways. First, it has a staff complementing system, which is designed to match staff resources as closely as possible with the work to be done. Secondly, management information systems provide regular monthly data of manpower utilization, the rate of clearance of work and the accuracy of benefit payments. Thirdly, surveys and detailed inspections of specific areas of work are carried out by staff from regional offices and by the Supplementary Benefits Commission's inspectorate. This is a small cadre of experts, who are able to undertake detailed examination of specific aspects of supplementary benefit work in order to guage the standard of its execution and the effectiveness of policy for supplementary benefits in practice. The local office work is also examined by audit teams independent of the line management. In addition, the Department also has annual performance reviews, whereby local managers discuss with their superiors their office's performance, identify problems and make plans for improvement next year. And senior staff pay frequent visits to local offices.

The Department also has a responsibility for measuring the efficiency of the National Health Service. Ideally, the department would like to be able to measure the contribution of the Health Service to the wellbeing of the community as a whole. This would require a complex cost-benefit analysis. As we have seen in chapter 4, however, such analyses run into the difficulty of measuring the direct and indirect social benefits of a general public service like health care. In the absence of such general assessments, the Department seeks to test the efficiency of the National Health Service by analysing particular activities. It measures performance where it can, and uses subjective assessments based on experience in other cases.

The Department accordingly uses six main tools to monitor the performance of the National Health Service, and to advise upon its improvement. They are as follows: accounting and auditing procedures, to draw attention to anomalies in the use of financial resources and variations in cost over time or between areas and regions; research, to throw light upon the relative effectiveness of different treatments; management services techniques, to identify improvements in management and administration; the professional judgement of specialists, to improve particular procedures and methods in the medical and health disciplines; statistical and economic analysis, to bring out significant trends and comparisons, adjusted where necessary for underlying variations; and the centralization of services, where economies of scale can be proved and where standard procedures can be demonstrated to be cost-effective.

As an example of this kind of work, comparisons of performance and cost information are regularly undertaken as follows:

(a) in hospitals: medical staff costs per case, and the costs of laundering per unit weight;
(b) in community services: the cost of health visiting per case, and the cost of immunization per thousand population;

(c) in regional services: the cost of the blood transfusion service and of the ambulance services per thousand population; and

(d) in primary care: the cost of general medical services per thousand population.

As examples of measuring technical efficiency the Department cite their system of measuring engineering maintenance standards against costs in order to improve the operation of launderies and boiler houses. They also mention their centralized services and standard procedures for the Health Service. Under these arrangements they place central contracts for nearly 25 per cent of the Health Service's expenditure on goods and services.

The Department also have a series of statistical indicators of efficiency, including the following:

(a) the cost per in-patient week, classified by seven types of hospital;

(b) the cost per in-patient case, classified by five types of hospital;

(c) the cost per in-patient attendance, classified by four types of hospital;

(d) the estimated average length of in-patient stay, classified by groups of medical specialities;

(e) the number of cases treated per available bed, classified by groups of specialities;

(f) the percentage of available beds occupied, classified by groups of specialities.

The Department point out that all comparisons of cost derived from such indicators have their pitfalls. It is necessary to set both inputs and populations in standard terms before significant relationships can be established. It is also necessary to take regional price variations into account, as well as changes in prices over time. Again, variations over time can result from improvements in the quality of health care derived, for example, from developments in surgical and medical treatment and techniques. For all these reasons, the conclusions based on statistical indicators need careful probing and analysis before action can reliably be taken on their basis. But the Department say that any substantial deviations from national averages are always a signal for enquiry. The reasons for them are investigated and, where necessary, improvements are made.

Monitoring and the planning process in local government

In 1965 the Secretary of State for the Environment invited local authorities bearing planning responsibilities for areas and regions to co-operate together and, in 1968, the counties of Nottinghamshire and Derbyshire and the urban authorities for Derby and Nottingham decided to produce a sub-regional planning study for the greater part of their four areas. This study was published in 1970. It set out a strategy for the region's social and economic development. The object of the strategy was to provide guide-lines for the local authorities who shared planning responsibilities. These guidelines would help them to take co-ordinated decisions, so that the region would develop in a planned and co-ordinated rather than a haphazard way. The strategy had 22 objectives and 12 main proposals. Examples of the objectives were as follows:

(a) to provide ample, attractive and substantial industrial sites conveniently located for the supplies of labour;

(b) to promote policies which have the effect of encouraging the growth of firms;

(c) to improve the appearance of the sub-region;

(d) to promote policies likely to encourage the conservation, improvement, or renewal as appropriate of the existing urban environment;

(e) to conserve good agricultural land and encourage full utilization of its potential.

Among the main strategy proposals were the following:

(a) to develop a substantial urban growth zone extending from Mansfield to Alfreton, with a population of over a quarter of a million by 1986 and perhaps 350,000 by the end of the century;

(b) to expand Nottingham's functions as a regional capital and office centre, and to guide its growth in a north-westerly direction. This would mean encouraging the movement of some industrial and other activities from the city to the Mansfield/Alfreton growth zone;

(c) to expand Derby's functions as a major centre of industrial technology and services, and to seek its development to the south and west.

The strategy recognized that long-term forecasts of population and employment cannot be made with certainty. The strategy therefore avoided postulating steady progress towards particular targets of growth and employment. Instead the strategy was conceived as the first stage in a developing body of objectives and proposals for the guidance of local authorities over a period of time. It was therefore necessary to keep the development of the strategy under careful review, not only to see how far it progressed but also to consider when its particular objectives needed revision and adjustment.

The four local authorities responsible for the sub-region accordingly set up a sub-regional management committee containing 16 members, four from each of the authorities. A monitoring and advisory unit was set up to report to this committee.[15] Its formal terms of reference were 'to see whether or not the adopted policies (of the strategy) are being followed'.

An important part of the work turned out to be the assessment of the implications of the likely decisions of the four member authorities for the strategy as a whole. Compromise and adjustment were necessary, and the advisory unit sought to promote this by studying such implications;

considering, where necessary, alternative possibilities more in accord with the general strategy; and drawing attention to them before irrevocable decisions had been taken by member authorities. Good communications and trust between the advisory unit and the four member authorities were vital.

The monitoring and advisory process employed by the unit is illustrated in Fig. 7.3.

Effective monitoring requires the measurement of progress. A number of performance indicators were accordingly devised. They were grouped into four categories:

(a) long-term forecasts of such factors as population growth, changes in employment and housebuilding requirements. These forecasts naturally needed revision during the development and application of the strategy;

(b) short-term forecasts of house building and changes in employment for each zone of the sub-region for each year in the period 1968 to 1975;

(c) 'strategic balances', by which the team meant crucial factors upon which the success of the strategy as a whole depended. These included the development of major retail centres in six major towns; the achievement and maintenance of high quality building standards; and the growth of employment in certain key zones;

(c) indices of such factors as unemployment and vagrancy for each of the employment office areas within the sub-region.

Using this monitoring process, and the performance indicators, the advisory unit was able to make a useful contribution to the strategy's development. For example, the unit was able to comment on proposals for a major out-of-town shopping centre and point out the importance of assessing the impact of the proposal on existing shopping centres and the plans for their development within the regional strategy. In the light of this analysis, planning permission for the proposal was refused. The unit was also asked to comment upon three possible sites for the construction of new houses for Nottingham. The unit was able to compare each one with the relevant elements of the strategy and advise Nottingham upon the most appropriate site.

The members of the monitoring and advisory unit do not claim that their work has been a complete success. They point out that a strategy for a large area is inevitably diffuse, vague and subject to change. Indeed, they see themselves as one of the major contributors to this change by their recommendations for the reassessment of the regional strategy in the light of changing events. They also recognize the difficult position of the unit in that it had to put forward suggestions and recommendations to four separate authorities. It is inevitable that these authorities will be conscious of their particular responsibilities to their own areas, and may not always give first priority to the requirements of the region as a whole.

Nevertheless, the monitoring and advisory unit has been useful. Public

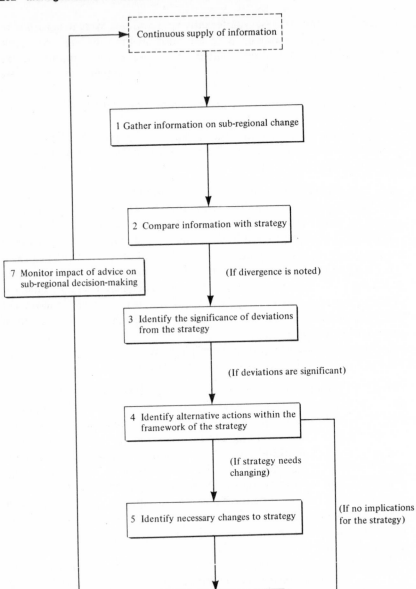

Fig. 7.3

administration will increasingly involve co-operation between a number of authorities, and better methods must be devised to ensure the co-operation between the constituent authorities and the monitoring of their joint endeavours. This monitoring and advisory unit has made a significant contribution to this difficult problem.

CONTROLS AND DEMOCRACY

The audit, review and control of government work is essential to the effective working of a democracy. It is only by viewing our past performance that we can start to obtain any reasonable guide to what our future activities ought to be. But the examination of past performance can easily become distorted. There are two main reasons for this.

First, the factors that can most easily be controlled and reviewed are those which are most easily measured. In spite of all the warnings about the need to design control systems which give the manager an insight into the achievement of his goals and purposes, it still remains the case that it is easier, for example, to calculate how many slum houses have been cleared and how many high-rise flats have been erected than it is to say whether the quality of life of the previous slum-dwellers has in fact been improved.

In their natural concern for the unhappy plight of slum-dwellers in our large cities, many local authorities took as their objective the destruction of old properties and the construction of new homes. These were often provided in high-rise flats, partly to reduce the amount of land needed to re-house a given number but also because of current architectural fashion. These policies have generated the skyline of so many of our large cities today. And a programme of re-housing in this form lends itself to simple measures of control and review, since it is easy to set targets of houses or flats to be built at standard prices and costs and to check up whether this has been done. Yet the very specificity of these measures of control and review tends to drive out the necessary attention to the question of whether these programmes do, in fact, improve the quality of the erstwhile slum-dwellers' lives.

In fact, many would argue today that some elements of quality and richness in the slum-dwellers' lives has been lost by breaking up their communities, and by requiring people to live on what might be described as the vertical rather than the horizontal plane, thus diminishing their opportunities for meeting and helping each other. We therefore need systems of control and review that pay full attention to these less tangible factors, and help us to anticipate the problems that may lie in apparently obvious solutions.

The second reason why control and review presents particular difficulties in government derives from the fact that political life is more concerned with the future than with the past. Politicians inevitably wish to concentrate upon the changes they themselves hope to plan and make during their period of office. Some attention and a good deal of publicity may be devoted to the alleged inadequacies of their predecessors. But more detailed attention is paid to the present administration's own policies. This is not to deny that attention is rightly paid to the glaring examples of misconception and mismanagement that lead to cancelled projects, public enquiries and court prosecutions. But insufficient attention is paid to the reasons for these failures and to the lessons that can be learned from them for the future. Insufficient attention is also paid to the reasons for our successful performances.

We need to devote more attention to analysing past performance to get a better understanding, for example, of how to carry out different systems of education and public health, to know the time and cost performances of our successful as well as our unsuccessful civil engineering projects and to analyse those of our defence projects which have not been cancelled as well as those that have. We need to know the reasons for comparative failure and success, to know snags and drawbacks and so to build up inventories of the reasons for good and bad practice and performance in various fields, and to make this information widely available within the relevant authorities in central and local government as the basis of planning for the future.

Management control systems of the kind we have discussed in this chapter can provide this kind of information and should be developed further. Control systems based on the other approaches we have studied in this chapter are also necessary and need further development. They do not provide comprehensive systems of audit review and control. But they serve other purposes, such as the protection of the individual, the prevention of fraud and the widening of public debate.

CONCLUSIONS AND SUMMARY

(1) Several approaches to the audit, control and review of government activities can be distinguished and this chapter has noted the political, legal, procedural, organizational, responsive and managerial.

(2) The first five of these approaches have a valuable contribution to make to the working of democracy and to the information and protection of the individual citizen. But none of them provides a comprehensive system of auditing, reviewing and controlling the work of central government departments and local authorities.

(3) The managerial approach seeks to provide this by concentrating upon the full range of managerial functions. It seeks to assess how far the objectives of an organization are being achieved, to determine the reasons for any shortcomings, and to propose appropriate and timely remedies.

(4) Comprehensive systems of audit, review and control based on the managerial approach should be further developed. The analysis of past performance has a useful contribution to make to the generation of future policy and the quality of its administration.

8
Conclusions

The purpose of this book has been to assess the contribution of management theory and practice to central and local government over the last 10 to 15 years. This chapter draws some general lessons from this experience, and makes suggestions for the future.

GENERAL LESSONS

The study of management has mainly been conducted on the basis that, by the analysis of past experience, it should be possible to determine models, theories and hypotheses about the way organizations work now, and how they can be made to work better in the future. These ideas should then be tested in practice. If they are successful, they can take their place within the developing body of management principles. In this way, the study and practice of management should serve to promote organizational health, in much the same way as the study of medicine is designed to promote bodily health.

This is an attractive prospectus. But experience over the years has revealed difficulties. It is often hard to set out the theories in a sufficiently precise form to test them. For example, statements like 'organizational arrangements should accord with the objectives sought' may sound reasonable. But they are ultimately incoherent. There can also be difficulties in deciding what is to count as a valid test, and what should be done if a theory fails its test. Should it be abandoned? Or should an attempt be made to amend it, and resubmit it to testing? Finally, even when experience seems to confirm a theory, there is still a judgement to be made about the areas of its application. Circumstances vary greatly. It is hard to decide whether theories which seem applicable in some areas, are also applicable in others which are generally similar but differ in some respects.

These problems are common to the social sciences. But if they could be overcome, difficulties would still remain for the study and practice of management. Organizations are not amenable to manipulation from outside in the way that is implied by this approach. They consist of people with a multiplicity of intentions and purposes. Ideas for change will be mediated in their application and effect by the necessity of applying them through the very people who will be affected by them.

Students of management may reply 'of course proposals for change must be explained and accepted'. But explanation and acceptance is not enough. The application of management ideas is possible only through the agency of the individuals concerned. The results will inevitably be a function of many factors. Understanding and acceptance of the theory will be two of them. But others will include the relationships between the members of the organization, their values, attitudes, past experience, appreciation of their present tasks, and their perception of the social, economic and political environment within which the organization is operating.

This is not to say that people will 'sabotage' proposed improvements, though this can happen. It is to affirm that changing the way people behave in their daily work is infinitely more complex than some originators of management ideas have suggested. Experience over the last 10 to 15 years has borne this out. Many of the examples quoted in this book are for ideas for management change that have turned out differently in practice from what their originators hoped to see. It has therefore become clear that the successful study and practice of management is less the generation and application of rules and principles and more the development and exchange of insights and ideas. Management theory does not put a minister or councillor or official in a position to say 'I must apply this principle and that rule'. It only allows him to say 'I now see things differently, and will try to act thus'.

This may sound a small dividend for all the books that have been written, the experiments made and the courses attended over the last 10 to 15 years. Yet it may still be worth having. For example, the great deal of attention paid to 'management by objectives' over the last decade may not have produced many long lasting schemes. And the exaggerated expectations that attended its translation from the private sector to many public authorities may have been counterproductive. Yet 'management by objectives' has encouraged many public servants to give greater thought and attention to the goals, purposes and objectives of their organizations, departments, branches and sections. This has been salutary, and has promoted self criticism and useful change.

The difficulty of translating management ideas into organizational practice also bears upon another point. Some of the original enthusiasm for managerial change was based upon the belief that if the right governmental organizations were devised, if they were staffed by the right kind of people, and if they employed the right techniques, then many of the social, political and economic problems that have dogged the United Kingdom since the end of the second world war would disappear and we should 'get

Britain moving again'. Certainly this idea—implicitly if not explicitly—was behind a great deal of the enthusiasm for many of the developments that have been studied in this book, including the introduction of 'giant departments', planning units, the recruitment of outside experts and special advisers, the institution of the Central Policy Review Staff, programme analysis and review techniques, output budgeting, cost-benefit analysis, corporate planning in local government, PPBS systems in central departments and local authorities, and many other innovations.

These innovations may produce some useful results. In particular, in this context, they may enable politicians and their advisers to see the choices before them more clearly. But management change is no substitute for political choice. We cannot 'get Britain moving' simply by reorganizing the Civil Service; we cannot find the public interest in the pluses and minuses of a cost benefit analysis; we cannot set out a list of objectives for 'Great Britain Limited'.

Governments can only survive by infringing many of the precepts of old-fashioned management thinking. They must entertain a variety of objectives and goals which cannot all be fully pursued without contradiction. They must rest upon shifting alliances and agreements with disparate groups. They must conciliate, explain and hedge. They must often rest content with coalition and not attempt consensus. Their task has become increasingly difficult with the rising number of pressure groups to be consulted about policies and their administration, and the increasing interest in popular consultation and participation. We may sometimes despair at the apparent muddle, confusion, delay and waste. The study and practice of management may be able to make a modest, but still useful contribution to their reduction. But it cannot remove them, without removing democracy itself. If political life proceeded upon the model of corporate management there would be less opportunity for participation, revision, second thoughts, the reaction to events and the accommodation of interests. But there would also be less liberty.

MANAGEMENT IN THE FUTURE

Experience has therefore shown that, whatever improvements may be secured by good management, policies at both central and local levels will still be difficult to select, subject to change and hard to implement. Good management cannot eliminate the need for political argument, dissension and discussion. Yet there is still a useful contribution for the study and practice of management to make in the following ways:

(*a*) There will be less need over the next decade for new general schemes of management thinking, akin to the scheme of planning, action and review that was explained in chapter 2 as informing the general approach to management over the last 10 to 15 years. There will also be less need for new general techniques like management by objectives and cost-benefit analysis. There will instead be a need for more detailed analysis of what people actually have to do in organizations so that, by greater self awareness and perception of the situation in which they are working, they will be able, hopefully, to make a more informed and effective contribution to getting work done. For example, we need to know more about the conditions for the successful conduct of negotiations, and how decisions can best be taken in conditions of extreme doubt and ambiguity, and when pressed for time.

(b) The greatest practical dividends are likely to continue to come from the application of the simplest and most straightforward techniques of organization and methods, personnel management and operational research, and from their progressive refinement and development. They may lack fashionable appeal; but they maintain their capacity to produce small scale but useful improvements in such fields as the design of forms, the handling of paper work and the revision of office duties.

(c) Useful dividends should also come from the further development and application of computers to administrative work. Distributed processing with microprocessors together with further communications development is likely to have important effects over the next decade. It will enable the data processing arrangements to fit into the natural organization of the job rather than vice versa. But there will also be new problems of training, organization and control.

(d) Experts in management services will therefore have a continuing role. But they will have to conduct their operations with increasing skill and perception. There will be fewer cases where they can successfully proceed by modelling themselves upon the surgeon, removing unnecessary growths and straightening twisted limbs. There will be more cases where their model should be the physician, discussing with the patient his style of life, habits and practices and thereby promoting a desire for self-discipline and the knowledge to effect it.

(e) There are several interconnected problems of management of particular significance to the public services that need further study:

(i) Relations between elected members and officials.

The relationship between ministers and civil servants on the one hand, and councillors and local government officers on the other is crucial to the success of public administration. The increasing complexity of government work requires that they should work closely together; old fashioned distinctions between policy making by politicians and execution by officials are outmoded. Yet their close co-operation does not mean identity of role. The connections between elected representatives and the public is now closer than it was in the past; the increasing time MPs, including ministers, spend in their constituency surgeries bears witness to this. There is consequently a need for a more detailed analysis and understanding of the various ways elected members of public authorities can work fruitfully with officials, and the potential snags and difficulties that might be avoided with greater understanding.

(ii) The tendency to complexity.

All organizations tend to become more complex over time. Rules proliferate, instructions pile upon each other, increasing amounts of time and energy become devoted to co-ordination and passing information between the members of the organization. In the private sector, market pressures can sometimes be relied upon to halt such growth dramatically. This sometimes happens in public administration too—organizations become so top heavy that they are abolished or cut down to scale. But such bloodletting is inherently wasteful. It is far better to be able to control the growth of such complexity by continuing attention to the signs of its early growth. The theory and practice of management can help here, by its emphasis upon the clarity of objectives and clear lines of command and.control—one instance where the stark oversimplifications of some aspects of contemporary management thinking can be helpful, as an antidote to excessive complexity. But further attention needs to be paid to methods of keeping complexity in check, especially bearing in mind that detailed and *ad hoc* attacks upon the problem through, for example, the separate examination of specific parts of an organization can produce separate solutions which complicate the working of the organization as a whole.

(iii) Over-centralization.

Another tendency in public administration is to try to produce detailed plans taking all possible relevant factors into account while, at the same time, seeking greater public participation in such planning and its administration. The difficulties inherent in this endeavour are further complicated by the tendency to change the objectives being sought and the rules by which such planning is to be undertaken before the process is complete. For example, vast amounts of time and energy have been devoted since the end of the Second World War at central and local level to producing plans for urban and regional development which have never been fully put into effect. Their preparation has often delayed the taking of decisions and the subsequent work on the ground, or caused the wasteful changing of horses in mid-stream with consequential extra delays and further costs as plans are altered before the completion of work. Students of management might usefully analyse such activities and processes, so as to warn ministers, councillors and officials of the difficulties and costs implicit in over centralized planning, and the limited extent to which experience shows that central standards can be combined with local initiative and variation.

(iv) Relations between separate organizations in the same area of activity.

We need a greater understanding of the way in which central government departments can work more effectively with local authorites, with nationalized industries and with the private sector. We also need a greater understanding of how various levels of activity conducted by different organizations, can be fruitfully combined. The different levels of activity conducted by the variety of organizations within the health and welfare services constitutes an example. At the present time, all these relationships are in principle governed by legal rules and administrative arrangements and instructions. Yet in practice they must always depend upon a network of concordats, working practices, customs and conventions. During the last 10 to 15 years there has been a great deal of change in public administration, as departments and local authorities have been reorganized and given new tasks. New relationships have followed quickly upon the heels of their predecessors. Close working arrangements have been sundered to be replaced by new formal rules. Confusion has arisen as officials are not quite sure how to approach their erstwhile colleagues—as 'members of the family'; as competitors; as 'foreign powers in treaty relationships'—and how much information to give them. There is consequently a need for greater understanding about how to conduct relations between different public organizations for the common benefit of all their clients.

(v) Audit, review and control.

Improved arrangements are necessary for the audit, review and control of the work of public authorities. As explained in the previous chapter, we need a clearer understanding of the purposes served by the various forms of political, legal, procedural, organizational, responsive and managerial audit, review and control. Students of management might usefully address themselves to this task of analysis and classification, and to suggesting ways in which different methods can be fruitfully combined for different types of work and different organizations.

(vi) Personnel management.

Finally, and perhaps most importantly, there is a need for continuing attention by students and practitioners of management to questions of personnel management in the public service. Attention must obviously be paid to pay, pensions, grading structures, recruitment, training, conditions of employment and similar matters. But above all attention must be paid to communications. It is through good communications that the enthusiasm and talent that is latent in every member of the public service can be evoked for their own benefit, and for action for the welfare of the people as a whole.

The study of management and the application of its ideas have made a useful contribution to the work of central and local government over the last 10 to 15 years. As this book has shown, however, many of the ideas have not developed as their originators imagined. There have been exaggerated claims; often, of course, the only way in which their originators could secure any attention at all. There have been false hopes, hurried applications, and failed schemes. There has also been valuable progress and, as the foregoing paragraphs have shown, there is much work to be done in the future, although a good deal of it could with advantage be devoted to new subjects and employ new methods and approaches.

The study of management cannot hope to promote a dramatic revolution in the conduct of public business. But it can encourage greater self-consciousness and understanding of others' viewpoints and consequently facilitate the development and application of human capacities within public administration. In short, it can help the public servant to follow the maxim 'know thyself'.

CONCLUSIONS AND SUMMARY

(1) Experience has shown that management theory cannot be applied directly to the analysis and improvement of organizations. Its effectiveness depends upon the extent and manner in which it is incorporated in the intentions and purposes of the individual members of organizations and their subsequent actions. Experience has also shown that political problems and choices cannot be painlessly resolved by the reorganization of the machinery of public administration and the application of management techniques.

(2) In particular, experience has shown that attempts to apply management theories and techniques do not always work out as intended and that the hopes expressed for them may be disappointed. It has also shown that theories based on experience outside government may be inappropriate to the management problems faced within central and local government, and that the way ahead in the public service is more likely to be by way of dialogue and discussion about possible improvements than by the rigid application of outside solutions.

(3) Nevertheless, the study and practice of management has produced some useful dividends for central and local government. There is a need for further work in the future on the following lines:

(*a*) less attention to general theories and techniques and more analysis and understanding of such day-to-day work as negotiating and taking decisions in conditions of ambiguity and when pressed for time;

(*b*) continued attention to simple and straightforward management ideas and techniques that effect modest but useful improvements in such activities as office procedures and the control of stocks;

(*c*) care and perception in the way that management experts carry out their assignments, so that their clients accept and believe in the improvements that are finally adopted;

(*d*) special attention to the following problems of particular importance to the public services:

(i) relations between ministers and civil servants on the one hand and councillors and local government officers on the other;

(ii) the tendency to complexity;

    (iii) over-centralization;

    (iv) relations between organizations operating in the same area of activity;

    (v) arrangements for audit, review and control;

    (vi) personnel management.

(4) The study of management cannot hope to promote a dramatic revolution in the conduct of public business. But it can promote a useful spirit of self questioning and a wider appreciation of factors relevant to the work in hand. In this way it can promote efficiency in public administration.

Notes to chapters

NOTES TO CHAPTER 2

1 *The Civil Service, Vol. 1: Report of the Committee 1966-1968.* Cmnd. 3638 p. 104, HMSO (1968).
2 There were in total nearly 1500 classes altogether, ranging in size from the clerical class containing over 190,000 members to some classes consisting of a very few such as organists at the Royal Hospital, Chelsea, which contained a single member.
3 Cmnd. 3638, Vol. 1, p. 104.
4 Cmnd. 3638, Vol. 1, pp. 104-105.
5-6 *Op. cit.* p. 105.
7 *The Reorganization of Central Government.* Cmnd. 4506 p. 4, HMSO (1970).
8 *Op. cit.* p. 5.
9 *Op. cit.* p. 5.
10 *Op. cit.* p. 5.
11 *Op. cit.* p. 5.
12 *Op. cit.* p. 14.
13 Cmnd. 3638, Vol. II, p. 18.
14 *The New Local Authorities: Management and Structure* p. XV, HMSO (1972).
15 *Op. cit.* p. 32.
16 *Op. cit.* p. XV.
17 *Op. cit.* p. 164.
18 *Op. cit.* p. 61.
19 *The New Scottish Local Authorities: Organization and Management Structure* p. 157 HMSO (1973).

NOTES TO CHAPTER 3

1 *The Control of Public Expenditure.* Cmnd. 1432, HMSO (1961).

2 *Output Budgeting for the Department of Education and Science,* para. 9, HMSO (1970).
3 *Op. cit.* paras. 10 and 11.
4 J. G. Bagley: 'Planning Programming Budgeting in DES,' *O and M Bulletin,* May 1972.
5 *Op. cit.* p. 80.
6 Sir William Pile:'Corporate Planning for Education in the Department of Education and Science,' *Public Administration,* Spring 1974.
7 The account of this document is based on the version published in *The Times Higher Education Supplement* 9 May 1975.
8 Lord Crowther-Hunt published three articles on planning in the Department of Education and Science in *The Times Higher Education Supplement* on 7, 14 and 21 May 1976.
9 *Tenth Report from the Select Committee on Expenditure* 1975-1976 session.
10 The tables are adapted from the *Statement on Defence Estimates 1978* Cmnd. 7099, HMSO (1978).
11 Mr J. J. B. (now Sir John) Hunt giving evidence to the Steering Sub-Committee of the Select Committee of the House of Commons on Expenditure on 27 January 1972.
12 *The Reorganization of Central Government.* Cmnd. 4506, p. 13, HMSO (1970).
13 Mr Edward Heath, giving evidence to the general sub-committee of the Select Committee of the House of Commons on Expenditure on 21 February 1977. Reported in *The Times* 22 February 1977.
14 The quotations are taken from an article *Turning Parliamentary Spotlight on Government's Special Advisers* by Peter Hennessy in *The Times* 26 January 1976.
15 *Government Observations on the Eleventh Report from the Expenditure Committee, Session 1976-77, HC 535,* p. 23, Cmnd. 7117, HMSO (1978).
16 The figures for 1967 come from *The Civil Service, Vol.4, Report of the Committee 1966-1968* (Fulton Committee). Cmnd. 3638, HMSO (1968), p. 185 and p. 189. The figures for 1976 come from *Civil Service Statistics,* p. 21, HMSO (1977).
17 The details of the output budgeting systems for Liverpool, Coventry and Gloucestershire are given in *Management in the Education Service by the Society of Education Officers.* Routledge and Kegan Paul (1975).
18 *Op. cit.* p.13.
19 *Op. cit.* p.15.
20 *Op. cit.* p.17.
21 See R. Butt: 'PPBS in British Local Government', in *Public Administration Committee Bulletin* (November 1970).
22 R. Greenwood, C. R. Hinings and S. Ranson: 'Contingency Theory

and the Organization of Local Authorities, Part I, Differentiation and Integration' in *Public Administration* (Spring 1975).
23 *Op. cit.* p.12
24 See *Cash Limits on Public Expenditure.* Cmnd. 6440, HMSO (1976).
25 For details of these and other recent changes in the PESC system in the light of economic difficulties see *The Government's Expenditure Plans.* Cmnd. 6721, 2 volumes, HMSO (1977).
26 *Inner Area Studies,* HMSO (1977).
27 H. Glennerster: *Social Service Budgets and Social Policy: British and American Experience.* Allen and Unwin (1975).
28 P. J. O. Self: *Econocrats and the Policy Process: the Politics and Philosophy of Cost-Benefit Analysis.* The Macmillan Press (1975).
29 Professor Dahrendorf's proposals were set out in a document circulated to the staff of the London School of Economics and to certain individuals in politics and industry. An account of the document appeared in *The Times Higher Educational Supplement* 14 May 1976.

NOTES TO CHAPTER 4

1 G.H. Peters: *Cost Benefit Analysis and Public Expenditure,* 3rd ed. The Institute of Economic Affairs (1973) and references cited therein.
2 *Op. cit.* and C.D. Foster and M.E. Beesley: 'Estimating the Social Benefit of Constructing an Underground Railway in London', *Journal of the Royal Statistical Society,* Series A, Vol. 126, Part 1 (1963).
3 *Commission on the Third London Airport.* HMSO (1970); G.H. Peters, *Op. cit.* C.M. Price: *Welfare Economics in Theory and Practice,* chapter 12. Macmillan (1977).
4 G.H. Peters, *Op. cit.* p.54.
5 V. Morris and A. Ziderman: 'The Economic Return on Investment in Higher Education in England and Wales', pp. xx–xxx. *Economic Trends.* HMSO (May 1971).
6 R.F.F. Dawson: *Cost of Road Accidents in Great Britain,* RRL Report LR 79. Road Research Laboratory, Crowthorne (1967) and G.H. Peters, *Op. cit.* pp. 59-60.
7 An account of recent practice in transport is contained in *The Economist* 18 December 1976.
8 *Report of the Advisory Committee on Trunk Road Assessment.* HMSO (1978).
9 This example is based on one quoted in M.S. Makower and E. Williamson: *Teach Yourself Operational Research* 3rd Ed. pp. 40-42. English Universities Press (1975). This book contains many examples of how to solve problems by operational research methods.
10 W. Russell: 'Peterhead Bay Harbour', *Management Services in Government,* Vol. 31, No.2, pp. 81-87 (May 1976).
11 Dr N.E. Hand: 'The Metropolitan Police M.S. Department', *Manage-*

ment Services in Government Vol. 29, No. 3, pp. 153-163 (August 1974).

12   Further details of this study and the other local government studies quoted are in the Local Government Operational Research Unit's *Information Bulletin No.14* Local Government Operational Research Unit, Reading and Manchester (1976).

13   F.E.R. Butler and Dr K. Aldred: 'The Financial Information Systems Project', *Management Services in Government* Vol. 32, No. 2, pp. 77-87 (May 1977).

NOTES TO CHAPTER 5

1   Joan Woodward: *Industrial Organization: Theory and Practice.* Tavistock (1965).

2   T. Burns and G.M. Stalker: *The Management of Innovation* 2nd ed. Tavistock (1968).

3   *The Reorganisation of Central Government* Cmnd. 4506, HMSO (1970).

4   S.D. Walker: 'The Management Review Programme', *Management Services in Government,* Vol. 32, No. 3, pp. 128-133 (August 1977).

5   For material on this subject, see the article by Peter Hennesey on 'The Treasury: Bank manager and probation officer rolled into one', *The Times,* 28 March 1977. This article is also the source of the two quotations from civil servants given in this section of this chapter. See also H. Heclo and A. Wildavsky: *The Private Government of Public Money.* Macmillan (1974).

6   See Sir R. Clarke, K.C.B., O.B.E. : *New Trends in Government.* HMSO (1971).

7   *Review of Overseas Representation* report by the Central Policy Review Staff, pp. x-xi. HMSO (1977).

8   T.P. Ogle and D.V. Orr: 'Centralization of Government Training Stores – An O and M Approach', *Management Services in Government,* Vol. 31, No. 4, pp. 217-224 (November 1976).

9   J.N. Archer: *A New Look for CSD Management Services, O and M Bulletin,* Vol. 26, No. 1, pp. 4-13 (February 1971).

10   J.N. Archer, *Op. cit.* pp. 7-8.

11   *The Civil Service: Volume 1: Report of the Committee 1966-68,* para. 150. Cmnd. 3638, HMSO (1968).

12   *Op. cit.* para. 154.

13   J.G. Cuckney: 'The Commercial Approach in Government Operations', *Management Services,* Vol. 29, No. 3, p. 123 (August 1974).

14   J.G. Cuckney, *Op. cit.* p. 124.

15   *Government Organization for Defence Procurement and Civil Aerospace.* Cmnd. 4641, HMSO (1971).

16   For the background to these proposed arrangements see the report of

the Committee on Government Industrial Establishments (the Malla-
bar Committee). Cmnd. 4713, HMSO (1971).
17 See for further information and background material G.M. Lamb
    Computers in the Public Service. George Allen and Unwin (1973).
18 Figures supplied by the Department of Health and Social Security and
    quoted by J. Rogaly: 'DHSS: the administrative nightmare', *The
    Financial Times,* 1 March 1977.
19 R.G.S. Brown: *The Management of Welfare,* p. 288 Fontana/Collins
    (1975).
20 J. Rogaly, *Op. cit.*
21 R.G.S. Brown, *Op. cit.* p.289.
22 R.G.S. Brown, *Op. cit.* p. 290.
23 R. Greenwood, M.A. Lomer, C.R. Hinings, S. Ranson: *The Organi-
    zation of Local Authorities in England and Wales 1967-75, INLO-
    GOV Discussion Paper Series L,* No. 5, 1975, University of
    Birmingham, Institute of Local Government Studies (1975).
24 R. Greenwood, C.R. Hinings, S. Ranson and K. Walsh: *In Pursuit of
    Corporate Rationality: Organizational Developments in the Post-
    Reorganization Period,* p. 2. University of Birmingham, Institute of
    Local Government Studies (1977). This research study has been of the
    greatest help in preparing this section of this chapter.
25 Quoted Greenwood, *et al., Op. cit.* p. 105.
26 Quoted Greenwood, *et al., Op. cit.* p. 123.
27 Greenwood, *et al., Op. cit.* pp. 125-126.
28 Greenwood, *et al., Op cit.* pp. 131-134.
29 I am indebted to Mr William Thornhill for this example.
30 *The Reorganization of Central Government,* para. 5 and 17. Cmnd.
    4506, HMSO (1970).

NOTES TO CHAPTER 6

1 Further details about 'hygiene factors' and 'motivational factors' are
   set out in F. Herzberg, B. Mausner, and B. Snyderman: *The Motivation to Work* New York. John Wiley and Sons (1959).
2 D. McGregor: *The Human Side of Enterprise.* New York McGraw
   Hill Book Company (1960).
3 R. Blake and J. Mouton: *The New Managerial Grid,* p.11. Houston, Gulf
   Publishing Company (1978). Reproduced by permission.
4 E. Sidney, M. Brown and M. Argyle: *Skills with People,* pp. 167-68,
   Hutchinson (1973).
5 E. Sidney, M. Brown and M. Argyle, *Op. cit,* pp. 169-70.
6 E. Jacques: *Equitable Payment.* New York, John Wiley (1961).
7 *The Civil Service, Vol. 1: Report of the Committee 1966-68,* p. 67,
   Cmnd. 3638, HMSO (1968).
8 *Op. cit.* pp. 104-105.

9   House of Commons Official Report (Hansard), Vol. 767, 26 June 1968, col. 456.

10   Civil Service National Whitley Council: *Developments on Fulton* (1969).

11   Civil Service National Whitley Council: *Fulton: A Framework for the Future*, p. 11, (1970).

12   Civil Service National Whitley Council: *The Shape of the Post Fulton Civil Service*, p. 2, (1972).

13   *The Civil Service Vol. 1 Report of the Committee 1966-68*, pp. 19-20, Cmnd. 3638. HMSO (1968).

14   Civil Service National Whitley Council: *Fulton: A Framework for the Future*, p. 16, (1970).

15   Eleventh Report from the Expenditure Committee of the House of Commons 1976-77, Vol. II, Pt 1, *The Response to the Fulton Report*, Memorandum by the Civil Service Department, para. 110.

16   *The Use of Accountants in the Civil Service*, report by Sir A. Burney and Sir R. Melville KCB. HMSO (1973).

17   Eleventh Report from the Expenditure Committee of the House of Commons 1976-77, Vol. 1, p. xxvi.

18   Government Observations on the Eleventh Report from the Expenditure Committee, Session 1976-77 HC 535, p. 7, Cmnd. 7117.

19   Eleventh Report from the Expenditure Committee of the House of Commons, Vol. II, Pt 1, *Op. cit.* p. 38.

20   *The Civil Service Vol. 3(1), Social Survey of the Civil Service* HMSO (1969).

21   *Report of the Committee of Inquiry into the Method II System of Selection for the Administrative Class of the Home Civil Service*, Cmnd. 4156, HMSO (1969).

22   *The Civil Service Vol 3(2) Surveys and Investigations*, R. A. Chapman *Profile of a Profession: The Administrative Class*, p. 9. HMSO (1968).

23   Eleventh Report from the Expenditure Committee of the House of Commons 1976-77, Vol. 1, p. lxx.

24   *Ibid*, pp. lxxi.

25   Government Observations on the Eleventh Report from the Expenditure Committee, *Op. cit.* pp. 4-5.

26   See, for example, P. Hennessy's article 'A Wit whose memoirs would earn a fortune' in *The Times* 1 April 1977. The article deals with Sir Derek Mitchell, a Second Permanent Secretary who resigned from the Treasury in 1977 to enter merchant banking, and who is reported as saying that his most difficult job in thirty years in the civil service was handling public service pensions.

27   Eleventh Report from the Expenditure Committee of the House of Commons 1976-77. Vol. 11, Pt 1, *Op. cit.* para. 6.

28   Eleventh Report from the Expenditure Committee of the House of Commons 1976-77, Vol. 1, p. lxxii.

29 *The New Local Authorities: Management and Structure*, p. xv. HMSO (1972).
30 *Ibid.*, p. 73.
31 R. Greenwood, C. R. Hinings, S. Ranson, K. Walsh, *In pursuit of Corporate Rationality: Organizational development in the post-reorganization period* University of Birmingham, Institute of Local Government Studies (1977).
32 *Ibid;* p. 30.
33 Eleventh Report from the Expenditure Committee of the House of Commons 1976-77, Vol. II, Pt 1, *Op. cit.* para. 68-74.
34 A full account of training in local government is given in chapter 11 of A. Fowler: *Personnel Management in Local Government.* Institute of Personnel Management (1975). This account has been of great help in preparing this section of this chapter.
35 D. M. Basey 'MbO in the Department of Education and Science' *Management Services in Government,* Vol. 30, No. 3 pp. 130-138 (August 1975).
36 S. V. Dulewicz, C. A. Fletcher, J. Walker: 'Job Appraisal Reviews Three Years On', *Management Services in Government,* Vol. 31, No. 3, pp. 134-143 (August 1976).
37 *Civil Servants and Change: Joint Statement by the National Whitley Council and Final Report by the Wider Issues Review Team,* p. 4. Civil Service Department (1975).
38 *Ibid.*, pp. 5-6.
39 *Ibid.*, pp. 11-12.
40 *Guide for New Managers.* Civil Service Department (1975).
41 D. Burden '"New Model Office" in the Department of Health and Social Security', p. 9. *Management Services in Government,* Vol. 31, No. 1.
42 Lord Helsby, who was Head of the Home Civil Service and Joint Permanent Secretary to the Treasury from 1963-68, entered the Civil Service during the War. He was previously a lecturer in economics at Durham University. Sir Richard Clarke was a financial journalist before joining the civil service in the war. He became Permanent Secretary of the Ministry of Technology. Lord Roll and Sir Henry Hardman were also university lecturers in economics before joining the Civil Service in the War. Lord Roll became Permanent Secretary of the Department of Economic Affairs, and Sir Henry was Permanent Secretary to the Ministry of Aviation and then to the Ministry of Defence. Sir William Nield did research for the Labour Party before the War. He joined the Civil Service in 1946, and became Permanent Secretary of the Department of Economic Affairs, in the Cabinet Office and of the Northern Ireland Office.
43 Eleventh Report from the Expenditure Committee of the House of Commons 1976-77, Vol. II, Pt 1, *Op. cit.* paras. 93-94.

44 See, for example, C de Paula 'A Businessman in Whitehall', *The Times*, 4 August 1970. Mr de Paula had been the co-ordinator of the industrial advisors to the Government and was the senior partner of Robson, Morrow and Co., Management Consultants, when he wrote this article. Another article 'Can Business live with the Bureaucrats' in *The Sunday Times* of 22 April 1973 gives the views of the following businessmen who had worked in government: Sir Richard Meyjes of Shell; Mr J. Sainsbury of J. Sainsbury Ltd.; Sir Derek Rayner of Marks and Spencer Ltd.; Mr R. Hutton of Hambros Bank Ltd.

45 Report of the Committee of Inquiry on Industrial Democracy, Cmnd. 6706. HMSO (1977).

46 See 'Councils uneasy about worker participation in local administration', *The Times*, 29 December 1976.

47 Peter Hennessy 'Worker-participation seen as key to Britain's recovery', *The Times* 11 January 1977.

NOTES TO CHAPTER 7

1 S.A. de Smith: *Constitutional and Administrative Law* 3rd ed. p. 516. Penguin Education (1977). © the Estate of S. A. de Smith, 1971, 1973, 1977. Reprinted by permission of Penguin Books Ltd.

2 *Government Accounting* Section E, para. 7. HMSO (1974).

3 See S.A. de Smith, *Op. cit.* p. 614 *et seq.* for a review of the work of the Parliamentary Commissioner.

4 Commission for Local Administration in England: *Your Local Ombudsman* (1977).

5 For details and comments see P. Hennessy: 'Whitehall gets guidance on way to open government', *The Times*, 5 August 1977.

6 *A New Partnership for our Schools*. The report of a committee under the Chairmanship of Mr T. Taylor on school governors and managers. HMSO (1977).

7 This example draws upon the discussion of network analysis in J. Argenti: *Management Techniques*, pp. 179-182. Allen and Unwin (1969).

8 Eleventh Report from the Expenditure Committee of the House of Commons, Session 1976-77, *The Civil Service, Vol. 1 - Report, Vol. II - Minutes of Evidence, Vol. III - Appendices*.

9 *Ibid.*, Vol. 1, para. 94.

10 *Ibid.*, para. 95.

11 Supplementary Benefits Commission: *Annual Report 1976* Cmnd. 6910. HMSO (1977).

12 'Prime Minister rules out reorganization of central government' by Peter Hennessy in *The Times* 16 March 1978 commenting on Government Observations on the Eleventh Report from the

Expenditure Committee Session 1976-77. H.C. 536, Cmnd. 7117. HMSO (1978).

13 Civil Service Department *Internal Audit in the Civil Service*. HMSO (1973).

14 Eleventh Report from the Expenditure Committee of the House of Commons, Session 1976-7, Vol. II, pp. 375-445.

15 Its work is described in J.D.S. Gillis, S. Brazier, K.J. Chamberlain, R.J.P. Harris, D.J. Scott *Monitoring and the Planning Process*. University of Birmingham, Institute of Local Government Studies (1974).

Bibliography

(1) THE THEORY AND PRACTICE OF MANAGEMENT

H. Koontz and Cyril O'Donnell: *Management: a systems and contingency analysis of managerial functions* 6th ed. Tokyo McGraw-Hill Koya-kusha (1972).

This is a comprehensive book on its subject. It takes broadly the same approach to management as that explained in chapter 2. The authors are American, and most of the examples are drawn from private business. It was first published in 1955. It is a good example of the general approach to the study of management during the last 10 to 15 years.

(2) MANAGEMENT IN CENTRAL AND LOCAL GOVERNMENT

R.G.S. Brown: *The Administrative Process in Britain*, revised edition. Methuen (1971).

A. Dunsire: *Administration: The Word and the Science*. Martin Robertson (1973).

J. Garrett: *The Management of Government*. Penguin Books (1972).

M.J. Hill: *The Sociology of Public Administration*. Weidenfeld and Nicolson (1972).

D. Keeling: *Management in Government*. George Allen and Unwin (1972).

P.J.O. Self: *Administrative Theories and Politics*, second edition. George Allen and Unwin (1977).

P.J.O. Self: *Econocrats and the Policy Process*. George Allen and Unwin (1975).

These are general works which deal in whole or part with the subject of this book. Detailed references to specific topics are given in the notes at the end of each chapter of this book.

Appendix 1
Output budgeting for the Department of Education and Science.

DETAILS OF THE COMPULSORY EDUCATION PROGRAMME

Main Objective

To provide the highest possible standard of education, according to the child's age, aptitude and ability, during the present years of compulsory schooling.

Measures or indicators of success

(a) Intra-educational	(b) Extra-educational
Reading tests	Employers' assessments of quality of 15-year-old school leavers
Mathematical ability	
Examination results	Social adjustment indicators, e.g. social behaviour of 15-year-old leavers after leaving school
Inspectors' assessments	
Social adjustment indicators e.g. truancy, juvenile delinquency, before leaving school	Appreciation of cultural values by school leavers

Particular policy objectives

	Programme No.	Additional measures or indicators of success
To reduce social and other inequalities, and to provide greater equality of opportunity, by reorganization of secondary schools	141	Social adjustment indicators for parents and families, as well as the children
		Educational performance, particularly of the less gifted

	Programme No.	Additional measures or indicators of success
To improve the standards of provision in the Educational Priority Areas	151 1611 and 1621	
To improve the staff/ pupil ratio to ( ) by 19( )	161	Changes in staff/pupil ratio

Coverage
In England and Wales:

(a) Primary Schools (excluding Nursery Classes)

(b) Secondary Schools, up to present compulsory school leaving age

(c) Special Schools, excluding classes for age groups outside the normal age of compulsory schooling

(d) Colleges and Departments of Education—that part of current and capital expenditure that can be attributed to providing teachers for this age group

(e) Schools Broadcasts and T.V. (part)

Branches of D.E.S. responsible
Schools

Architects and building

Teachers I and II

Special services

No.	Programme	Coverage	Intermediate measures or indicators of success	Remarks
11	Maintenance of existing pattern and scale of provision	In schools, current expenditure on present numbers		
111	For existing numbers	In colleges of education etc. *pro rata* to 'steady state' requirements for present number of		

No.	Programme	Coverage	Intermediate measures or indicators of success	Remarks
		teachers in schools. Elsewhere: current levels of expenditure on schools broadcasts. T.V. etc.		
112	For population change	For schools, building and subsequent current expenditure on teachers etc. In colleges of education etc. *pro rata* to 'population increase' element of requirement for teachers	Numbers taught	
13	For population shift	School building directly linked to geographical re-distribution of the population	'Outturn' of population shift. Reduction of over-crowding and closure of sub-standard schools in 'emigration areas'	Schools provided for this will also contribute to Pro-gramme 15
12	Reducation of the cost of provision to existing standards		Cost reduc-tion at 'constant prices'	This will have a negative 'net cost'
121	Reducing the 'real cost' of new school building			Probably no longer significant
122	Increased utilization of buildings in colleges of education			
123	Other	Other methods of increased efficiency		

No.	Programme	Coverage	Intermediate measures or indicators of success	Remarks
		not necessarily related to buildings		
13	Changes in the participation rate			A 'nul' programme unless there is a significant shift to or from private education
14	Changes in school organization			
141	'Secondary reorganization'	Specific provision in school building programme. Any resultant change in current costs	Social adjustment indicators for both children and families. Educational performance both overall, and of particular ability levels	
142	Other changes			The Plowden proposals on age of transfer are one example
15	Changes in the standards of accommodation		Improvement in the stock of school buildings	Programmes 112 and 113 will also contribute to this
	Improvement of the stock of school buildings			
151	(a) in E.P.As*	Improvement element in school building		
152	(b) elsewhere			

*Educational priority areas

No.	Programme	Coverage	Intermediate measures or indicators of success	Remarks
		programme and some minor works and adaptations		
155	Changes in the standards of new school building	Additional cost/ saving on all new buildings in programmes 112, 113 14 and 152		
16	Changes in the availability and training of teachers			'Availability' relates to the total time which teachers spend in contact with pupils
161	Changes in staffing ratios	In schools: expenditure on salaries, plus costs of associated requirements for buildings and schools In Colleges of education etc.: share of 'improving' staffing ratio element of teacher output Recruitment expenditure Changes in salary scales and structures designed to change recruiting pattern	Increase in staffing ratio	The programme budget forecasts of expenditure will usually be at 'constant prices'. Salary increases— differential or across the board— in excess of the movement in the general level of wages and salaries given in order to improve teacher supply would be included in this item

1611   (a) in E.P.As.
1612   (b) elsewhere

No.	Programme	Coverage	Intermediate measures or indicators of success	Remarks
162	Changed provision of teachers' aides	Salaries etc., plus training costs		
1621	(a) in E.P.As.			
1622	(b) elsewhere			
163	Change in the provision of in-service training and teachers' centres		Inspectors' assessments of teaching performance	This will complement programme 17
164	Other	Increased secretarial assistance to reduce teachers' time on administration, changes in the quality and length of the initial training of teachers		This would be analysed in detail in a 'dummy' programme
17	Improving teaching methods and curriculum			
171	Curriculum development	Research projects, including experiments, into the development of curriculum for the compulsory age groups		
172	Educational technology	Research into educational technology. Purchase of equipment and teaching programmes Increases in expenditure on schools broadcast and T.V.		
18	Other changes in the scale of provision of inputs	Net change in the provision of materials, books equipment (not included above) school outings, music teaching, etc.		

No.	Programme	Coverage	Intermediate measures or indicators of success	Remarks
10	Other (Compulsory Education)	That part of inputs such as administration and inspection which can be allocated to 'Compulsory Education' but not to specific programmes or sub-programmes		

Source: *Output Budgeting for the Department of Education and Science*, pp. 109–116, HMSO (1970).

Appendix 2
PPBS in Liverpool: the education programme structure.

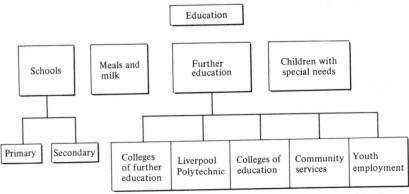

Each programme and sub-programme has a 'prime objective' and is divided into a number of 'elements', each element having its own 'element objective'.

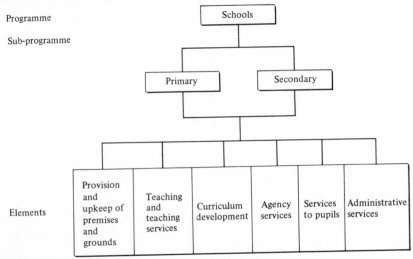

SUB-PROGRAMMES: PRIMARY
SECONDARY

(Activities similar for each sub-programmes except where indicated: *Primary activities; §Secondary activities only.)

Prime objective for both sub-programmes

To provide suitable full-time education for Liverpool children of primary* and secondary§ school age whose parents wish them to attend maintained (county or voluntary) schools, and to make adequate provision for the needs of children below* above§ statutory school age.

Element objective	Activities
1 To provide premises that are adequate in quantity and quality for modern educational needs	1.1 Assessment of pupil numbers and distribution
	1.2 Formulation of an appropriate organizational structure
	1.3 The design and improvement of new buildings, existing buildings and grounds
	1.4 To discuss provision for community use with other sectors of the service
	1.5 To provide furniture and equipment
	1.6 Maintenance of buildings and grounds
2 To provide general and specialist teachers of suitable quality and quantity according to national standards and to deploy them to the best advantage	2.1 Assessment of pupils numbers and desirable staffing ratios
	2.2 To recruit qualified teachers according to need
	2.3 In association with governors and managers, to appoint teachers to individual schools within the overall policy of the Education Committee
To provide support staff and material resources for teaching	2.4 To recruit and allocate non-teaching support staff;

Element objective	*Activities*
	nursery assistants*; welfare assistants*; technical assistants
	2.5 Supply of material resources according to national standards; books, stationery and materials; and educational equipment
3 To conduct research and development in the field of teaching method and practice and to propagate the material results thereof	3.1 Establishment of suitable premises for research and development in both primary and secondary centres
	3.2 Employment of appropriate professional staff
	3.3 Employment of appropriate non-teaching support staff
	3.4 Supply of material resources; books; stationery and education equipment
	3.5 Organization of in-service training; period secondment to attend extra-authority courses; and short-term secondment to attend Liverpool courses
4 To provide school places to meet educational and parental demands not available within the normal provision of a Local Education Authority	4.1 To negotiate reciprocal places with neighbouring L.E.A.s
	4.2 To provide selective places in direct grant schools
	4.3 To provide places for specialist education in independent schools
5 The provision of additional services to enable children to attend appropriate schools, engage in a variety	5.1 Provision of transport to and from school in accordance with local standards

Element objective	Activities
of extra-curricular activities and travel for activities conducted away from the school site	5.2 Provision of fees and expenses in connection with the curriculum
	5.3 Arrangement of outside activities to enrich the normal school curriculum
	5.4 Provision of transport to schools and the Authorities' detached establishments
6 To provide administrative services in schools	6.1 Employment of appropriate Clerical staff in accordance with locally determined standards
	6.2 Adequate provision of stationery, telephones and administrative equipment

Source: *Management in the Education Service,* the Society of Education Officers, Routledge & Kegan Paul (1975).

Appendix 3
PPBS in Coventry: the education programme area.

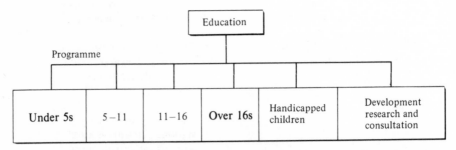

The objectives of the education programme in Coventry were set out in terms of user groups differentiated mainly by age. The full list of objectives, sub-objectives and activities is not given here but the nature of the scheme should be clear from these examples.

PRIME OBJECTIVE OF THE EDUCATION PROGRAMME AREA

To enrich the lives of people by the optimum personal development of each individual in the community.

The prime objective is approached through six objectives:

Objective 1

To ensure, in the light of parental wishes, adequate educational provision appropriate to the needs of infants below the age of five years.

Objective 2

In association with parents and voluntary bodies to ensure the provision for all children other than handicapped children and aged between five and 11 years of full time education appropriate to their different ages, abilities and aptitudes and to their particular needs and to secure their participation therein.

Objective 3

In association with parents and voluntary bodies to ensure the provision for all children other than handicapped children and aged between 12 and 16 years of full time education appropriate to their different ages, abilities, aptitudes and other needs and to secure their participation therein.

Objective 4

In association with other bodies (local, regional and national) to secure the provision of facilities for students over 16 years of age to develop further their interests, skills and intellectual attainments to achieve the highest possible degree of competence and satisfaction in their vocation and in their personal life.

Objective 5

In association with parents and voluntary bodies to ensure the provision for handicapped children up to 16 years of age of full-time education appropriate to their different ages, abilities and aptitudes and to their particular needs and to secure their participation therein.

Objective 6

To ensure the progressive development of the education service; to identify the changing needs by the initiation and support of research; and to secure an effective consultative partnership of all participants within the service.

Each of these objectives is further broken down and the example of the sub-objectives and activities subsumed under Objective 3 will suffice to show the way in which this has been done.

Sub-objectives	Activities
3.1 To provide and maintain, with other bodies, a sufficient pattern of secondary schools appropriate in number, character and location	3.11 The provision and maintenance of secondary schools
3.2 In association with parents, governors and teachers and in accordance with the Articles of Government to ensure an appropriate standard and variety of instruction and training for all secondary pupils	3.21 The provision of teaching staff for secondary schools
	3.22 The provision of educational materials to aid instruction and training
	3.23 The provision of inspection and advice to schools

Sub-objectives	Activities
	3.24 The improvement in the quality of the teaching force through in-service training and teachers' centres
	3.25 The encouragement of the development of educational thinking and practice through support for educational research generally and curriculum development in particular
3.3 With parents to secure the regular attendance of pupils at school and to ensure that they are in a fit condition to benefit from the education provided	3.31 The provision of facilities to improve the mental and physical health of all pupils
	3.32 Assistance in the transport of pupils to and from schools
	3.33 The provision of facilities to improve the standard of nutrition of all pupils
	3.34 The provision of assistance so that no child is withdrawn from school because of financial difficulties
	3.35 Improvement in the attendance of children at school
	3.36 Enforcement of the regulations governing the employ- of juveniles
3.4 With parents, governors, teachers and voluntary bodies to ensure appropriate provision for extra-mural activities to promote the social and other development of children	3.41 The provision of facilities for cultural development, outdoor pursuits and school journeys and outings
	3.42 The provision of facilities for school clubs, hobbies

Sub-objectives	Activities
	and out-of-school sports activities
	3.43 The provision of youth clubs and assistance to voluntary youth organizations
3.5 To ensure that appropriate guidance is available to pupils concerning opportunities in Further Education and careers	3.51 The provision of careers and educational advisory services

Source: *Management in the Education Service,* the Society of Education Officers, Routledge & Kegan Paul (1975).

Appendix 4
PPBS in Gloucestershire:
Gloucestershire's educational
hemisphere.

Further details are given below of the programme for older children. This should serve as an example of Gloucestershire's approach.

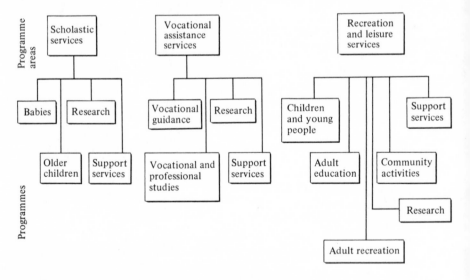

THE PROGRAMME FOR OLDER CHILDREN

The overall objective of the education service for children is

To assist parents in the upbringing of their children in such a manner as to promote their proper spiritual, moral, mental and physical development.

In the case of older children, the objective is also

To develop basic abilities and attitudes enabling individuals to become active members of society.

The activities or means employed towards this end are then described as follows:

238

1. By providing and maintaining schools. Costs to be broken down for each school by subject or groups of subjects. To include costs of extra-curricular activities when possible.

2. By maintaining schools provided by other bodies. As above.

3. By assisting parents with grants to enable them to send their children to schools not maintained by the authority (including schools maintained by other Local Education Authorities).

4. By providing, and encouraging others to provide facilities supplementary to school curricula.

   (a) Milk and meals in schools
   (b) Swimming facilities
   (c) Field centres
   (d) Musuems
   (e) Short-term residential facilities
   (f) Children's libraries
        (i) Schools
        (ii) Community
   (g) Other facilities

5 By taking measures designed to enable children to derive full advantage from their education.

   (a) Identification of children with physical, mental or social handicaps and provision of advice and remedial measures.
        (i) welfare work and school attendance
        (ii) school medical service (part)
        (iii) school psychological service
   (b) Protection of school children from influences and activities harmful to their schooling.
        (i) restriction of employment
   (c) Financial assistance with costs of education for parents in need
        (i) school uniform grant
        (ii) grants towards costs of extra-curricula activities.
   (d) Transport between home and school

6. By assisting and encouraging thinking about education-

   (a) By providing and maintaining teachers' centres.
   (b) By enabling teachers and others to attend conferences courses and seminars.
   (c) By making grants for educational research.
   (d) By grant-aiding bodies having educational objectives.
   (e) By the services of a staff of organizers and advisers.

Source: *Management in the Education Service,* the Society of Education Officers, Routledge & Kegan Paul (1975).

Appendix 5
Discounting and present values.

A basic problem in measuring and comparing the value of different projects arises from the fact that their costs and benefits fall at different points in time. At its simplest, we have to answer three questions.

(*a*) Is £1 received a year today worth less now than £1 received today?

(*b*) If so, why is it worth less?

(*c*) How much less is it worth?

The answers depend upon the alternative uses to which the £1 received today could have been put. Suppose the £1 could have been invested with certainty at 6 per cent to produce £1.06 one year today. Then it is clear that we are really being offered a choice between £1 now and £1.06 a year today. Whether we choose £1 now or £1.06 a year today is, of course, a different question and depends upon whether we decide that the satisfaction we get from spending £1 now will exceed what we shall get from spending £1.06 in a year from today.

However that may be, the answers to the questions are:

(*a*) £1 received a year today is worth less now than £1 received today;

(*b*) it is worth less because £1 received today could be invested at 6 per cent per annum to grow into £1.06 a year today;

(*c*) in order to receive £1 a year today we should need to invest £0.943 (£1/1.06) today. Thus £1 received a year today is worth £0.057 less than £1 received today.

Generalizing this result for any future series of cash flows and any interest or discount rate we have

$$PV = \frac{1}{(1+r)^n}$$

where PV equals the value today of £1 to be received at the end of the year n, discounted at r per cent. Thus at 12 per cent the present value of £1 to be received four years from today is

$$PV = \frac{1}{(1+.12)^4} = \frac{1}{1.574} = £0.6355$$

In order to save the effort of making these detailed calculations, present value tables are available showing the present value of £1 at various discount rates for various numbers of periods.

It may be helpful to extend this basic formula in the following ways:

(a) the present value of any amount (An) to be received at the end of n years discounted at r per cent is

$$PV = \frac{An}{(1+r)^n}$$

Thus the present value of £1000 at the end of four years when discounted at 12% is

$$PV = \frac{1000}{(1+.12)^4} = £635.5$$

(b) the present value of a series of payments to be received at the end of each of the next n years, discounted at r per cent is

$$PV = \sum_{t=1}^{n} \frac{At}{(1+r)^t}$$

For example, suppose A_1 to be received at the end of the first year is £500, A_2 to be received at the end of the second year is £1000, A_3 to be received at the end of the third year is £1000, and A_4 to be received at the end of the fourth year is £2000. Then, if the discount rate is 12 per cent;

$$PV = \frac{500}{(1+.12)} + \frac{1000}{(1+.12)^2} + \frac{1000}{(1+.12)^3} + \frac{1000}{(1+.12)^4}$$

$$= £446.43 + £797.19 + £711.78 + £1,271.04$$

$$= £3,226.44.$$

We can also look at the problem from a different point of view. We are often interested in finding the discount rate which will equate the present value of the cash outflows with the present value of the cash inflows of a project. Suppose we have a project with a series of cash flows (inflows would be positive and outflows would be negative) over the next n periods designated A_0, A_1, A_2....An. For a simple investment, incurring costs in the first period and benefits thereafter, A_0 will be negative and A_1,....An will be positive. We are seeking the rate of discount r such that

$$A_0 + \frac{A_1}{(1+r)} + \frac{A_2}{(1+r)^2} + \ldots + \frac{An}{(1+r)^n} = 0$$

$$\text{or} \sum_{t=0}^{n} \frac{At}{(1+r)^t} = 0$$

The rate of discount in this calculation is called the internal rate of return.

As a final example, let us take a project with the following cash flows:

	Cash Inflow +	Cash Outflow −	Net Cash Flow
Period 0	0	£900,000 (construction costs)	− £900,000
Period 1	£352,000 (receipts)	£100,000 (running costs)	+ £252,000
Period 2	£367,000 (receipts)	£100,000 (running costs)	+ £267,000
Period 3	£367,000 (receipts)	£100,000 (running costs)	+ £267,000
Period 4	£322,000 (receipts)	£100,000 (running costs)	+ £222,000
Period 5	£292,000 (receipts from services provided and from disposal of investment)	£100,000 (running costs)	+ £192,000

The internal rate of return r would be the value that satisfies the following equation

$$0 = -900,000 + \frac{252,000}{(1+r)} + \frac{267,000}{(1+r)^2} + \frac{267,000}{(1+r)^3} + \frac{222,000}{(1+r)^4} + \frac{192,000}{(1+r)^5}$$

In this example, r would be 11%.

If the discount rate were set at 10 per cent the net present value would be

$$NPV = -900,000 + \frac{252,000}{(1+.1)} + \frac{267.000}{(1+.1)^2} + \frac{267,000}{(1+.1)^3} + \frac{222,000}{(1+.1)^4} + \frac{192,000}{(1+.1)^5}$$

$$NPV = + £21,198.$$

In short, if the discount rate is 10 per cent then this project has a positive net present value of £21,198.

Two points should be made in conclusion. First, the net present value and internal rate of return methods do not always rank a set of projects in the same order. Generally the net present value method is the better. This is because the internal rate of return method assumes that the cash flows arising during the life of the project are re-invested over its remaining life at the internal rate of return. As this assumption cannot be guaranteed it is often a handicap to the practical application of the method.

Secondly, there is the problem of selecting the discount or interest rate to be used in the calculations. Ideally, we should hope to find one rate that reflects both the opportunity cost of the capital employed and coincides with the rate expressing society's preference between present and future consumption. But this is unlikely; the capital market is not perfectly competitive, as it would have to be to meet these requirements and, even if it were, the yields on private sector projects would still vary because of the different degrees of risk attaching to them when they were undertaken. The effect of taxation is also relevant in that the actual rates of return are higher than those quoted on the market and the structure of the tax system means that different kinds of project bear different rates of tax.

Finally, there may be a distinction between private and social time preferences. As individuals, the return we expect on investments relates to our lives and, perhaps, those of our children. If this rate were to be used as the investment criteria for the community as a whole, it might well rule out projects such as land conservation schemes which yield only a small return and are mainly designed to benefit future generations.

It follows that no one rate of discount can be recommended as certainly correct. Analysis can suggest a range of figures and this is a useful contribution. But the final decision cannot be a technical judgement alone, and must also include wider considerations including those based on political principles and value judgements. Indeed, it is not a question of whether or not these wider considerations should be included. They will necessarily be included, because technical considerations will not in themselves be enough to determine one outcome rather than another. The real question is whether these wider considerations should be set out for all to see, or if they should be concealed beneath technical jargon. Clearly, the former course is the right one.

Note

For further reading, and instruction on carrying out the calculations described above, for example, the calculation of the internal rate of return, see

(a) J.R. McGuigan and R.C. Moyer: *Managerial Economics: Private and Public Sector Decision Analysis.* Holt, Rinehart and Winston, the Dryden Press, Hinsdale, Illinois (1975).

Some of the illustrations in this appendix draw upon those set out in this book.

(b) E.J. Mishan: *Cost-Benefit Analysis,* 2nd ed. George Allen and Unwin (1975).

Appendix 6
Management by objectives.

The attached notes set out some practical examples of the kind of documentation used in a management by objectives exercise in local government. The exercise relates to the work of an architectural section leader in a county architects department and includes the following papers:

(*a*) a management job description
(*b*) a statement of key result areas and key activities
(*c*) a job improvement plan.

These documents refer to a hypothetical example, though they are based on actual cases. They have not been completed in full, but only to the extent that is necessary to understand how they should be fully filled in. Finally, there is no claim made that all management by objectives exercises must use documents exactly like these (although it would be difficult to carry one out without something very similar). The object of presenting these documents is to give some practical idea of how a management by objectives investigator might proceed, and the kind of factors that need to be considered. With a little imagination the reader will be able to see how such an exercise might be carried out in other areas—indeed, as an exercise, he or she might like to see how it could be applied to his or her own department, section or job.

(*a*) MANAGEMENT JOB DESCRIPTION

Job   Architectural Section Leader   Name _____

Rank   Assistant County Architect   Date _____

Unit   Section 1 _____

1 *Main Purpose of Job*

   (*a*) Definition

      To utilize available resources with maximum efficiency to achieve the Section's building programme on time, on cost, and to a satisfactory design and functional quality.

   (*b*) Depth and Breadth of Job

(i) Level of management or staff	Third
(ii) Committees involved	Police, Health, Educational, General Purposes
(iii) Funds involved	Capital loan
(iv) Main direct resources	Staff of Section
(v) Main indirect resources	Specialists

   (*c*) Summary of Personal Key Result Areas

      (i) Resource planning in section (ii)Time achievement (iii)Productivity and profitability of section (iv)Cost/effectiveness (v)Quality (vi)Staff development and training

2 Position in Organization

   (*a*) Responsible to

(i) Directly and primarily to	County Architect
(ii) For specified departmental KRAs stages or other aspects to	

(*b*) Staff primarily and directly responsible to job holder	Section staff

   (*c*) Other staff with whom you have frequent working contact

(i) In a primarily senior role:	Officers in other
(ii) Mainly lateral contact:	Departments of the
(iii) In a primarily junior role:	Authority

   (*d*) Main working contacts outside department

3 Scope of Job

   [E.g. (*a*) Value of annual budgets or work and number of jobs or orders per Committee and/or type of building; (*b*) Funds; (*c*) Services; (*d*) Number of staff directly supervised; (*e*) Number of staff supervised by people under (*d*) above; (*f*) Other mainly direct resources controlled or influenced e.g. Private firms, internal budgets, etc.]

Staff : 11   Salary : £35,000

Annual output : £1,000,000

(b) KEY RESULT AREAS AND KEY ACTIVITIES
State the key result areas and key activities of the job where, if the overall purpose of the job is to be achieved, you must obtain results.

Ref No.	KRAs and Key Activities	Standard of Performance (Description of conditions that exist when the activity is well done) (Please state existing standard, where different from required standard)	Control used to measure Performance (the means by which actual level of performance is judged and the frequency of measurement)	Comments, suggestions and problems
(1)	(2)	(3)	(4)	(5)
2	I *Resource planning* To agree to a realistic programme for the Section having regard to the resources available	(i) Section fully loaded at all times for at least the next three months	Report on allocation (loading and capacity)	Capacity and loading calculation only now being introduced
3	II *The achievement* To ensure that all stages of the building programme are achieved on time	(i) Realistic time programme available for whole Section and updated monthly (ii) Programmes agreed with all concerned for all stages (iii) Time achievement at least (a) Tenders 100% (b) All stages 95%	Section programmes and progress reports	Major changes to programmes notified to Specialists without delay and agreed

4	III *Productivity and profitability* To utilize manpower and resources most effectively	(i) Agreed net expenditure plan achieved (ii) Output per man to be not less than £30,000 per annum per £1000 gross salary	Report on expenditure, national income and notional profit Report on output, capacity and allocation	Section budget and cost accounts now being introduced Value of output to be based on work content
5	IV *Building cost-effectiveness* To provide maximum value with cost limits compatible with the brief plus quality requirements	(i) Cost plan within cost limit (ii) Tender figure within cost limit. (iii) Final accounts within tender figure	Schedule of compliance with cost limits. „ „	Necessary for the architect to ensure that cost plan is properly updated where this relates to a project which, for whatever reason, has been deferred since its preparation
6	V *Quality* 1 To design buildings to the maximum functional and technical quality compatible with cost limitations	(i) Design reflects the contents of the brief. (ii) Design satisfies departmental design policy and standards (iii) Design agreed with client and ministry	Project review Project review Clients and Ministries agreement	More architect participation in preparation of brief with Client department (Inadequate briefs too often result in revised requirement at a late date. Better machinery for securing approval necessary. (Possibly by pre-arranged meeting on particular day)

Ref No.	KRAs and Key Activities	Standard of Performance (Description of conditions that exist when the activity is well done) (Please state existing standard, where different from required standard)		Control used to measure Performance (the means by which actual level of performance is judged and the frequency of measurement)	Comments, suggestions and problems
(1)	(2)	(3)		(4)	(5)
2	To prepare drawings schedules and specifications to acceptable standards and with maximum relevant information content	(i)	All relevant information provided to specialists and to contractors.	Regular appraisal of drawings and schedules	At least 90% of drawings checked before being passed to quantity surveyor or contractor
		(ii)	Not more than 5% of provisional measured information supplied to contractor at commencement of contract	Report on provisional documentation and remeasurement	
3	Carrying out effective supervision of the contract to ensure the work is completed to the reasonable satisfaction of the County Architect	(i)	Drawings, specifications and contract requirements complied with by contractor	Critical check of each project	Are architects sufficiently well trained to ensure that acceptable level of supervision is achieved? Identity of authorized supervising officer to be established and made clear to site management and by whom all instructions or orders must be given
		(ii)	User satisfied with functional requirements	Committee and client comments	

7   VI *Development and training*
To ensure that staff are effectively developed and trained

(i) Management job descriptions available and agreed with all scheduled staff.

(ii) Job reviewed and improvement plans available and agreed for the above

(iii) Training programme takes account of training needs identified from reviews and achievements

MBO progress report

Training report (training plans and review of achievement)

Department policy regarding exact responsibilities of junior staff needs to be clearly stated

Vacancies not to remain unfilled for more than one month.

(c) JOB IMPROVEMENT PLAN Job Holder ....

Sheet .... of ....   Position .... A.C.A. ....

Date ....

To cover period fm .... to ....

Review No.	1	2	3	4
Planned Review Date				
Actual Review Date				

OBJECTIVE	ACTION PLAN	By whom	By when
	(S) denotes supporting action needed		
1 To improve the programming system within the Section	(1) Receive workload realistically related to resources and at an earlier date		
	(2) Prepare programme for each project		
	(3) Fully involve 2 i/c in overall programming of workload		
	(4) Agree programmes with specialist sections		
	(5) Review of section programme at weekly intervals and revise as necessary		
2 To increase the average output per £1000 of salary within the Section from £23,000 to at least £30,000	(1) Achieve objective No. 1		
	(2) Ensure that projects are allocated within the section to individual project architects on a selective basis in relation to known capabilities		
	(3) Suitable projects to be incorporated within total annual workload (S)		

COMMENTS

Workload to be allocated by September preceding starts year and briefing to be completed within 2 months of allocation

Section to be fully loaded at all times for at least the next three months

Better and more regular clerical support

RESULTS REVIEW

Review number

Was objective achieved? Fully/substantially? Partly/Hardly

Was shortfall in Officer's control? Yes/No

Was agreed support provided? Yes/No

What further action is necessary?

Objectives 1, 2 and are top priority

	(4) Set realistic but tighter targets (5) Accurate up-to-date information required from management services at monthly periods (S)	
3 To achieve more effective co-ordination with specialist sections	(1) Agree detail programme (S) (2) Major changes to programme notified to specialists without delay (3) Structural specialist project to engineers to provide continuity of support until completion of specialist element including completion of all drawings (4) Further develop multi-professional team working by locating structural engineer in section for duration of his involvement on project (S)	Collaboration with the structural section is at best intermittent The degree of support depends upon the pressure brought to bear by the architect rather than resulting from voluntary co-operation As a result, control of the programme is difficult and achievement of target dates cannot be assured
4 To improve effective building cost control	(1) Agree procedure for preparation of cost plan (2) Check that cost plan is properly updated when necessary (3) Contain cost plan within financial position of project (4) Obtain cost statement showing financial position of project (5) Contain final account within tender figure (6) Check on cost statement	Need for frequent feed back from divisional offices on maintenance problems encountered

Appendix 7
Motivating

Extract from pp. 18–24 of revised edition of *Guide for New Managers*, Civil Service Department (1979).

By this we mean that the manager's job is to inspire his staff so that they will want to:

give of their best in following his lead;
contribute as a team to the purpose of the organization;
be loyal to each other, to him and to the organization;
achieve satisfaction from their work.

This concerns the manager's colleagues as people; how he deals with them and they with him; how he shows his concern for their careers and their welfare.

Now that the manager can no longer be that remote figure who barks 'Jump', it is difficult to write about providing the driving force for a group of staff without resorting to clichés about 'leadership', 'participation' and 'setting an example' and so on. But there are some specific things you can do as manager to stamp your own management style on the organization and to show that you recognize members of your staff as individuals.

TEAMWORK

Every office has a staff side, formal or informal, and people often think of management and staff (the official side and the staff side) in terms of opposing sides. On many issues, however, management and staff will find themselves united on a solution. Remember this, and wherever the interests of staff and management coincide use that combined strength to good purpose. But conflicts will undoubtedly arise from time to time and it is your job as manager to resolve as many of these locally as he can.

The Civil Service is noted for the amicable relationships that normally exist between its management and its staff. Recently an agreement was published on extending the facilities, such as accommodation, telephones and leave of absence, made available to trade union representatives. As a local manager, you should do all you can to foster effective methods of negotiation, consultation and communication with your staff side representatives within the spirit of your own departmental guidance.

Communication is one of the great human problems. Make a statement to any 10 people and 10 versions of what you meant will emerge. Yet each manager's position in the chain of communication between top management and the coal-face is critical. It is through him that policy is translated into action and (by what he reports back) that the effects of the policy should become known. And, in his middle-position, he must always keep in mind the need to be objective and to distinguish comment from fact.

Failure to communicate can have disastrous effects on one's colleagues. Where their careers, work, welfare, status, wellbeing are concerned people are quick to take offence or fear the worst because they don't know. This can happen even where the reason for an action is to make life easier for them. For example, a private, discreet search for better premises to improve the lot of staff housed in a black-listed hovel came back to the manager as a firm statement that the office was to be closed and the staff dispersed within the year. Keep your colleagues informed about what is going on.

One way to avoid such misunderstandings is to ensure that all staff are consulted in the decision-making process. This means that manager and staff explore the task to be carried out and together consider the problems and various possible courses of action.

Better by far to have meetings when there is something specific to talk about than to programme a fixed series of regular meetings. That is an invitation to people to look for (or even make up) something to talk, grumble or quarrel about.

Participation is in no sense an abnegation of the manager's responsibility. In the end it is you who must say if no consensus emerges 'I have listened to all you have to say and after considering all the facts this is the way we are going to do it'. Indeed even if a consensus does exist, you may well have to disagree and make a decision to the contrary. If so, do explain why.

If all you want from life is to be loved by all and to hurt no one, then perhaps management is not for you because every decision you take is going to upset someone. You cannot be a good manager and be 'Popularity Jack'.

In talking about your staff to a third person, 'colleagues' is a useful and accurate word to use. Moreover, its use keeps in mind the importance of treating them as colleagues whose interests you share.

It is worth remembering that, as a manager, you are always on parade. This can be a bit wearing but it can can also be turned to advantage. Be yourself and assert your individuality. People prefer to work for someone who has s style of his own rather than for someone who plays 'The Manager'. Don't take yourself too seriously. Be prepared to take a joke against yourself—and to join in the laughter.

You must set the standards—of behaviour, of punctuality, of quality of work—and you must be the first to conform to them. And you must be consistent.

Opinions differ about the job of the manager in periods of heavy pressure. Some argue strongly that the manager's job is to remain in detached overall control; others that he should take off his coat and buckle to with his staff. How you approach the problem will depend very much on your own management style. But there is no doubt about the good and lasting effects of morale of the direct contribution of the manager who rolls up his sleeves—provided he does not make too many mistakes or do it so often that he either interferes or loses sight of his main purpose.

Often the methods of work in an office have been evolved with much care and thought. Nevertheless the staff regularly carrying out procedures can spot weaknesses and suggest remedies. Encourage this and see that *they* get the credit.

By the same token, if your section has made a mistake, accept the blame yourself and see that it is put right.

INDIVIDUALS AT WORK

Most of us know from our own family life how necessary it is to treat people as individuals and neither try to mould them into a pattern nor ride rough-shod over their views. The same sensitivity to the feelings of others should be the keynote in dealing with staff.

Consideration for others and consistency are essential ingredients in creating an atmosphere in which people can give of their best.

Patience and courtesy are not synonymous with weakness. If they characterize your normal staff relations then sternness when called for will be the more effective.

Without prying you should get to know something about the personal background and interests of each member of your staff. This will help you to gauge their likely reactions to you and your background and to events both within the department and at large.

Don't expect the same reactions when you approach different people in the same manner. For example, the same remark may bring out quite different reactions from the man of your own age whose enthusiasms you share, the elderly lady who has only recently come out to work for the first time and the young boy or girl straight from school.

One notable example of how easy it is to get it wrong is the way in which you address colleagues. Whether you do so formally or by using first names will depend on a number of things; your age and theirs, departmental practice, how long they have worked with you. But it is a pretty safe bet that if you really want to upset people you will address them by surname only.

And how should the staff address you? Does this really matter (other than to you) provided that they all address you in a similar way and you do not encourage some to use your first name while calling for formality from others? What really matters is your standing with them and this will depend on their regard for you as a person, the way you know your job and your attitude and behaviour.

Favouritism destroys team-spirit insidiously but surely. You will inevitably respond more to some colleagues than to others. Again you must be consistent. It will help you to be so if you consciously try to deal with them all on the basis of their work, not their politics or religion (or lack of it) or the football team they support or the composers they prefer.

These attitudes are of particular importance if, as a young manager, you are put in charge of staff older than you. This is no new problem. It is one all managers will have faced at some time in their careers. Some of the staff will inevitably be hurt by, even resentful over, your appointment.

There is no easy answer to this. Be frank and acknowledge that many of them are expert at the job they do. Listen and learn from them. Concentrate on the work because, in the last analysis, it will not be until you can show you are at least their equal in that, that you will gain their respect.

Above all, avoid open confrontation and do not 'pull rank' unless you are driven to it. If you are, be polite but firm and make it clear that the decision is for you to take, that this is what you have decided and that you will accept full responsibility for it.

Management calls for moral courage. Where it is appropriate you cannot afford *not* to remonstrate, admonish, report. Don't tell yourself 'It does not matter this time'.

Inevitably there will come a time when you are faced with a confrontation either between two members of the staff or between one of them and you. You cannot walk away from it. All your effort should be directed towards cooling the situation and introducing reasoned discussion. To preserve the self-respect of the officer involved and, indeed, your own (and this is particularly important if any question of reproof arises) get the confrontation out of the arena and make it private. Be patient and quiet and search for facts on which you can base a judgement. In the extreme case you may well have to send home the officers concerned after arranging to see them again first thing the following morning.

Your basic philosophy should be that of pride in consuming your own smoke. If, as in the work itself, you come to regard it as a personal failure when you are unable to bring about a solution within your own area of control, then you are developing the right attitude of responsibility for the team as a whole.

If, however, a disciplinary infringement is so serious that you clearly must refer it up for decision, then, as you would with a question for guidance about the work, state the facts, set out the pros and cons for each possible course of action and say what, if it were within your gift, your decision would be and why. But you should have alerted your own manager long before that stage is reached.

There is another, brighter side to reporting to higher authority. Where one of your staff has carried out a particularly meritorious job of work involving outstanding effort or skill, or where one of them has obtained an outside qualification of some standing, make sure that you send forward a request for a note to be made on his service record. You might also suggest that a letter of commendation from, say, the Establishment Officer or Regional Director would not come amiss.

Always be ready to praise an officer who has done well—but don't devalue the currency.

Perhaps the most important task the manager has in relation to his staff as individuals is that of completing their staff reports and, where he is the countersigning officer, conducting their job appraisal reviews. These must reflect performance over the year as a whole and it is often difficult to distinguish the overall pattern from a series of isolated incidents, good and bad.

So that the overall impression should not be unduly coloured by the most recent incident, it can be helpful to keep a small personal note on each member of staff and to jot down a judgement on overall standards at fairly regular intervals (say, once a quarter) as well as making a note of specific commendations or criticisms.

Take time over staff reports. Complete them first in pencil. Leave them for a week and read them afresh, amending up or down as necessary. Compare each member of the staff, item by item, to make sure that the markings are accurate relatively. For example, is Miss A's judgement really that much better than Mr B's or Mrs C's?

Then, finally, wherever this is appropriate, it is helpful if the countersigning officer calls the reporting officers together to compare overall markings and promotion potential of the staff as a whole. This helps solve the perpetual problem of ensuring uniform reporting standards throughout the organization.

Objective staff-reporting is in everyone's interests. If an unsatisfactory rating is deserved, you cannot funk giving it. It is not kindness to mark an officer up in an attempt to give him a run for his money at a promotion board. To lower your standards in this way is unfair to staff who receive and deserve high markings. And make no mistake, it damages your reputation with your own managers—and with your staff.

In this process it is not only the immediate past that is under review but the future development of staff and their most effective deployment. Career development interviews conducted by central management form an essential link in a chain which must begin with the local manager and involve him throughout.

In particular be honest with staff. If an officer is not recommended for promotion because of deficiencies in his work or character, he is entitled to an explanation—an honest and constructive one. The case is easier if you can produce evidence of unsatisfactory work or conduct.

If one of your staff faces a promotion board then it is in your interests (and those of the rest of your staff) that he should be seen to do himself justice and merit the markings he has been given. Why not draw on your own greater experience and spend a short while advising him about the sort of questions he is likely to get and how best to tackle them? Remind him of some of the more important or controversial aspects of the department's work to which he would be expected to have given some thought. If he has not appeared before a board before, it would be helpful, too, to advise him about its make-up and procedures. A word of caution might also be given to the effect that it would be a mistake to link the chance of success to a great deal of last-minute swotting. Finally, make the point that promotion is competitive and depends on an assessment of the whole person: how he will react in the face of personal disappointment should he not succeed will be very revealing of his character.

THE MANAGER AND HIS MANAGERS

Do you know how your own manager will judge your effectiveness?

At an early stage discuss with your own manager what he expects of you and what the limits of your discretion are. What separate areas of responsibility can you agree, for example? What delegations can you expect? What Whitley agreements, departmental and local, impinge on your authority? What authority have you to grant leave or time off, to change staff duties, to work overtime? At what stage should you report arrears of work? What disciplinary infringements should be referred up?

The new manager cannot expect to be completely self-reliant from the outset. But he can, by establishing such limits clearly, take the first steps towards becoming so.

As a manager, it is sometimes difficult, but necessary, to remember that you are part of management as a whole because at times your local interests will conflict with those of the large organization. For example, if you publicly denigrate your own manager when he moves one of your staff to strengthen a weaker unit, it is management as a whole (including you) that suffers. Try to be philosophical about it and console yourself with the thought that your staff, in whose training you played a part, are beginning to be recognized as being of good quality and of value to the organization as a whole. This is not to say that, if you consider you are being unfairly dealt with by your own manager, you should not stand up for yourself.

Few things so quickly and irrevocably destroy your standing with both your own managers and your staff as disloyalty. This is because it stems from lack of courage to accept responsibility for the mistakes of your subordinates—and for your own shortcomings as their manager.

WELFARE

The welfare of your staff is, first and foremost, your responsibility. This is so, although there is always a staff welfare officer, or welfare liaison officer, available to give specialist help in personal and group problems. There may be many problems you can solve on your own, but do not leave it too long or try to take a problem too far before considering a talk with the welfare officer.

Remember, however, that there will be occasions when the last person an officer will want to confide in will be his manager. Respect this and, if he wishes, make every effort to ensure that he sees as soon as possible whoever he thinks can best help him. Encourage him, for example, to use the departmental welfare service and his trade union representative.

In sickness

When did you last visit—or at least telephone—a colleague on sick leave? It can be demoralizing for him to think that no one at work cares whether the returns or not.

In long-term illness, why not organize a weekly rota for visiting? Put yourself down for an early visit. And for the first contribution towards some small token for the visitor to take.

If one of your colleagues should die, make sure the staff welfare officer is informed as quickly as possible as he is trained to help in these cases. But what practical steps can you take to help? Can you assist with form-filling and making sure that the family receives all the help, benefit and assistance it is entitled to? Can you help any member of the family to get a job?

and in health

There is a tendency to think of welfare as relating primarily to sickness. But just as important must be your concern for the day-to-day welfare of your staff.

If a colleague has a problem at home he will bring it to the office and his work will be affected: to that extent his problems are your problems. You should always be prepared to listen and to offer suggestions if asked (but be careful not to seem to interfere). In that way you will help him decide for himself how best to deal with his problem.

As a manager, you should make a point of receiving the new recruit the day he joins the organization and introducing him to his new colleagues. One of the most persistent criticisms of managers is that of remoteness. See that it does not apply to you. It does not need long, a week or two later, to make a point of finding out how he has settled in, what problems he has, how he feels he is coping with the work, his ambitions and interests, etc.

Talking about personal problems can be embarrassing in the presence of other colleagues. As far as you can, try to arrange for any talk of a sensitive nature to take place in private. If you have no room of your own, is a colleague away or would your manager let you use his room?

Many activities in the Civil Service are governed by rules designed partly to ensure that equitable treatment is given as between person and person, grade and grade. From time to time, however, these rules prove to be unsatisfactory and even unjust in particular instances. The influence of a manager is much greater than that of an individual member of his staff. Where he senses injustice the manager should use that influence in bringing the facts to light and pressing hard to remedial action.

Some of us have to work in accommodation that is far from ideal. It is the job of management to house its staff decently. We mention elsewhere some of the steps a manager can take to make the best of his premises. He should see to his own accommodation similarly—but only after the comfort of his staff has been dealt with.

Appendix 8
Specimen internal control questionnaire for departmental organization

Source: *Internal Audit in the Civil Service*, pp. 28–31, Civil Service Department, HMSO (1973)

ICQ No. I : ORGANIZATION

Explanatory note. This ICQ covers the overall organization of the department to be audited and its functions. It should normally be the first ICQ completed so that a broad understanding of the organization can be gained before the internal control in each function is assessed. It may be useful to complete this part of the questionnaire for sections within the department. Any matters arising from its completion which are considered to be of special relevance to the assessment of the system of control over other functions should be noted in the 'Remarks' column provided below. This column should also be used to record the action taken regarding any unsatisfactory features.

General organization of the department

	Audit File ref	Remarks

1 (*a*) Is there in existence an up-to-date organization chart showing the overall structure and management of the department and the duties, lines of responsibility and accountability of its key personnel (if so, obtain copies)? *Yes/No*
(*b*) If not, prepare an organization chart, supplemented by brief notes as necessary, showing:
   (i) the principal divisions or branches of the department (with a description of their functions) and their respective complements
   (ii) the title, rank and, where appropriate, the name of each responsible official showing the lines of responsibility
(*c*) Review the charts or notes obtained or prepared in (*a*) or (*b*) above and consider whether the definition of duties and responsibilities for the department as a whole appears to be adequate:
   (i) as between divisions and branches
   (ii) as between posts		

Audit File ref	Remarks

2 List on a separate schedule the number and addresses of the department's
  (i) headquarters offices
  (ii) regional offices
  (iii) stores depots
  (iv) trading or manufacturing centres
  (v) other premises
describing briefly the activities undertaken at each.

Organization of Accounts Branch

3 (a) Is there in existence an organization chart (or written job descriptions) showing in detail the duties, lines of responsibility and accountability of the accounts branch staff (if so obtain a copy)?
  Yes/No

(b) If not, prepare such a chart or some brief notes illustrating as clearly as possible the lines of responsibility within the accounts branch, including:
  (i) the principal sections of the branch (with a description of their functions), and the approximate number of persons in each
  (ii) the titles, ranks and, where appropriate, the names of the senior officers within the branch and the extent of their responsibility.

(c) Review the charts or notes obtained or prepared in (a) or (b) above and consider whether
  (i) the definition of duties and responsibilities, and
  (ii) the overall segregation of duties (eg as between accounting records and cash handling) within the branch appear to be adequate, bearing in mind the scale on which the branch operates.

4 (a) Are there clear instructions relating to the arrangement or delegation of duties in the event of members of the staff being absent?
  Yes/No

(b) Are the accounts branch staff required to take their main annual leave according to a settled rota?
  Yes/No

Accounting manuals, instructions and Accounts

5 (a) Are there in existence

	Audit File ref	*Remarks*

(i) any accounting manuals or instructions (if so, obtain copies)?

Yes/No

(ii) any indices of account classifications (eg Vote Subheads) and code numbers (if so, obtain copies)?

Yes/No

(*b*) If so, review the manuals or instructions and consider their overall adequacy in relation to the size of the department and the complexity of its work, paying particular attention to:

(i) internal control systems and procedures

(ii) procedures to ensure consistency of accounting treatment

(*c*) Consider whether the distribution of the manuals or instructions is adequate (the distribution should extend to each section responsible for raising or handling documents which are used for accounting purposes).

6. (*a*) Which branch or section is responsible for periodically reviewing and revising the accounting manuals, instructions and account classifications?

(*b*) At what intervals is this carried out?

(*c*) Who authorises any revisions considered necessary?

7 List the principal accounting records maintained by the department, indicating which section is responsible for them and where they are kept.

Specimen signatures

8 Obtain specimen signatures and initials of all the officials responsible for authorizing documents under the system of internal control. Where the number of authorized signatories makes this proposal impracticable, the department's system of internal control should provide for separate lists to be kept up to date within the various divisions or branches of the department.

Index

Racecourse Betting Control Board, 3
Ranson, S., 44, 109, 214, 217, 219
Rayner, Sir Derek, 97–8, 220
Redcliffe-Maud, Lord, 12, 14
Reports on
the Civil Service 1968 (Fulton),
7–9, 140–51
the Civil Service 1854 (Northcote-
Trevelyan), 7
the Civil Service 1977 (Report of
the Expenditure Committee),
145, 147–8, 150, 193–6
the Control of Public Expenditure
1961 (Plowden), 7, 24
the Future of the United Kingdom
Power Plant Industry 1976, 36
a Joint Framework for Social
Policies 1975, 36
Local Government—Royal
Commission 1966–1969
(Redcliffe-Maud), 14
Management in Local Government
1961 (Maud), 12–13
the Method II System of Selection
for the Administrative Class of
the Home Civil Service 1969
(Davies), 146
the New Local Authorities:
Management and Structure
1972 (Bains), 14–16, 110
the New Scottish Local Authorities:
Organisation and Structure
1973, 17
the Reorganization of Central
Government 1970, 9–11
the Review of Overseas
Representation 1977, 88–91
the Third London Airport 1971
(Roskill), 55–60
the Use of Accountants in the Civil
Service 1973 (Melville/Burney),
144–5
Research
in central government, 39–40
in local government, 44
in personnel management, 127–39
Reynolds, D.J., 61
Rogaly, J., 4, 217
Roll, Sir Eric (now Lord), 219
Roskill, Rt. Hon. Sir Eustace (now
Rt. Hon. Lord Justice
Roskill), 55
Ross, Professor C.R., 35
Rothschild, Lord, 10, 35

Royal Institute of Public
Administration, 158
Royal Mint, 98
Royal Ordnance Factories, 7, 83,
98–9, 171
Russell, W., 215

Sainsbury, J., 220
Scottish Office, 10
Select Committee on Expenditure,
176–7
Report on Civil Service 1977, 145,
147–8, 150, 193–6
Self, Professor P.J.O., 47, 215, 222
Senior Policy Advisers, 9, 39
Serota, Baroness, 181
Shell Group of Companies, 10
Sidney, E., 217
Smee, J. Odling, 91
de Smith, Professor S.A., 220
Snow, Lord, 6
Snyderman, B., 217
Special advisers, 37–9
Staff associations (See Trade unions)
Stalker, G.M., 80, 216
Statisticians
in the Civil Service, 39, 142
Stewart, Professor J.D., 111, 112
Strathclyde, University of
Centre for the Study of Public
Policy, 47
Supplementary Benefits Commission,
195
Systems—Organizations as, 77–82

Taylor, T., 220
"Theory X and Theory Y"
Management, 129–31
Thornhill, W., 217
Tornado aircraft
project team for, 83
Trade unions, 124
in central government, 141–3, 151,
169–71
in local government, 158, 183
and participation, 169–71
Trading funds, 98–9
Training
in central government, 154–5
in local government, 152–3,
156–8
Training Services Agency, 82, 95
HM Treasury, 3, 10, 84–8, 150
TSR 2 aircraft, 7